D1470403

The Royal Book of Lists

An Irreverent Romp through Royal History from Alfred the Great to Prince William

by Matt Richardson

A HOUNSLOW BOOK
A MEMBER OF THE DUNDURN GROUP
TORONTO › OXFORD

Design: Bruna Brunelli
Printer: University of Toronto Press

Canadian Cataloguing in Publication Data

Richardson, Matt
    The royal book of lists: an irreverent romp through royal history from Alfred the Great to Prince William

ISBN 0-88882-238-3

1. Great Britain—Kings and rulers—Biography. 2. Great Britain—History. I. Title.

DA28.1R52 2001   941'.009'9   C2001-901941-6

1   2   3   4   5   05   04   03   02   01

THE CANADA COUNCIL | LE CONSEIL DES ARTS
FOR THE ARTS | DU CANADA
SINCE 1957 | DEPUIS 1957

Canada

ONTARIO ARTS COUNCIL
CONSEIL DES ARTS DE L'ONTARIO

We acknowledge the support of the **Canada Council for the Arts** and the **Ontario Arts Council** for our publishing program. We also acknowledge the financial support of the **Government of Canada** through the **Book Publishing Industry Development Program, The Association for the Export of Canadian Books,** and the **Government of Ontario** through the **Ontario Book Publishers Tax Credit** program.

Dundurn Press	Dundurn Press	Dundurn Press
8 Market Street	73 Lime Walk	2250 Military Road
Suite 200	Headington, Oxford,	Tonawanda NY
Toronto, Ontario, Canada	England	U.S.A. 14150
M5E 1M6	OX3 7AD	

Contents

THE GREAT BEYOND

Eight Royals Who Believed in the Supernatural
Three Royals Who Had Personal Psychics
Five Royal Superstitions
Six Significant Royal Predictions
Four Royals Believed to Possess Healing Powers
Six Royal Omens
12 Terrifying Royal Hauntings
Three Deceased Royals on Public Display
The Author's Six Predictions Regarding the Monarchy's Future

CROWNING GLORY

Four Ongoing Royal Ceremonies and Traditions
Five Royal Traditions That Have Been Abandoned
Three Important Annual Events Related to Royalty
Three Unusual Royalty-Related Job-Descriptions
Five Royal Orders
Three Memorable Princely Investitures
Seven Royal Crowns
Eight Examples of Royal Regalia
13 Monarchs Who Were Never Crowned
Eight Royals Who Were Also Emperor (Or Empress) of India
11 Unforgettable Coronations

WAR AND DISASTER

Nine Royals Who Served in the Navy
Five Notable Royal Regiments
Four Tragic Warships Named For Royals
Five Kings Who Were Killed in Battle
Three Royal Crusaders
Four Conquering Kings
Three Royal Responses to Terrible London Disasters
Eight Thoroughly Unmilitary Royals
Three Monarchs Who Made Frontline Visits
Two Royal Decorations
Three Wartime Sacrifices Made By Royals
Five Examples of Dynastic Warfare

13 Monarchs Whose Bodies Were Lost, Stolen or Destroyed

Eight Royal Forays Among the Common People
Nine Monarchs Who Faced Outright Rebellions

12 Unrealised Royal Ambitions
Four Common Royal Misconceptions
Five Things Lost or Destroyed by Royals
Physical Peculiarities of 15 Royals
Charles I's 12 Good Rules To Live By
12 Curious Facts About Queens
Four Well-Known Royal Anecdotes that are (unfortunately) Untrue
Three Unusual Places to Find British Royals
Three Reasons Why It's Good to be the King (or Queen)
Three Drawbacks to Being Royal

The Five Longest Reigns
The Five Shortest Reigns
The Five Oldest Sovereigns to Ascend to the Throne
The Five Youngest Sovereigns to Ascend to the Throne
Five Monarchs Who Died Youngest
Five Monarchs Who Lived the Longest
The Five Best Sovereigns
The Five Worst Sovereigns
The Five Most Underrated Sovereigns
The Five Most Overrated Sovereigns
28 Royal Firsts and Lasts

Acknowledgments

I'd like to particularly thank my parents for their unending support, along with my agent David Johnston at Livingston-Cooke / Curtis Brown Canada, and Kirk Howard, Tony Hawke, Barry Jowett, Jennifer Scott, Kerry Breeze, Beth Bruder, and Bruna Brunelli at Dundurn. Also instrumental in this project were Garry Toffoli and Claudia Willetts at the Canadian Royal Heritage Trust, who allowed me access to their extensive archives. My appreciation goes out as well to the staff at Unionville Library (especially Bob Henderson, Pat Boon, and Katya Whelan). Finally, I'd like to thank my friends Mark Godfrey, Doug Sweetman, and John Pigott for putting up with me all these years while I struggled to find my voice. It goes without saying that everyone else can kiss my ass…

Sex
and
Scandal

NINE GAY OR BISEXUAL ROYALS

1. WILLIAM II, "RUFUS" (C. 1056–1100)

Accused of homosexuality by hostile contemporary chroniclers, who alleged that the king surrounded himself with boys who "(rivalled) young women in delicacy." Although this may be merely guilt by association, it is nevertheless true that William remained a lifelong bachelor.

2. RICHARD I, "THE LIONHEART" (1157–99)

Richard's sexual orientation has always been the subject of much speculation. During his lifetime chroniclers linked him romantically with his father's arch-enemy, King Philip Augustus of France, while churchmen tended to lecture him on the fate of the Biblical Sodom. He is also said to have preferred the queen's brother to her. Yet, despite these facts, he did manage to produce at least one (and possibly two) illegitimate sons.

3. EDWARD II (1284–1327)

The king's first presumed homosexual lover, a Gascon knight named Piers de Gaveston, irritated the English court to no end with his obnoxiousness and was ultimately murdered in 1312. Edward's next "favourite," Sir Hugh Despenser, was somewhat more tolerable, although he too would ultimately be killed after allegedly plotting against the queen.

4. RICHARD II (1367–1400)

Although twice married, Richard was nevertheless known for his effeminate court and foppish clothing (not the least of which being a fabulous gemstone-covered ball gown). Among the men that he was known to have had an openly homosexual relationship with was Robert de Vere, whom he made the first English marquis.

James I

5. JAMES I (1566–1625)

James evidently found it difficult to keep his hands off the handsome young men chosen as his bedroom attendants, and was once observed by a court diarist strolling with one, his fingers unashamedly "fiddling about his cod-piece." While the bisexual king surrounded himself with his effeminate "favourites," his wife Anne of Denmark lived a happy and for the most part separate life.

6. WILLIAM III (1650–1702)

England's last-known gay king — or was he? Though no direct evidence exists of actual homosexuality, it is nevertheless true that, while living in his native Holland, William surrounded himself with a coterie of young male aides whose sexual proclivities were invariably suspect. It was a lifestyle that he would quickly return to after the death of his wife Mary in 1694, and in his later years the king particularly favoured a young captain of the cavalry named Arnout Joust van Keppel, whom he eventually elevated to a dukedom.

7. ANNE (1665–1714)

Though more-or-less happily married, Anne was for years infatuated with Sarah Churchill, her lady of the bedchamber. So close were the two women, in fact, that they even developed their own secret language for communicating with one another. When this relationship eventually went sour the queen formed an equally intense "friendship" with a woman named Abigail Masham.

8. ALBERT VICTOR, DUKE OF CLARENCE (1864–92)

Although the first-born son of Edward VII enjoyed enormous success with women, it was widely rumoured that he enjoyed the company of men as well, particularly during his lengthy stint in the Royal Navy. He is also believed to have had a long-term homosexual affair with his tutor at Cambridge, J. K. Stephen; indeed, when the effete prince died from pneumonia in 1892 at the age of 28 the latter was so devastated that he starved himself to death.

9. GEORGE, DUKE OF KENT (1902–42)

The highly effeminate, perfume-wearing George had a decided preference for fair-haired German boys, and was once arrested during a raid on a London gay club known as the Nut House. He was afterwards held by police until his identity as the king's son could be confirmed.

SEVEN EXAMPLES OF ROYAL VULGARITY

1. CAROLINE OF BRUNSWICK-WOLFENBÜTTEL (1768–1821)

After separating from her husband, the future King George IV, the princess spent several years travelling around Europe and generally making a spectacle of herself. A portly and prematurely elderly woman who surrounded herself with handsome young men, she was said to enjoy dancing topless at parties.

2. WILLIAM IV (1765–1837)

A career sailor before becoming king, William had a filthy mouth and was once arrested for brawling.

3. EDWARD VII (1841–1910)

Once, in Paris, Edward was persuaded to dance an undignified and quite enthusiastic cancan at the Moulin Rouge.

4. GEORGE VI (1895–1952)

Enjoyed leading conga lines at the end of palace balls.

5. PHILIP, DUKE OF EDINBURGH (1921–)

Once vomited into a top hat in the middle of a state funeral.

6. CHARLES, PRINCE OF WALES (1948–)

Once caught staring "long and hard" down Prime Minister Pierre Trudeau's wife's top during a state dinner.

7. Sarah, Duchess of York (1959–)

Instances of public vulgarity on the part of "Fergie" are legion. Her specialties include food throwing, public flirtation, bawdy storytelling and the goosing of strangers.

EIGHT CELEBRATED ROYAL MISTRESSES

1. Rosamund Clifford (c. 1133–c. 1176)

Known as "Fair Rosamund"; Henry II is said to have built a secret bower in the middle of a maze for her at Woodstock Palace to facilitate their trysts. The great love of his life, she was most likely poisoned by an agent of his wife, Queen Eleanor.

2. Alice Perrers (c. 1348–1400)

Long before the death of his good-natured but homely wife Queen Philippa, Edward III had acquired a sexy young mistress named Alice Perrers by whom he had at least three illegitimate children. Noted for her political meddling, the latter was said to occasionally share the king's bed with her daughter and not surprisingly earned the enmity of the court. When Edward died suddenly of a stroke she stole the rings from his fingers and fled.

3.–5. Eleanor "Nell" Gwynne (1650–87), Louise De Kéroüaille (1649–1734) and Francis Stuart (1647–1702)

Nell Gwynne began her mistressing career as a humble, 14-year-old Cockney orange seller at the Theatre Royal in Drury Lane, where she came to the attention of Charles II. The king called her "Nelly," while her name for him was "Charles the Third," owing to the fact that two of her previous lovers also went by that name. The king's other favourite mistress was a witty and attractive Frenchwoman, who had originally been sent to his court as a spy by Louis XIV. After successfully ingratiating herself, the latter was subsequently created Duchess of Portsmouth and had one of her sons by the king styled Duke of Richmond. Being a Catholic, however, she quickly became unpopular with the English people, thus prompting Nell Gwynne's notorious reply to an angry crowd that had confused the two and attacked her carriage: "Pray good people desist — I am the *Protestant* whore!" Yet another of Charles II's countless romantic interests, Francis Stuart, is remembered today as the model for the "Britannia" featured on British coins and medals.

6. MELUSINE VON DER SCHULENBERG (1667–1743)

Legally divorced by the time he assumed the English throne in 1714, George I instead brought along from Germany his favourite middle-aged courtesan, whom he later created the Duchess of Kendal. A remarkably tall and slender woman who had lost all her hair to smallpox, she was quickly dubbed "the Maypole" by the court. A second mistress was said to have stayed behind in Hanover, in order to provide the king with sex on his frequent visits home.

7. ALICE KEPPEL (DATES UNKNOWN)

The striking, chestnut-haired wife of the Earl of Albermarle, Alice was a gracious and tactful courtier who was admired not only by her lover Edward VII but also, incredibly, by his wife Queen Alexandra as well. Indeed, in an act of astonishing generosity, the latter actually invited her to visit Edward on his deathbed for a farewell. Out of all the king's innumerable mistresses (which included such notables as Lady Randolph Churchill — the mother of Winston) Alice came closest to being considered his "second wife." She made the famous observation, "A royal mistress should curtsey first, and then jump into bed."

8. CAMILLA PARKER-BOWLES (1947–)

The daughter of a wealthy land developer (and the great-great-granddaughter of another royal mistress, Alice Keppel), Camilla first dated Prince Charles in 1972 and their affair would continue — despite their respective marriages — until the present day. Like most royal mistresses she is far from beautiful (Princess Diana's nickname for her was "the Rottweiler"); nevertheless, now that she and the prince are once again single it would appear that marriage is inevitable.

SEVEN FEMALE ROYALS RUMOURED TO HAVE HAD AFFAIRS

1. ELEANOR OF AQUITAINE (1122–1204)

Said to have had a torrid romance with the Muslim leader Saladin.

2. ISABELLA OF FRANCE (1292–1358)

The only medieval queen positively known to have been an adulteress.

3. CAROLINE OF BRUNSWICK-WOLFENBÜTTEL (1768–1821)

In 1799 the then Princess of Wales was believed to have had an affair with future Prime Minister George Canning. Later, during her long separation from her husband, Caroline is definitely known to have had an intimate relationship with her chamberlain, Bartolomeo Pergami.

4. MARGARET, COUNTESS OF SNOWDON (1930–)

The princess first met Roderic ("Roddy") Llewellyn, an effeminate landscape gardener 18 years younger than herself, at a house party in 1973. Although still married to Lord Snowdon at the time she was immediately taken with him, and was not put off either by persistent rumours of his bisexuality or the fact that he then lived in a hippy commune. Needless to say the relationship didn't last, and after a brief but highly embarrassing career as a pop singer Roddy seemingly disappeared from the face of the earth.

5. PRINCESS MICHAEL OF KENT (1945–)

Once caught leaving the house of her Texan lover, Ward Hunt, disguised in a wig and sunglasses.

6. SARAH, DUCHESS OF YORK (1959–)

Claimed to have had her various, well-publicized affairs out of boredom and loneliness; her husband Prince Andrew was frequently-away for long periods because of his naval career.

8. DIANA, PRINCESS OF WALES (1961–97)

Numerous, mostly brief affairs with a succession of cads

FIVE ROYALS WHO VISITED PROSTITUTES

1. GEORGE IV (1762–1830)

Not averse to visiting the brothels of London if the need arose, in particular one that specialized in flagellation. His own household servants were also considered fair game.

2. WILLIAM IV (1765–1837)

During his long years of service in the Royal Navy the future William IV was a devotee of brothels, with a decided preference for native Caribbean women.

3. EDWARD VII (1841–1910)

A frequenter of the Parisian brothel Le Chabanais, and known to have utilized the services of the famed Spanish whore Caroline "La Belle" Ortero.

4. ALBERT VICTOR, DUKE OF CLARENCE (1864–92)

Linked to a scandal involving a homosexual brothel in London.

5. GEORGE V (1865–1936)

Despite his carefully crafted image as a virtuous family man, throughout his marriage the king utilised the services of prostitutes in boarding houses at Bognor and other seaside resorts.

TEN SEXUALLY PROFLIGATE ROYALS

1. EDWY (C. 942–959)

The 15-year-old Edwy shocked his advisors during his coronation feast, after slipping away at one point to his chambers in the company of a young woman and her mother. He was later discovered by two distinguished clerics in the midst of an enthusiastic *ménage à trois*, the crown of England having been thrown carelessly upon the floor. The youthful king was promptly reprimanded with a smack upside the head.

2. JOHN (1166–1216)

A notorious lecher, it was John's abduction and rape of a young noblewoman that finally persuaded his barons to bring him to heel by having him sign the *Magna Carta*.

3. EDWARD IV (1442–83)

Renowned for his licentiousness and complete lack of standards.

4. CHARLES II (1630–85)

Highly sexed, though discriminating in his partners. Not one to merely cast off his old mistresses, the king would generally provide them with a title and a pension, and steadfastly refused to divorce his wife despite the fact that she was incapable of having children.

5. GEORGE II (1683–1760)

The king considered himself a great lover and often boasted about his sexual prowess. Amazingly, his wife Queen Caroline not only approved of his extra-marital affairs but actually selected his mistresses for him.

6. GEORGE IV (1762–1830)

Despite being physically repulsive "Prinny" still managed to bed a considerable number of women. Toward this end he would use any unscrupulous method he could think of to win them over, his approach generally consisting of equal amounts of bribery and whining. Should the object of his affections fail to be swayed by either of these he would often resort to more dramatic measures, such as pretending that he was terminally ill or threatening suicide. He also had an unusual means of keeping track of his sexual conquests, in that he would invariably ask for a lock of the lady's hair and place it inside a labeled envelope. When his brothers were going through his belongings after his death, they discovered some 7,000 envelopes, containing enough hair to stuff a mattress.

7. WILLIAM IV (1765–1837)

Raped one of his mother's maids-of-honour at the age of fourteen.

8. EDWARD VII (1841–1910)

A compulsive adulterer; slept with about three different women per week for nearly half a century.

9. EDWARD VIII (1894–1972)

The future king was an international playboy throughout the jazz age and the subject of a popular American song: "I've Danced With a Man Who Danced With a Girl Who Danced With the Prince of Wales." He also had an alarming preference for older, married women — the uglier the better. No doubt reluctant to give up his status as the world's most eligible bachelor, he was 41 years old and still unmarried when he came to the throne.

10. ANDREW, DUKE OF YORK (1960–)

Among the seemingly endless list of women that "Randy Andy" was associated with prior to his marriage was the American porno-star Koo Stark; the queen was said to have liked her very much, though this didn't prevent her from commanding the affair to be ended. Since his divorce the prince has begun to reassert his jet-setting ways, and is often to be seen in the company of beautiful women.

SEX-RELATED CURIOSITIES OF THREE FEMALE ROYALS

1. ELIZABETH I (1533–1603)

In her later years the queen had a habit of revealing her bare breasts to her assembled courtiers.

2. VICTORIA (1819–1901)

Had no idea that lesbianism existed until an anti-homosexual bill was brought before her to sign in 1885. Even then she refused to recognise its existence, however, and promptly removed all female references — thus making male homosexuality illegal (up until the 1960s), but lesbianism legal.

3. ANNE, THE PRINCESS ROYAL (1950–)

During the 1976 Olympic Games, the equestrienne daughter of Elizabeth II was the only female competitor not given a sex test.

THREE FEMALE ROYALS
WHO HAVE BEEN PHOTOGRAPED NUDE

1. SARAH, DUCHESS OF YORK (1959–)

In the summer of 1992 photos appeared on the cover of the *Daily Mirror*, showing a bare-breasted Duchess of York on holiday in the South of France having her toes sucked by a man who wasn't her husband. "Fergie" had the double misfortune of being on vacation with the queen at Balmoral when the scandal hit.

2. DIANA, PRINCESS OF WALES (1961–97)

Various nude pictures, purporting to be of the princess, abound on the internet.

3. SOPHIE, COUNTESS OF WESSEX (1965–)

In 1999 the royal family scored a much-needed public-relations coup with the marriage of Prince Edward to Princess Diana look-alike Sophie Rees-Jones. Unfortunately, this good feeling was soon marred by the appearance in print of some embarrassing photos of the latter, which depicted her in a most un-regal manner.

SIX POSSIBLE LOVERS OF ELIZABETH I ("THE VIRGIN QUEEN")

The last of the Tudor monarchs, Elizabeth never married but, rather, used the prospect of marriage as a diplomatic lever. Although generally considered to have died a virgin, she was not, however, without her romantic attachments.

1. ROBERT DUDLEY, EARL OF LEICESTER (C. 1532–1588)

> "So the Queen of England is to marry her horse-keeper, who has killed his wife to make room for her."
>
> Mary, Queen of Scots

Elizabeth's one true love, Robert Dudley was the brother of Guilford Dudley, who had been executed along with his wife Queen Jane in 1554. Though they would never formalise the relationship, Dudley nevertheless filled the role of unofficial consort to the queen and kept apartments next to hers at all her principle residences. He was ultimately banished from court owing to a pernicious rumour that he had murdered his wife, and would eventually marry another. For this Elizabeth never truly forgave him, even if her feelings for him remained strong. Indeed, the queen kept Dudley's final note to her in a little chest by her bedside for the remainder of her life. Across it she had written the poignant words: "His last letter."

2. SIR CHRISTOPHER HATTON (1540–91)
Another of the queen's handsome favourites; in 1587 Hatton was elevated to lord chancellor, despite the fact that he had only a very limited knowledge of the law and did not want the job in any case. It was just one of many such "favours" that the queen lavished upon him throughout his many years of loyal service.

3. FRANCIS, DUKE OF ANJOU (D. 1584)
Francis, the heir to the French throne, was a froglike dwarf with a face deformed by smallpox, whom the queen most likely used to keep other suitors at bay. There is some evidence to suggest however that the two had a romantic liaison in 1573, at the Crown Inn in Canterbury.

When he died a decade later Elizabeth reportedly declared that she had "loved him so entirely" she could never marry another, though this fact didn't prevent her from quite literally dancing for joy at the news.

4. ROBERT DEVEREUX, EARL OF ESSEX (1567–1601)

The stepson of Robert Dudley, Robert was just 19 when he began his affair with the 53-year-old queen. After he later plotted against her she was forced to have him executed.

5. EDWARD DE VERE, EARL OF OXFORD (1550–1604)

It was this same Edward de Vere who, bowing low to the queen on one occasion, accidentally let go with a most undignified passing of wind. So embarrassed was he that he thereafter left the country for seven years. On his return he was welcomed back by Elizabeth with the comforting words, "My Lord, I have forgot the fart."

6. SIR WALTER RALEIGH (1552–1618)

Renowned author, explorer and military commander. The popular story that Raleigh first came to queen's attention by laying down his cloak in a mud puddle for her to walk through is untrue, although he did come to be a royal favourite for ten years (in spite of the fact that he was far from handsome). He eventually earned her displeasure through an illicit affair with one of her maids of honour, and was imprisoned for a time in the Tower of London. In 1603 he was tried for conspiracy against James I and condemned to death, although the sentence would not be carried out for another 15 years.

EIGHT ROYALS WHO HAD FLINGS WITH ACTORS OR ACTRESSES

1. GEORGE IV (1762–1830)

The pretty actress Mary Robinson, better known by her stage name Perdita (earned from a successful stint in a David Garrick production of *The Winter's Tale*) was the subject of a brief but intense infatuation on the part of the then Prince of Wales. Rather older and wiser than her suitor, Robinson managed to extract a £20,000 bond from him, to be paid when he came of age. This he did in due course, despite the fact that by then he had lost all interest in her.

2. WILLIAM IV (1765–1837)

For twenty years the future king lived with (and was frequently supported by) Dorothea Bland, a highly successful Irish comic actress in her day who went by the stage name Mrs. Jordan. She was ultimately dumped for someone more suitable when it became clear he would inherit the throne, and died alone and destitute in France. Their ten greedy children (known as the "little FitzClarences") would remain a source of irritation to William for the remainder of his life.

3. EDWARD VII (1841–1910)

Lost his virginity at the age of 19 to the sluttish actress Nellie Clifden. Later, he was positively known to have had affairs with the noted English stage actresses Lillie Langtry ("the Jersey Lily") and Margot Tennant, and widely suspected of having had one with Sarah Bernhardt. Edward's fling with Langtry was particularly contentious; on one occasion he was heard to complain to her, "I've spent enough on you to buy a battleship," to which his mistress shot back, "And you've spent enough in me to float one!"

4. ALBERT VICTOR, DUKE OF CLARENCE (1864–92)

Sarah Bernhardt claimed that the prince was the father of her son.

5. GEORGE, DUKE OF KENT (1902–42)

During the 1920s the duke was involved with a number of celebrities and aristocrats of both sexes, perhaps the most notable being the actor / playwright Noël Coward.

6. PHILIP, DUKE OF EDINBURGH (1921–)

Merle Oberon, best-known for her roles in such '40s-era movies as *The Scarlet Pimpernel* and *Wuthering Heights*, had a long-term friendship with the prince that (at least according to her) at times became rather more intimate.

7. MARGARET, COUNTESS OF SNOWDON (1930–)

One of the more notable flings the queen's sister has had over the years was with Danny Kaye, the American comedian and actor.

8. ANNE, THE PRINCESS ROYAL (1950–)

During the 1980s the princess was rumoured to be having an affair with Anthony Andrews, a British actor best known for his role in the mini-series *Brideshead Revisited*.

FIVE ROYAL PRUDES

1. HENRY VI (1421–71)

A true puritan, according to a contemporary the king was "wont utterly to avoid the unguarded sight of naked persons." He also took it upon himself to personally defend the chastity of every member of his household, and refused to allow anyone to use obscene language in his presence.

2. ELIZABETH I (1533–1603)

Imprisoned a man once for kissing one of her maids-of-honour.

3. GEORGE III (1738–1820)

Once, when a kilted Scottish officer was bowing to the king during a reception at St James' Palace, the latter suddenly noticed, to his horror, that the garment appeared to be riding up alarmingly. He immediately jumped to his feet and began shouting, "Keep the ladies at the back! Keep the ladies at the back!"

4. ALBERT, PRINCE CONSORT (1819–61)

Contrary to popular belief, it wasn't Victoria so much as her husband who was responsible for the stifling attitude towards sex that we now associate with "Victorianism." Indeed, the queen herself can be said to have had a rather forward-looking view of the subject, as evidenced by oft-expressed enjoyment of the act of lovemaking.

5. GEORGE V (1865–1936)

The king hated kissing scenes in films, and would often shout out "Get on with it, man!" at the screen. He also forbade his wife from wearing shorter, more fashionable skirts.

*Love
and
Marriage*

SEVEN FIRST MEETINGS OF FUTURE ROYAL COUPLES
(AND ONE RECONNAISSANCE)

1. HENRY VI MEETS MARGART OF ANJOU

The king was apparently able to inspect his bride-by-proxy personally without her knowledge. It seems that when the queen first arrived in England from her native France, Henry and one of his dukes disguised themselves as squires and set out to meet her, under the ruse that they were bearing an important letter for her to read. While she was so occupied, the king was thus able to find out what she was really like.

2. HENRY VIII MEETS ANNE OF CLEVES

Upon discovering his arranged bride to be markedly unlike her flattering portraits, the king was moved to ask his courtiers if they had brought him the "Flanders Mare."

3. CHARLES I MEETS HENRIETTA MARIA OF FRANCE

On first meeting her husband (whom she had unwisely married by proxy), the Bourbon princess immediately burst into tears.

4. GEORGE IV MEETS CAROLINE OF BRUNSWICK-WOLFENBÜTTEL

Seeing his fat and dumpy arranged-wife for the first time, George immediately turned to an aide and gasped, "Harris, I am not well; pray get me a glass of brandy."

5. THE PRINCE OF WALES MEETS WALLIS SIMPSON

Approaching Wallis Simpson at a private party in 1931, the future King Edward VIII casually inquired of the Baltimore native (who was then suffering a head cold) if she missed central heating. "I'm sorry, Sir, but you disappoint me…Every American woman who comes to your country is always asked the same question. I had hoped for something more original from the Prince of Wales."

6. Princess Elizabeth meets Prince Philip of Greece

Prince Philip of Greece was still a cadet at the Royal Naval College when George VI took his family there for a visit in 1939. This was when his 13-year-old daughter Elizabeth first saw her handsome, 18-year-old future husband, playing tennis. "How good he is, Crawfie!" she remarked to her governess with genuine enthusiasm, as if assessing a fine thoroughbred racehorse. "How high he can jump!"

7. Prince Charles meets Lady Diana Spencer

The 29-year-old prince first exchanged words with his 16-year-old future wife, briefly, in the middle of a ploughed field in November 1977 while a guest at the Spencer family estate.

AND ONE RECONNAISSANCE

Henry VII (1457–1509)

Before consenting to an arranged marriage with the widowed Queen Joan of Naples, the king sent out envoys to find out certain pertinent information about her appearance. Aside from the obvious questions regarding height and complexion, he particularly wanted them to "mark her breasts and paps whether they be big or small" and determine "whether there appear any hair about her lips or not." One final instruction was felt to be among the most important of all; that they "approach as near to her mouth as they honestly may, to the intent that they may feel the condition of her breath, whether it be sweet or not." Henry, incidentally, opted to pass on the match.

EIGHT MEMORABLE ROYAL WEDDINGS

Up until the twentieth century royal weddings were wholly private affairs, which were usually held in one of the chapels at Buckingham Palace or Windsor Castle. Westminster Abbey has since become the more usual venue, with the level of pomp steadily increasing. At the conclusion to each ceremony the bride's bouquet is placed on the Tomb of the Unknown Warrior.

1. PRINCE ARTHUR MARRIES KATHERINE OF ARAGON

Nothing in the whole of Henry VII's reign matched the series of festivities that marked the marriage of his first-born son Arthur to the daughter of the King of Aragon in 1501. Highlighting the day's events were a knight's procession with parade floats and banquet entertainments that included, among other things, the first court masque ever held in England.

2. CHARLES II MARRIES KATHERINE HENRIETTA OF BRAGANZA

In 1662 the fun loving, newly crowned king married (for political reasons) the pious, dangerously inbred daughter of the king of Portugal, whose dowry included the valuable possessions of Tangier and Bombay. Because the bride was a Catholic it was necessary in fact to have two ceremonies — one private and one public. Despite the seeming mismatch the marriage would prove to be a successful one, Charles continuing to enjoy his numerous mistresses while the queen dutifully looked the other way.

3. THE WEDDING OF WILLIAM AND MARY

An arranged marriage between the king's niece and Prince William of Orange. During the ceremony, which took place in 1677, the princess wept openly while the groom, for his part, wore funereal black.

4. FREDRICK, PRINCE OF WALES MARRIES PRINCESS AUGUSTA

During the ceremony the bride was so nervous that she threw up over the queen's skirt.

5. THE DOUBLE ROYAL WEDDING OF 1818

After George IV's sole heir Princess Charlotte died in 1817, several of his younger brothers immediately put aside their respective mistresses in favour of more suitable royal matches. This scramble to provide their own heir to the throne ultimately culminated in a bizarre, money-saving ceremony at Kew in July 1818, during which the aging dukes of Clarence and Kent hooked up with a pair of standard-issue German princesses.

6. THE PRINCE OF WALES MARRIES PRINCESS ALEXANDRA

The wedding of the future Edward VII to Alexandra of Denmark in 1863 was marred by a particularly lengthy sermon by the archbishop, prompting the orchestra at one point to begin tuning up out of boredom.

7. THE DUKE OF WINDSOR MARRIES WALLIS SIMPSON

The largely mythical "love story of the century" culminated on June 3, 1937, when the newly abdicated Edward VIII married his plain old American divorcée Wallis Simpson. The rather pathetic service, which took place at the Château de Candé in France, was entirely boycotted by other members of the royal family.

8. Prince Charles marries Lady Diana Spencer

The most memorable royal wedding of them all took place on July 29, 1981, in front of a live worldwide audience estimated at 750 million. Not surprisingly, it was also one of the more unusual, taking place as it did in St Paul's rather than in the more traditional Westminster Abbey, and presided over by an archbishop of Canterbury wearing a retro-futuristic silver cope. All went off without a hitch however (except when Diana repeated the groom's multiple middle names in the incorrect order), and as the couple emerged from the cathedral afterwards bells began to peal out across the country. Perhaps tellingly for a marriage that was destined to go so terribly wrong, Diana was the first royal bride in history to omit the word "obey" from her wedding vows.

FOUR MEMORABLE ROYAL WEDDING NIGHTS

1. William III and Mary II

While getting to know his new wife in a biblical sense, the somewhat stuffy Dutch prince was surprised when King Charles II suddenly drew back the curtains of the bed and yelled out, "Now nephew, to your work! Hey! St George for England!"

2. George IV and Caroline of Brunswick-Wolfenbüttel

On his wedding night in 1795 George found it necessary to get blinding drunk in order, as he put it, to endure his wife's "personal nastiness" long enough to consummate the union. For her part Queen Caroline later complained that, amongst other atrocities committed by him on the occasion (before he ultimately passed out in the fire grate), he had forced her to smoke a pipe.

3. Queen Victoria and Prince Albert

"Close your eyes and think of England."
(*Honeymoon advice, attributed to Victoria*)

Victoria spent much of the couple's wedding night lying on a sofa, complaining of a "sick headache." Interestingly, though it would be her husband who would ultimately wear the pants in the family, it was the queen who made the marriage proposal.

4. PRINCE MICHAEL OF KENT AND PRINCESS MICHAEL OF KENT

In 1978 the prince abided by his Catholic bride's wishes and refrained from consummating the marriage on their wedding night. She wanted to remain in a "state of grace" until receiving Holy Communion the following morning.

FIVE MESSY ROYAL MARRIAGE BREAK-UPS

Interestingly, in recent years there has been a far greater incidence of divorce among British royals than in the general population.

1. HENRY II AND ELEANOR OF AQUITAINE

An acrimonious break-up, largely owing to the king's many infidelities.

2. EDWARD II AND ISABELLA OF FRANCE

The gay King Edward is said to have carried a knife in his hose with which to kill his treacherous wife Isabella. The latter, unfortunately, had similar designs and was able to beat him to it.

3. GEORGE IV AND CAROLINE OF BRUNSWICK-WOLFENBÜTTEL

George, as Prince Regent, had only agreed to marry this vulgar German princess after parliament had agreed to pay off his enormous debts if he did so. Their dislike was instantaneous and mutual, and after just two weeks together the marriage was effectively over. Within a year George made a request to his father for a formal separation, and Caroline ultimately went off to live in Europe. She returned in 1820, at which point her husband instituted official divorce proceedings on the grounds of her adultery (then a treasonable crime on the part of his consort). For several months the country was alternately scandalized and enthralled by the sordid details of the couple's private lives. In the end, however, a bill to dissolve the marriage was ultimately dropped.

4. PRINCE CHARLES AND PRINCESS DIANA

After a lengthy (and often vicious) media war between the Prince and Princess of Wales and their respective supporters, in August 1996 the once-unthinkable divorce finally became official. Aside from the complex financial arrangements involved, under the terms of the £20 million settlement Diana retained many royal privileges as mother of a future king but was stripped of her royal title. Regarding this last fact she was (at least outwardly) philosophic; instead of becoming queen of England, she stated, her new desire was to become "queen of people's hearts."

5. PRINCE ANDREW AND SARAH FERGUSON

Despite the fact that Prince Andrew himself remained on more or less good terms with his ex-wife Fergie after their 1996 divorce (indeed, there has occasionally even been talk of a reconciliation), both the queen and Prince Philip steadfastly refused to allow her to join in the social life of the royal family, at, for instance, their annual Christmas celebrations at Sandringham.

THREE ROYALS WHO MARRIED CHILDREN

1. EDWARD I (1239–1307)

In 1254, the 15-year-old king married 10-year-old Eleanor of Castile. His second marriage was arguably even more remarkable, the king being over forty years older than his bride, Margaret of France.

2. RICHARD II (1284–1327)

Richard II's second wife was seven-year-old Isabella of Valois, the daughter of French King Charles VI. When his courtiers protested that she was simply too young to marry, Richard is said to have politely reminded them "that every day would make her older."

3. RICHARD, DUKE OF YORK (1473–C. 1483)

In 1478 Prince Richard, the five-year-old son of Edward IV married his six-year-old first cousin Anne Mowbray. The pope is said to have given special permission for the union.

FIVE ROYALS WHO MARRIED THEIR COUSIN

1. *HENRY VII (1457–1509)*

Married his cousin Elizabeth of York in 1486, after first securing a dispensation from the pope. The union is remembered today as the event that finally brought together the Houses of Lancaster and York and thus ended the Wars of the Roses.

2. *GEORGE IV (1762–1830)*

Married his first cousin, Caroline of Brunswick-Wolfenbüttel.

3. *VICTORIA (1819–1901)*

Victoria and Albert were first cousins.

4. *GEORGE, DUKE OF KENT (1902–42)*

Wed his beautiful cousin, Princess Marina of Greece, in 1934. In fairness it should be noted that the marriage was strictly one of convenience, being deemed necessary to resurrect the duke's tainted public image.

5. *ELIZABETH II (1926–)*

The then Princess Elizabeth married her third cousin Philip Mountbatten in 1947.

NINE ROYALS WHO (MAY HAVE) MARRIED SECRETLY

1. *EDWY (C. 941–959)*

Greatly antagonized high religious officials by his secret marriage to his stepmother's daughter. The marriage was later annulled.

2. *EDWARD IV (1442–83)*

Kept his marriage to Elizabeth Woodville — a beautiful older widower and commoner with two sons of her own — under wraps for five months because of concerns regarding her unsuitability at court. The secret was only revealed when the king came under pressure to make a diplomatic match.

3. *HENRY VIII (1491–1547)*

Due to the complications involved, Henry's marriage to his pregnant mistress Anne Boleyn in 1533 was held secretly and at an undisclosed location (most likely York Place, London or the Palace of Westminster).

4. CHARLES II (1630–85)

The Jacobite pretender James Scott, Duke of Monmouth based his claim to the throne on a supposed marriage between his mother, Lucy Walter, and the king.

5. GEORGE III (1738–1820)

During his first year on the throne George is alleged to have secretly wed a Quaker woman named Hannah Lightfoot, the daughter of a shoemaker, who later bore him a son. Documents relating to the supposed marriage, which is said to have taken place in 1759, were impounded a century later by government officials and judged to be genuine. Since that time however permission to examine the papers, which now reside in the Royal Archives, has invariably been refused. Should the charge ever be fully substantiated it could prove to be rather tricky for the royal family, as it would mean that the king was a bigamist and every one of his successors since that day a usurper.

6. GEORGE IV (1762–1830)

In 1785 the then Prince of Wales secretly married a Catholic widow six years his senior named Maria Fitzherbert, in a private ceremony in London. The union (which was illegal under British law but recognized by Papal Brief in 1800) produced no issue and the couple lived apart for the most of their married life; nevertheless, had it been widely known George would certainly have been barred from succeeding to the throne.

7. EDWARD, DUKE OF KENT (1767–1820)

While Queen Victoria's martinet father was stationed in Quebec he is believed to have secretly married a French-Canadian prostitute named Julie de St Laurent. Although the royal family has always denied this, what is beyond dispute is that he lived with her for almost three decades.

8. ALBERT VICTOR, DUKE OF CLARENCE (1864–92)

Said to have married a commoner named Annie Crook sometime during the 1880s, by whom he had a daughter.

9. GEORGE V (1865–1936)

George V's reign was dogged by a persistent (if rather improbable) rumour that, in 1890, he had secretly married the daughter of a British admiral in Malta, by whom he had several children. The allegation — first made by a journalist who was later jailed for libel — further asserted that, when his older brother unexpectedly died and left him heir to the throne, the then prince callously ditched his wife and kids and bigamously remarried.

EIGHT SOVEREIGNS WHO NEVER MARRIED

1. *ATHELSTAN (C. 895–939)*
2. *EDRED (C. 923–955)*
3. *EDWARD THE MARTYR (C. 963–978)*
4. *HARTHACANUTE (C. 1018–1042)*
5. *WILLIAM II, "RUFUS" (C. 1056–1100)*
6. *EDWARD V (1470–C. 1483)* *
7. *EDWARD VI (1537–53)* *
8. *ELIZABETH I (1533–1603)* *

* *Believed to have died a virgin.*

THE SIX WIVES OF HENRY VIII

Divorced, beheaded, died,
Divorced, beheaded, survived.

(Mnemonic device,
celebrating the fate of Henry VIII's wives)

1. KATHERINE OF ARAGON (1485–1536)

The daughter of Ferdinand II of Aragon and Isabella of Castile, and widow of Prince Arthur, the king's elder brother. After marrying Henry in 1509 Katherine (who was six years older than her husband) conceived a total of eight times, although the only one of the resulting offspring to survive infancy was the future Mary I. When it became obvious that she would never be able to give her husband the male heir he needed an annulment was sought, with the pope's refusal to grant it ultimately leading to the Reformation. After their historic, Anglican-sanctioned divorce in 1533 Katherine ended her days under guard at Kimbolton Castle, where she soon died of cancer. Her devotion to Henry undimmed, her final letter to him ended: "Lastly, I make this vow, that mine eyes desire you above all things."

2. Anne Boleyn (c. 1500–36)

Originally Henry's mistress, the bewitching, black-eyed Anne was pregnant when he married her in 1533. Like Katherine of Aragon she would leave only a single surviving child (the future Elizabeth I). This failure to provide the king with a boy — in addition to some spurious accusations of adultery — ultimately led to her beheading for treason on May 19, 1536.

3. Jane Seymour (c. 1505–37)

Henry's favourite queen was the delicate if somewhat plain Jane Seymour, a former lady-in-waiting to Katharine of Aragon, whom he married just two weeks after Anne Boleyn's execution in 1536. Tragically, she was to die soon after giving birth (by caesarian section) to the king's long-desired male heir, a sickly boy who was destined to become the short-lived Edward VI. Jane was the only one of his dead wives for whom the king wore black.

Queen Jane Seymour, the third of Henry VIII's six wives. (Imperial Gallery, Vienna)

4. ANNE OF CLEVES (1515–57)

Married Henry in 1540. An arranged, purely diplomatic match, Anne unfortunately proved to be much homelier in person than in her pre-nuptial portrait. The marriage was annulled seven months later, without ever having been consummated, and Anne lived the remaining 17 years of her life on a farm in Surrey.

5. KATHERINE HOWARD (C. 1525–42)

Henry married this beautiful but promiscuous young niece of his right-hand man, the duke of Norfolk, three weeks after his annulment from Anne of Cleves. Like Anne Boleyn she would ultimately be accused of infidelity (though in her case she was actually guilty), and was executed a year and a half later.

6. KATHERINE PARR (C. 1513–48)

A sensible, unprepossessing widow, Katherine married Henry in 1543 and served more as a nurse than a wife. Perhaps best remembered as the stepmother to two future queens of England (Elizabeth I and Lady Jane Grey) she also had the unique distinction of outliving the king, though only by a year.

Family
Life

SEVEN QUEENS WHO HAD CHILDREN LATE IN LIFE

1. ELEANOR OF AQUITAINE (1122–1204)

The queen (who was eleven years older than her husband Henry II) was forty when her first child was born, and forty-five when she finally gave birth to the future King John.

2. ELEANOR OF CASTILE (1244–90)

Wife of Edward I. Gave birth to her fifteenth and final child at the age of 46.

3. PHILIPPA OF HAINAULT (1314–69)

Wife of Edward III. Gave birth to her twelfth child when she was 43.

4. CHARLOTTE OF MECKLENBURG-STRELITZ (1744–1818)

Wife of George III. Was 38 when she gave birth to her fifteenth and final child.

5. VICTORIA (1819–1901)

The queen was nearly 38 when she gave birth to her ninth and last child in 1857.

6. MARY OF TECK (1867–1955)

Gave birth to her mentally and physically unsound youngest child, Prince John, at the age of 38.

7. ELIZABETH II (1926–)

Her youngest child, Prince Edward, was born when she was just shy of 38.

FOUR UNUSUAL ROYAL BIRTHS

1. RICHARD III (1452–85)

A breech birth. Tudor propaganda stated that he had been two years in the womb and arrived in the world with shoulder-length hair and teeth. Shakespeare, for his part, claimed he had been born prematurely, a "foul undigested lump."

2. ALBERT VICTOR, DUKE OF CLARENCE (1864–92)

Born almost three months premature.

3. PHILIP, DUKE OF EDINBURGH (1921–)

Born on the dining-room table at the palace of *Mon Repos*, on the Greek island of Corfu. The former Prince of Greece has always been quick to disown any deeper connection with that country, however, and is in actual fact largely German with a bit of Danish.

4. ELIZABETH II (1926–)

Born (by Caesarean section) in a private house at 17 Bruton Street in London. Her mother had to be artificially inseminated with a turkey baster owing to George VI's erectile problems.

16 BRITISH ROYALS BORN IN FRANCE

1. *WILLIAM I, "THE CONQUEROR" (c. 1027–87)*
2. *MATILDA OF FLANDERS (c. 1031–83)*
3. *WILLIAM II "RUFUS" (c. 1056–1100)*
4. *STEPHEN (c. 1097–1154)*
5. *MATILDA OF BOULOGNE (c. 1103–52)*
6. *HENRY II (1133–89)*
7. *ELEANOR OF AQUITAINE (1122–1204)*
8. *ISABELLA OF ANGOULÊME (1186–1246)*
9. *ELEANOR OF PROVENCE (1222–91)*
10. *MARGARET OF FRANCE (1282–1318)*
11. *ISABELLA OF FRANCE (1292–1358)*
12. *RICHARD II (1367–1400)*
13. *KATHERINE OF VALOIS (1401–37)*
14. *MARGARET OF ANJOU (1430–82)*

15. EDWARD IV (1442–83)
16. HENRIETTA MARIA OF FRANCE (1609–69)

TEN BRITISH ROYALS BORN IN GERMANY

1. ANNE OF CLEVES (1515–57)
2. GEORGE I (1660–1727)
3. SOPHIA DOROTHEA OF CELLE (1666–1726)
4. GEORGE II (1683–1760)
5. CAROLINE OF BRANDENBURG-ANSBACH (1683–1737)
6. FREDERICK, PRINCE OF WALES (1707–51)
7. CHARLOTTE OF MECKLENBURG-STRELITZ (1744–1818)
8. CAROLINE OF BRUNSWICK-WOLFENBÜTTEL (1768–1821)
9. ADELAIDE OF SAXE-MEININGEN (1792–1849)
10. ALBERT, PRINCE CONSORT (1819–61)

FIVE BRITISH ROYALS BORN IN SCOTLAND

1. MATILDA OF SCOTLAND (1080–1118)
2. JAMES I (1566–1625)
3. HENRY, PRINCE OF WALES (1594–1612)
4. CHARLES I (1600–49)
5. MARGARET, COUNTESS OF SNOWDON (1930–)

THREE BRITISH SOVEREIGNS BORN IN WALES

1. EDWARD II (1284–1327)
2. HENRY V (1387–1422)
3. HENRY VII (1457–1509)

THE SEVEN LOATHSOME SONS OF GEORGE III

Famously described by the Duke of Wellington as "the damnedest millstones about the necks of any government that can be imagined," each of the king's seven surviving sons grew to become a highly dysfunctional embarrassment to his family. Much of the blame for this can no doubt be attributed to an overly strict upbringing.

1. GEORGE, PRINCE OF WALES (1762–1830)

Although remembered by history (with a certain degree of accuracy) primarily as a drunken wastrel — a cartoonist's dream — there was, however, another side to George IV. Even the Duke of Wellington was forced to admit that the prince was "the most extraordinary compound of talent, wit, buffoonery, obstinacy, and good feelings; in short, a medley of the most opposite qualities, with a great preponderance of good — that I ever saw in any character in my life." A generous philanthropist (it was he, for instance, who donated his father's vast book collection to the nation to form the British Museum Library), he was also a man of almost oceanic arrogance and vanity whom many of his contemporaries actually considered to be certifiably insane.

2. FREDERICK, DUKE OF YORK (1763–1827)

Known to history as "the Grand Old Duke of York" owing to a popular jingle that celebrated his military incompetence, George IIIs' second-eldest son was a bloated and depraved buffoon. Despite that fact, for a time in the late eighteenth century proponents of the monarchical system actually considered placing him on a proposed American throne. He instead became commander-in-chief of the British army in 1795, from which position he was later forced to resign over a patronage scandal.

3. WILLIAM, DUKE OF CLARENCE (1765–1837)

The future William IV was, in every measurable sense, a complete idiot. It has been said that his only contribution to history as king was that, by lowering popular expectation of the monarchy to such an extent, he was actually able to make people forget just how bad his predecessor George IV had been.

William IV (as Duke of Clarence), from a miniature by J.P. Fisher.

4. EDWARD, DUKE OF KENT (1767–1820)

Perhaps the most odious of all George III's sons was Queen Victoria's father, a man better known by his nickname "the Beast." Once described by court diarist Charles Greville as "the greatest rascal who ever went unhung," Edward was a vicious bully who used his position as a colonel in the Royal Fusiliers to unleash his sadistic sexual proclivities on unsuspecting servicemen. His favourite pastime, from which he received ill-disguised pleasure, was in flogging men to the point of death for the most trivial of offences, and even by the brutal standards of the day his behaviour quickly earned him the reputation of a psychopath. After single-handedly driving his men to the point of mutiny while serving as commander of the garrison at Gibraltar he was ultimately relieved of his post and packed off to Canada, only to wreak similar havoc there. Amazingly he was then returned to Gibraltar as governor-general, where he was at last successful in inspiring an open revolt. Lucky to escape with his life, he was permanently recalled to England.

5. ERNEST, DUKE OF CUMBERLAND (1771–1851)

According to court diarist Charles Greville, in 1800 the duke incestuously raped and impregnated his own sister Sophia; ten years later, he was accused of slashing his valet's throat with a razor. Neither incident, however, prevented his becoming King of Hanover in 1837. His wife, it is worth noting, was no angel either, and is widely believed to have murdered her two previous spouses.

6. AUGUSTUS FREDERICK, DUKE OF SUSSEX (1773–1843)

Described by most who knew him as a complete non-entity, Augustus Frederick did in fact have one trait that set him apart from virtually every other member of the royal family throughout history — a genuinely left-leaning political view. Indeed, although all of the sons of George III were attracted to the Whig cause at some point in their lives, the appeal for them was mainly in its power to irritate their father rather than any actual political conviction. The Duke of Sussex, however, remained a staunch supporter of the anti-monarchist party throughout his life, and insisted upon being buried among commoners in London's Kensal Green Cemetery.

7. ADOLPHUS, DUKE OF CAMBRIDGE (1774–1850)

With his trademark blonde wig and shrill, babbling speech, George III's youngest son was, to put it kindly, an eccentric. The

Duke of Wellington's assessment was more indelicate ("as mad as bedlam").

SIX ROYAL BRATS

1. EDWARD VII (1841–1910)
As a boy Edward was known to make faces, spit and throw stones at one tutor, and tug on the beard of another. When reprimanded he would stamp his legs and scream "in the most dreadful manner."

2. EDWARD VIII (1894–1972)
Once purposely fed a tadpole sandwich to his hated French teacher.

3. MARGARET, COUNTESS OF SNOWDON (1930–)
An odd child, Margaret used to amuse herself by endlessly placing acorns in unattended shoes and by hiding the gardener's broom. If caught she would invariably put the blame on her imaginary friend, Cousin Halifax.

4. ANNE, THE PRINCESS ROYAL (1950–)
After learning as a child that Buckingham Palace guards had to present arms every time she walked past, the princess would often rush backwards and forwards in front of them to make them repeatedly snap to. She was eventually discovered and ordered to desist.

5. ANDREW, DUKE OF YORK (1960–)
The prince enjoyed tying together the shoelaces of unwitting royal sentries, and once tobogganed down the palace stairs on a silver tray.

6. PRINCE WILLIAM (1982–)
A spoiled child who fought constantly in school, William once shoved a classmate's head down a toilet.

THREE ROYALS WHO MAY HAVE BEEN ILLEGITIMATE

1. WILLIAM I, "THE CONQUEROR" (C. 1027–87)
The illegitimate son of Robert II, Duke of Normandy, by a tanner's daughter. Prior to earning his fearsome epithet "The Conqueror,"

the first Norman King of England was popularly known as William the Bastard.

2. ALBERT, PRINCE CONSORT (1819–61)

Rumoured to have been the product of an adulterous affair between his mother and a Jewish court chamberlain.

3. PHILIP, DUKE OF EDINBURGH (1921–)

Widely believed to be the illegitimate son of Earl Louis Mountbatten of Burma. At any rate it was the latter's surname that the prince assumed in 1947, after renouncing his Greek citizenship and German title.

11 KINGS WHO HAD ILLEGITIMATE CHILDREN

1. HAROLD II (C. 1021–66)

Had five or six illegitimate children by his mistress, Edith "Swan-neck."

2. HENRY I (1068–1135)

Believed to hold the record for the most bastard children sired by any British king; he had about two dozen in total, in addition to the four legal ones by his consort Matilda of Scotland. In 1120 Henry was devastated when his only two legitimate sons, William and Richard, drowned in the wreck of the *White Ship* in the Channel.

3. HENRY II (1133–89)

Fathered at least a dozen bastards by various women. It was one of these latter sons, incidentally, of whom the king declared (after all his legitimate sons had plotted against him): "Baseborn indeed have my other children shown themselves; this alone is my true son!"

4. RICHARD III (1452–85)

Approximately seven illegitimate children, all by unknown mothers.

5. HENRY VIII (1491–1547)

At least two bastards by two different mothers, only one of whom was ever acknowledged.

6. CHARLES II (1630–85)

Although he only admitted to fathering about 14 illegitimate children, some historians count as many as twenty.

7. JAMES II (1633–1701)

This most self-righteous of kings had at least seven illegitimate children.

8. GEORGE I (1660–1727)

At the age of sixteen the first Hanoverian King of England accidentally impregnated his sister's governess. Nothing is known about the fate of either the child or its mother, and George was always careful in the future to never acknowledge his bastards. He was, however, known to have had two illegitimate children by his mistress Melusine von der Schulenberg.

9. GEORGE IV (1762–1830)

Although he only ever accepted paternity of two illegitimate children during the course of his life (both of which were sons), this notoriously unselective womanizer is also widely believed to have sired a daughter by a boarding-house keeper from Weymouth. This relatively small number of bastard offspring may be attributed more perhaps to George's premature impotence, rather than to restraint.

10. EDWARD VII (1841–1910)

The last reigning British monarch to acknowledge a bastard son.

11. EDWARD VIII (1894–1972)

Believed to have fathered at least one illegitimate son by the wife of a friend, whose resemblance to the king was striking.

TEN GREAT ROYAL HOUSES

The concept of kingship arrived in England along with the first wave of Germanic immigration in the fifth century AD, in the form of tribal chieftains said to be descended from the god Wotan. Over the next few centuries the country would be made up of a loose association of these small, warring, primarily Anglo-Saxon kingdoms, which gradually became converted to Christianity.

1. THE HOUSE OF WESSEX (To 1066)

The first great royal house of a unified country (later to be known as England), the Kingdom of the West Saxons (Wessex) had its origins in King Egbert's victory over the Mercians in 829. Aside from the brief interludes during which parts of the country were overrun by Danish raiders, the House of Wessex would continue to rule more or less effectively right up until the Norman Invasion.

2. THE HOUSE OF NORMANDY (1066–1135)

Descended from sturdy Viking stock that had assumed the religion, language and customs of France, the Normans were the most fearsome warriors of the eleventh century. They were also accomplished builders, with many of the castles that they used to maintain control in England after their invasion still standing to this day.

3.–5. THE HOUSES OF ANJOU, LANCASTER AND YORK (1154–1485)

The Angevins originated with Geoffrey of Anjou in the twelfth century, and ruled over an empire that stretched at one point from the Scottish border to the Pyrenees. His son Henry II would become the first of the so-called "Plantagenet" kings; this rather broad nickname, incidentally, (which includes the three related families of Anjou, Lancaster and York) originated from Geoffrey's habit of wearing a sprig of broom flower *(planta genista)* on his helmet.

6. THE HOUSE OF TUDOR (1485–1603)

Overcoming their rather questionable claim to the throne, the Tudors would go on to become, arguably, the most successful family dynasty in English history. Indeed, during their sixteenth century glory days they would produce three remarkably gifted rulers — Henry VII, Henry VIII, and Elizabeth I — who between them would reign for over a hundred years.

7. THE HOUSE OF STUART (1603–1714)

Though highly successful in Scotland, the Stuart (or Stewart) dynasty would never have much luck in England. All four Stuart kings had serious flaws in their character, and the period in which they ruled was dominated by civil war and social instability. Two of them — Charles I and James II — would be destined to lose the crown itself. After the deaths of the pretender Bonnie Prince Charlie and his brother Henry the direct Stuart line became extinct, with the mantle eventually passing to the ruling house of Bavaria. Thus it was that one of the descendants of the Stuart kings of Britain, Crown Prince Rupprecht, actually fought as a general in the German army during World War I.

8. THE HOUSE OF HANOVER (1714–1901)

> I sing of Georges four
> Since Providence could stand no more
> Some say that far the worst
> Of all was George the First
> But yet by some 'tis reckoned
> That worse still was George the Second
> And what mortal ever heard
> Any good of George the Third?
> When George the Fourth from the earth descended
> Thank God the line of Georges ended
>
> Walter Savage Landor

By the beginning of the eighteenth century it had become abundantly clear that Queen Anne would never provide an heir to the British throne. In 1701 therefore the Act of Settlement was passed to prevent a Jacobite restoration, the crown consequently, on her death, bypassing the 57 Catholic royals who had a better claim to its ownership to land in the unlikely hands of George Guelph, the Protestant ruler of the German state of Hanover. Although generally ridiculous, he and his successors would unintentionally do much to further parliamentary democracy. Indeed, it was the almost complete lack of interest in English affairs on the part of the first two Hanoverians that ultimately led to the appointment of a council of ministers — the beginning of the cabinet system of government.

9. THE HOUSE OF SAXE-COBURG-GOTHA (1901–17)

Incredibly, by the end of his reign not one of the seven sons and five daughters of George III had yet produced a single legitimate heir. The throne would ultimately pass to his fourth son's daughter Victoria, who in 1840 married Prince Albert of Saxe-Coburg-Gotha. Her son and successor, Edward VII, was the only representative of this House (sometimes called the House of Wettin).

Four generations of royals: Queen Victoria with the future kings Edward VII, George V, and Edward VIII, in 1894.

10. THE HOUSE OF WINDSOR (1917–)

In July 1917, with the First World War still raging and anti-German sentiment understandably running very high, George V decided it politically expedient to change the family's Teutonic surname to something more typically English. At the suggestion of his private secretary, Lord Stamfordham, the name Windsor was finally chosen, after the venerable castle that is such a symbol of British royalty. On hearing of the change, the normally humourless German Kaiser is said to have joked that he was looking forward to a performance of Shakespeare's *The Merry Wives of Saxe-Coburg-Gotha*. It should be noted that, in accordance with the wishes of the present queen, the family name (beginning with the third generation of her male descendants) will officially become the House of Mountbatten-Windsor, in belated recognition of her husband.

Succession

THE 22 ENGLISH PRINCES OF WALES

In 1284 Edward I bestowed the title "Prince of Wales" on his son, the future Edward II. Ever since that day, the firstborn son of each sovereign has been given the same title to indicate his right to the English throne as heir apparent. The precise point at which the title is bestowed, however, remains very much at the discretion of the sovereign, the age ranging anywhere from five days (in the case of George III) right up to later adulthood.

1. EDWARD OF CAERNARVON (1284–1327)
Son of Edward I; became Edward II.

2. EDWARD OF WOODSTOCK (1330–76)
Son of Edward III. Popularly known as "the Black Prince" he died a year before his father, having been worn out by constant campaigning.

3. RICHARD OF BORDEAUX (1367–1400)
Grandson of Edward III; became Richard II.

4. HENRY OF MONMOUTH (1386–1422)
Son of Henry IV; became Henry V.

5. EDWARD OF WESTMINSTER (1453–71)
Son of Henry VI. Killed at the Battle of Tewkesbury.

6. EDWARD OF YORK (1471–C. 1483)
Son of Edward IV; became Edward V.

7. EDWARD OF MIDDLEHAM (C. 1473–84)

Only son of Richard III. Died shortly after being invested as Prince of Wales, at the age of 11.

8. ARTHUR OF WINCHESTER (1486–1502)

Son of Henry VII. Created Prince of Wales in 1489 and invested as such the following year, but died before he could take the throne.

9. HENRY OF GREENWICH (1491–1547)

Son of Henry VII; became Henry VIII.

10. HENRY OF RICHMOND (1 JAN. 1511–22 FEB. 1511)

Though one of three short-lived sons of Henry VIII by Katherine of Aragon, Henry was the only one to be *styled* Prince of Wales.

11. HENRY OF STIRLING (1594–1612)

Son of James I. Died of typhoid at the age of 18.

12. CHARLES OF DUNFERMLINE (1600–49)

Son of James I; became Charles I.

13. CHARLES OF ST. JAMES'S (1630–85)

Son of Charles I; declared in 1630 but never formally created Prince of Wales. Became Charles II.

14. JAMES FRANCIS EDWARD OF ST. JAMES'S (1688–1766)

Son of James II. *Styled* Prince of Wales in 1688, he was later attainted by Act of Parliament in 1702 and forfeited all his British titles.

15. GEORGE AUGUSTUS OF HANOVER (1683–1760)

Son of George I; became George II.

16. FREDRICK LEWIS OF HANOVER (1707–51)

Son of George II. Died of pleurisy while still Prince of Wales.

17. GEORGE WILLIAM FREDRICK OF NORFOLK HOUSE (1738–1820)

Grandson of George II; became George III.

18. GEORGE AUGUSTUS FREDRICK OF ST. JAMES'S (1762–1830)

Son of George III; became George IV. Amazingly, George didn't actually visit his own principality until the 44th year of his holding the title, and then only briefly.

19. ALBERT EDWARD OF BUCKINGHAM PALACE (1841–1910)

Son of Queen Victoria; became Edward VII. The longest-serving Prince of Wales, having held the title for 59 years.

20. GEORGE FREDRICK ERNEST ALBERT OF MALBOROUGH HOUSE (1865–1936)

Son of Edward VII; became George V.

21. EDWARD ALBERT CHRISTIAN GEORGE ANDREW PATRICK DAVID OF WHITE LODGE, RICHMOND (1894–1972)

Son of George V; became Edward VIII after a quarter of a century as Prince of Wales.

22. CHARLES PHILIP ARTHUR GEORGE OF BUCKINGHAM PALACE (1948–)

Son of Elizabeth II. Proclaimed Prince of Wales in 1958, in his mother's pre-taped, closing-ceremony message for the Commonwealth Games in Cardiff.

SIX ENGLISH MONARCHS WHO ALSO REIGNED IN IRELAND

It is one of the great ironies in history that a pope, Alexander III, gave Ireland to Henry II in an effort to eradicate native Celtish customs. English rule in the Emerald Isle subsequent to that time would mostly be an indirect one, with the country continuing to be ruled by local nobles and chiefs who acknowledged the king without ever actually setting eyes on him. Gradually even this rule came to be resented, and in 1922 the mainly Catholic / Republican southern counties formed the independent Irish Free State and later left the Commonwealth altogether. The six counties that make up Northern Ireland remained in the United Kingdom, and continue to acknowledge Elizabeth II as sovereign.

1. HENRY II (1133–89)

Fearing the creation of an independent Norman kingdom in Ireland, in 1171 Henry went there in person to assert his authority. He had brought along with him a large army but did not need it; the native Irish chiefs receivied him warmly and most readily acknowledged his overlordship.

2. JOHN (1166–1216)

Declared king of Ireland in 1177 by his father. Unfortunately, he would later be recalled from his first expedition there after mocking the beards of the chieftains who had come to pay him homage.

3. RICHARD II (1367–1400)

During his two visits to Ireland Richard made various efforts to anglicise the local kings, to little avail.

4. HENRY VIII (1491–1547)

The first English king to style himself "King of Ireland." From Henry's reign onward English interference in Irish affairs would steadily increase.

5. GEORGE III (1738–1820)

Proclaimed King of Great Britain and Ireland in 1801on the passing of the Act of Union.

6. WILLIAM IV (1765–1837)

Known as William II in Ireland.

THREE ENGLISH ROYALS WHO REIGNED
(BY ANOTHER NAME) IN SCOTLAND

Throughout the Middle Ages English kings tried — and invariably failed — to either conquer "barbarian" Scotland for good or at least bring it to heel. This seemingly endless conflict was at last resolved with the Act of Union in 1707. Although Scotland lost its own distinct monarchy as a result of this new "United Kingdom," along with its parliament (until the reign of Elizabeth II), it was however able to retain its unique religious and legal systems. British monarchs continue to be crowned in a separate ceremony in Scotland as well to this day, though only as a formality.

1. JAMES I (1566–1625)

The son of the ill-fated Mary Queen of Scots, James was declared King of Scotland at the age of one year after his mother lost the support of her lords and abdicated. He continued to rule the country as James VI until assuming the English crown in 1603 as well. Although technically "shared" thereafter by the subjects of both kingdoms, he rarely set foot again in Scotland.

2. JAMES STUART, "THE OLD PRETENDER" (1688–1766)

Son of the deposed James II. Proclaimed "James VIII" of Scotland while in exile in France.

3. WILLIAM IV (1765–1837)

Known as William III of Scotland.

FIVE ENGLISH KINGS WHO CLAIMED TO BE KING OF FRANCE

From the time of the Norman invasion of England in 1066 until the fifteenth century, each king of England was also technically a prince of France. Some took this futile French claim more seriously than others.

1. EDWARD III (1312–77)

In 1340 Edward became the first English king to formally assume the title King of France.

2. HENRY V (1387–1422)

Revived the French wars and ultimately won complete victory (not to mention Charles VI's daughter), though not before causing many thousands of deaths on both sides. Under the terms of the resulting Treaty of Troyes in 1420 Henry was designated regent and heir to the throne of France; ironically, he did not live long enough to enjoy his inheritance.

3. HENRY VI (1421–71)

Succeeded his grandfather, the mad Charles VI of France, as King of France in 1422. He was officially crowned at the cathedral of Notre Dame in Paris in 1431 and assumed personal rule in 1437.

4. EDWARD IV (1442–83)

After his attempt to reclaim the French territory lost by his predecessor bogged down, Edward agreed to withdraw his forces back to England, though not before accepting a hefty payment to do so.

5. GEORGE III (1738–1820)

The last English monarch to style himself King of France; by the time of George's coronation the claim had become so nominal that he was obliged to hire actors to impersonate the dukes of Normandy and Aquitaine, in order to obtain their fealty. The title would be renounced for good on January 1, 1801.

NINE ROYAL REACTIONS ON HEARING OF THEIR ACCESSION

1. JANE (1537–54)

Bursting into tears, the young Lady Jane Grey is said to have exclaimed: "The Crown in not my right, and pleaseth me not. The Lady Mary is the rightful heir."

2. ELIZABETH I (1533–1603)

(In Latin) "This is the Lord's doing and it is marvellous in our eyes."

3. ANNE (1665–1714)

"It is a fine day."

4. GEORGE II (1683–1760)

"Dat is vun beeg lie!"

5. WILLIAM IV (1765–1837)

"I shall go back to bed. I have never slept with a queen before." It would appear, incidentally, that the king did not mourn for his dead brother George IV at all.

6. VICTORIA (1819–1901)

(On discovering, at the age of 10, that she was heir to the throne) "I will be good."

7. EDWARD VII (1841–1910)

When told (at the same age that Victoria had been) that he was one day destined to sit on the throne, he was quite unable to grasp what this meant and had to turn to his mother for an explanation.

8. GEORGE VI (1895–1952)

Woefully unprepared to be king, either by training or desire; on realising the inevitability of his position George VI is said to cried out, "This can't be happening to me!" He then put his head on Queen Mary's shoulder and wept for an hour.

9. ELIZABETH II (1926–)

Learned of her father's death while staying at Treetops, a tree-house safari lodge in the wilds of Kenya. Though she traditionally is said to have taken the news "bravely, like a queen," she in fact cried the whole way back to England.

SIX SECOND SONS WHO SUCCEEDED TO THE THRONE

1. RICHARD II (1367–1400)

Second son of Edward "the Black Prince." His elder brother died in childhood.

2. HENRY VIII (1491–1547)

It has been speculated that, being the second son of Henry VII, an inferiority complex may have been at the heart of the king's legendary egotism. Succeeded to the throne after his elder brother Arthur, Prince of Wales, died in 1502, and later married his widow Katherine of Aragon.

3. CHARLES I (1600–49)

Succeeded his father James I after the death of his elder brother Henry, Prince of Wales.

4. CHARLES II (1630–85)

The king was actually the second son named Charles by his parents; the first, unfortunately, survived for only a single day.

5. GEORGE V (1865–1936)

The second son of Edward VII. After the unexpectedly early death of Prince Albert Victor in 1892 from pneumonia, his younger brother George was expected to assume all of his duties as the new heir to the throne. Among these included marriage to the dead man's fiancée, Mary of Teck.

6. GEORGE VI (1895–1952)

The second son of George V. Succeeded after the abdication of his elder brother, Edward VIII.

SIX BRITISH ROYALS WHO REIGNED IN HANOVER

The Hanoverian dynasty that was to assume the English throne in 1714 continued to hold the title elector (later, king) of their native country as well until the accession of Queen Victoria. The latter, as a woman, was prevented from continuing the tradition under German Salic law, with the result that the German title passed to the next male descendant of George III instead.

1. GEORGE I (1660–1727)
2. WILLIAM, DUKE OF CUMBERLAND (1721–65)
3. GEORGE III (1738–1820)
4. GEORGE IV (1762–1830)
5. WILLIAM IV (1765–1837)
6. ERNEST, DUKE OF CUMBERLAND (1771–1851)

SEVEN SUCCESSFUL ROYAL USURPERS

1. CANUTE (C. 995–1035)
Claimed the English throne by right of conquest in 1016, and managed to hang on to it for two decades.

2. WILLIAM I, "THE CONQUEROR" (C. 1027–87)
In 1066 the then Duke of Normandy was outraged when he learnt that his old friend and cousin, King Edward the Confessor, had nominated his Danish brother-in-law Harold, Earl of Godwin as heir to the throne. William believed that the English crown had already been promised to him, and that further it was legitimately his by right of blood. After Harold II formally proclaimed himself king on his predecessor's death, William felt he had no choice but to press the Norman claim by force at Hastings, where Harold's brief reign was brought to a violent end.

3. STEPHEN (C. 1097–1154)
When Henry I died suddenly in 1135 Stephen, Count of Boulogne had the good fortune to be nearer to London than any other possible claimant. With the help of the English barons he seized the vacant throne, at the same time disregarding his oath of fealty to the legitimate heir, Henry's daughter Matilda. Stephen could have had the latter arrested when she finally arrived on the scene in 1141 but chose not to, and when

her forces quickly managed to gain the upper hand Stephen was briefly deposed and imprisoned. He was soon restored by the populace, however, who weren't quite ready to accept a female ruler — especially one as haughty as Matilda. Yet the civil war between the two factions would continue on for another eighteen years, until a workable compromise was at last reached — Stephen would retain the throne for the remainder of his lifetime, but would be succeeded by Matilda's son, Henry II.

4. HENRY BOLINGBROKE (1366–1413)

He deposed Richard II in August 1399 and proclaimed himself Henry IV, thus beginning the deadly rivalry between the houses of York and Lancaster.

5. EDWARD IV (1442–83)

Deposed Henry VI on March 29, 1461 at the bloody Battle of Towton. The latter was restored to the throne with the help of the Earl of Warwick ("the Kingmaker") in 1470, only to be deposed again by Edward and his mercenaries the following year after their victory at Tewkesbury.

Richard III

6. RICHARD, DUKE OF GLOUCESTER (1452–85)

The story of the "little princes in the Tower" remains, to this day, one of the most famous murder mysteries of all time. In April 1483 the uncrowned boy king, Edward V, and his brother Richard were left in the care of their uncle Richard of Gloucester for "protection" after the death of their father, Edward IV. They were never seen again, and the uncle was subsequently crowned Richard III; not surprisingly, it has been widely assumed since that time that he murdered his nephews as a means of obtaining the throne. Some historians, however, think that the real culprit was actually Henry VII, the king who ruled after Richard.

7. HENRY TUDOR (1457–1509)

Successfully claimed the throne after defeating his cousin, Richard III, at the Battle of Bosworth Field, styling himself Henry VII. As king he would be highly effective in both consolidating his power and in re-establishing the heredity principle of monarchy.

FOUR MEMORABLE REGENCIES

According to the Regency Act of 1943, an heir to the throne must be at least 18 years of age to rule in his or her own right.

1. EDWARD III (1312–77)

After Queen Isabella and her lover, Roger Mortimer, successfully plotted to have her husband Edward II deposed and murdered, the two shared regency until such time as the young Edward III attained his majority. When the latter did so, however, his first act was to have the pair overthrown, with Mortimer being executed and his mother allowed an honourable retirement from public life.

2. HENRY VI (1421–71)

The first baby to inherit the throne of England, Henry VI presided over his first parliament while sleeping in his mother's arms. During his periods of madness in later life the reins of government would once again be turned over — this time to a "protector of the realm."

3. EDWARD VI (1537–53)

Only nine years old on the death of his father Henry VIII, Edward was entrusted into the care of his uncle Edward Seymour, who became lord protector in his stead. Seymour was displaced two years later by Robert Dudley, Duke of Northumberland, who was able to manipulate the frail and pedantic boy king to his own advantage until the latter's untimely death at age fifteen. It is from the duke's urgings that the crown was left to Edward's Protestant cousin Lady Jane Grey, rather than to his half-sister Mary, the legitimate Catholic heir.

4. GEORGE III (1738–1820)

After his father lapsed into his final period of incapacity George was created prince regent by act of parliament in 1811, a title he would hold until his accession as George IV in 1820. This so-called Regency period was a distinctive one in British history, the name lending itself to a characteristic style of architecture and furniture.

FOUR YEARS THAT SAW THREE KINGS ON THE THRONE

1. 1016 (Ethelred II, Edmund II, and Canute)

2. 1066 (Edward the Confessor, Harold II, and William the Conqueror)
3. 1483 (Edward IV, Edward V, and Richard III)
4. 1936 (George V, Edward VIII, and George VI)

THE ROYAL LINE OF SUCCESSION (AS OF 2000)

According to the eleventh-century law of primogeniture, the British throne devolves upon the firstborn son of the deceased sovereign, and thence to his issue. Female children of the sovereign stand to inherit only if no male heirs are present.

1. CHARLES, PRINCE OF WALES (B. 1948)
2. PRINCE WILLIAM (B. 1982)
3. PRINCE HENRY (B. 1984)
4. ANDREW, DUKE OF YORK (B. 1960)
5. PRINCESS BEATRICE (B. 1988)
6. PRINCESS EUGENIE (B. 1990)
7. EDWARD, EARL OF WESSEX (B. 1964)
8. ANNE, THE PRINCESS ROYAL (B. 1950)
9. PETER PHILLIPS (B. 1977)
10. ZARA PHILLIPS (B. 1981)
11. MARGARET, COUNTESS OF SNOWDON (B. 1930)
12. DAVID, VISCOUNT LINLEY (B. 1961)
13. LADY SARAH ARMSTRONG-JONES (B. 1964)
14. RICHARD, DUKE OF GLOUCESTER (B. 1944)
15. ALEXANDER, EARL OF ULSTER (B. 1974)
16. LADY DAVINA WINDSOR (B. 1980)
17. LADY ROSE WINDSOR (B. 1980)
18. EDWARD, DUKE OF KENT (B. 1935)
19. GEORGE, EARL OF ST ANDREWS (B. 1962)
20. LORD NICHOLAS WINDSOR (B. 1970)
21. LADY HELEN WINDSOR (B. 1964)
22. LORD FREDERICK WINDSOR (B. 1979)
23. LADY GABRIELLA WINDSOR (B. 1981)
24. PRINCESS ALEXANDRA (B. 1936)
25. JAMES OGILVIE (B. 1964)
26. MARINA OGILVIE (B. 1966)
27. GEORGE, EARL OF HAREWOOD (B. 1923)

What's in a Name?

FOUR MEMORABLE ROYAL CHRISTENINGS

Formerly, all royal babies were christened with a container of water taken from the Jordan River that had been in the family since the time of Queen Victoria (unfortunately, the supply has since run out). In recent years the ceremony has usually taken place in the music room at Buckingham Palace, where either the archbishop of Canterbury or the dean of Westminster presides, with the child wearing a frilly heirloom gown of Honiton lace.

1. ETHELRED II, "THE UNREADY" (C. 968–1016)
At his baptism the future king piddled in the font, thereby defiling the holy water. It was understandably taken to be a bad omen.

2. JAMES STUART, "THE OLD PRETENDER" (1688–1766)
It was the provocative christening of this son of James II into the Catholic faith that was largely responsible for sparking the Glorious Revolution, which led to the king's deposition and exile. Protestants in England were appalled by the event; indeed, many believed at the time that the baby wasn't royal at all, but had actually been smuggled into the palace in a warming pan in order to guarantee a Catholic succession. Circumstances weren't helped much either when Pope Innocent XI agreed to stand as godfather.

3. EDWARD VII (1841–1910)
The bill for Edward VII's christening came to £200,000.

4. DIANA, PRINCESS OF WALES (1961–97)
The princess's future husband Charles was one of the guests on hand for her christening in the early 1960s.

13 ROYALS WHO PREFERRED A MORE INFORMAL NAME

1. *FREDERICK, PRINCE OF WALES (1707–51)* ("Fretz")
2. *EDWARD VII (1841–1910)* ("Bertie")
3. *ALEXANDRA OF DENMARK (1844–1925)* ("Alix")
4. *ALBERT VICTOR, DUKE OF CLARENCE (1864–92)* ("Eddy")
5. *MARY OF TECK (1867–1955)* ("May")
6. *EDWARD VIII (1894–1972)* ("David")
7. *GEORGE VI (1895–1952)* ("Bertie")
8. *EARL LOUIS MOUNTBATTEN OF BURMA (1900–79)* ("Dickie")
9. *ELIZABETH II (1926–)* ("Lillibet")
10. *MARGARET, COUNTESS OF SNOWDON (1930–)* ("Margot")
11. *EDWARD, DUKE OF KENT (1935–)* ("Ted")
12. *PRINCE WILLIAM (1982–)* ("Wills")
13. *PRINCE HENRY (1984–)* ("Harry")

NINE ROYAL NICKNAMES BESTOWED BY COMMONERS

1. *"THE BLACK PRINCE"*

Edward, Prince of Wales (son of Edward III) was not called "the Black Prince" during his lifetime, though it is by this name that he is now universally known. The first recorded use of the term came two centuries after his death, and probably referred to his legendary foul temper rather than to his supposed wearing of black armour.

2. *"BLUFF KING HAL"*

Henry VIII's informal nickname, after syphilis and marital disappointments had turned him into an ogre.

3. *"OLD ROWLEY"*

A name bestowed upon Charles II by his court (after a well-known royal stud horse). He was also known as "the Merry Monarch," for much the same reason.

4. *"MRS MORLEY"*

The pet name given to Queen Anne by her lesbian lover Sarah Churchill; Anne's name for Sarah was "Mrs Freeman."

5. "FARMER GEORGE"

It is to George III, with his three experimental farms in Windsor Park, that we owe the concept of the British monarch as dignified country squire.

6. "PRINNY"

A widely used, semi-derogatory name for George IV. He was also known as the "First Gentleman of Europe."

7. "THE GRANDMOTHER OF EUROPE"

Thanks to the tireless P.R. efforts of her prime ministers Disraeli and Gladstone, by the 1870s Queen Victoria's image would be miraculously transformed from that of reclusive madwoman to serene, all-knowing empress. Certainly it is true that, through the marriages of her nine children, virtually every royal house in Europe would come to be related to her hemophilia-tainted blood.

8. "TUM TUM"

A term of affection for Edward VII by his friends, in honour of his over-fondness for good food and drink.

9. "BAT LUGS"

The name given to the future George VI while attending Dartmouth Naval College, in reference to his gigantic, "sticky-outy" ears. His similarly afflicted grandson Prince Charles, meanwhile, was often called "Jug Ears" by his classmates.

SIX NOTABLE ROYAL EPITHETS

1. ALFRED THE GREAT (C. 849–899)

Earned his unique title (though not until the sixteenth century) through his military skill, administrative reforms, and scholarship.

2. EDWARD THE MARTYR (C. 963–978)

In the case of this king the term "Martyr" was actually intended to mean "unpopular."

3. ETHELRED II, "THE UNREADY" (C. 968–1016)

Not as insulting as it sounds; the epithet is actually a play on the name "Ethelred," meaning "noble council," to which was added "un-red" ("without council"). The latter was subsequently mistranslated as "unready."

4. EDMUND II (C. 990–1016)
Known as Edmund Ironside owing to his considerable courage.

5. WILLIAM II, "RUFUS" (C. 1056–1100)
So-named because of his ruddy complexion.

6. RICHARD I (1157–99)
Popularly known as *Coeur de Lion* ("the Lionheart").

FOUR GEOGRAPHICAL FEATURES NAMED FOR QUEEN VICTORIA (AND HER RELATIVES)

1. AFRICAN LAKES
Lake Victoria — the source of the Nile — was discovered by the explorer John Hanning Speke in 1860 and named for Queen Victoria. Another large East African Lake (Lake Albert) was fittingly named in honour of Victoria's husband, the prince consort.

2. WATERFALLS
The spectacular Victoria Falls were discovered by African explorer David Livingstone in 1855. In Guyana, the King George waterfall is among the world's highest.

3. CANADIAN ISLANDS
The island province of Prince Edward Island, Canada, was originally named for Edward, Duke of Kent (the father of Queen Victoria). Other major Canadian islands named for royals include the Queen Charlotte's off the coast of British Columbia, and Victoria Island in the far north (the latter being the tenth largest in the world).

4. A DESERT
Named for Queen Victoria in southwestern Australia.

TWO MASCULINE TITLES BELONGING TO ELIZABETH II

"By the Grace of God, of the United Kingdom of Great Britain and Northern Ireland, and of Her other Realms and Territories, Queen, Head of the Commonwealth, Defender of the Faith."

1. LORD OF MAN
2. DUKE OF LANCASTER

FOUR MISCELLANEOUS THINGS NAMED FOR ROYALS

1. A POPULAR COCKTAIL
The "Bloody Mary" (named for Mary I) was first invented by a Parisian bartender in 1920.

2. A GENTLEMEN'S CLUB AND A BREED OF DOG
London's Wig Club was named for the singular item that served as its mascot of sorts — a wig made entirely out of pubic hair from Charles II's many mistresses.

3. A RUDE GESTURE
The classic "thumb-on-nose-with-fingers-fluttering-and-tongue-stuck-out" gesture was originally known as a Queen Anne's Fan.

4. A FLOWER
"Sweet Williams" were named for William "Butcher" Cumberland (son of George II) by the women of England, to commemorate his massacre of Jacobites at Culloden.

THE THREE CUNARD QUEENS

During the twentieth century the Cunard Shipping Line launched three famous luxury liners, each named for a different English queen.

1. THE QUEEN MARY
Launched in 1934. The first ship to exceed 75,000 metric tons, the *Queen Mary* actually derived her name through a misunderstanding. It

seems that Cunard had originally wanted to call her the *Queen Victoria*, but the chairman had dug himself into a hole by informing George V that the new ship was to be christened "after one of England's most noble queens." The king assumed that he was referring to his own wife, and *Queen Mary* it was. After a career of making regularly scheduled trips across the Atlantic, she was retired in 1967.

2. *The* QUEEN ELIZABETH

The sister ship of the *Queen Mary* and (until recently) the largest ocean liner ever built, the *Queen Elizabeth* was launched in 1938 and plied the seas for the next thirty years.

3. *The* QUEEN ELIZABETH 2

Launched in 1969. Smaller but more powerful than the original *Queen Elizabeth*, the QE2 was designed for round the world cruising.

SIX AMERICAN STATES NAMED FOR BRITISH ROYALS

1. *VIRGINIA (for the "Virgin Queen," Elizabeth I)*
2. *MARYLAND (for Henrietta Maria, wife of Charles I)*
3. *NORTH CAROLINA (for Charles I)*
4. *SOUTH CAROLINA (for Charles II)*
5. *NEW YORK (for James II, while still Duke of York)*
6. *GEORGIA (for George II)*

SIX MONARCHS WHO LENT THEIR NAME TO AN AGE

1. *HENRY VII (1457–1509)*

Hastened in the Tudor Age by his encouragement of the *nouveau riche* class.

2. *ELIZABETH I (1533–1603)*

The Elizabethan Age (roughly, 1560-1600) was a time of unprecedented artistic creativity, exploration and national peace. All of this, however, actually had very little to do with Elizabeth herself, a woman personally resistant to change. Yet there can be no question that "Good Queen Bess," as she was known to her subjects, was a much loved and admired monarch.

3. JAMES I (1566–1625)

The first 15 years of James I's rule — a time of important artistic and architectural developments — are remembered as the Jacobean Age ("Jacobean" being taken from the Latin form of the king's name).

4. GEORGE I (1660–1727)

The Georgian Age, which spanned the reigns of the four Hanoverian Georges, was characterised by classical influences in architecture and the arts.

5. VICTORIA (1819–1901)

Thanks in large measure to the inspired leadership of the prince consort and a succession of outstanding prime ministers, during the nineteenth century Britain rose to become the greatest power the world had ever known. A time of colonisation, industry and scientific discovery, this so-called Victorian Age was also marked by a firm belief in the merits of hard work and rigid morality.

6. EDWARD VII (1841–1910)

Although he reigned for a mere nine years, the king was the very personification of the elegant period in which he lived — a time that would come to be known as the Edwardian Age.

Edward VII, from a painting by Sir Arthur S. Cope.

*Sickness
and
Health*

SIX ROYALS WHO SUFFERED AT THE HANDS OF QUACKS

1. ELIZABETH I (1533–1603)

Almost died from smallpox in 1562. Doctor's attributed her eventual cure (and lack of blemishes) to their standard, sixteenth century treatment — wrapping the patient in a scarlet cloth and placing her before a fire.

2. HENRY, PRINCE OF WALES (1594–1612)

The popular son of James I died unexpectedly of typhoid fever at the age of 18. Evidently, the doctor's recommended course of treatment (having the bottoms of the prince's feet pecked by pigeons) failed to achieve the desired results.

3. CHARLES II (1630–85)

Though technically speaking the king died from a stroke, in actuality it was far more likely to have been as the result of his medical treatment. No less than a dozen doctors were involved in these misguided ministrations, which included massive bleedings, huge doses of emetics, and constant, 14-ingredient enemas. When these failed to have the desired effect the king's scalp was shaved and singed with burning irons, his nose was filled with sneezing powder and his body covered in hot plasters (which were then painfully torn off again). His feet were daubed with an emollient of resin and pigeon feces, he was forced to drink 40 drops of an extract made from a dead man's skull, and finally, with the patient sinking, holes were drilled into his skull in a last-ditch effort to "purge the toxins from his body." To his credit Charles kept his famous sense of humour throughout, even going so far as to apologise to his courtiers for taking so long to die.

4. George III (1738–1820)

The king's first attack of "madness" in 1788 was characterised by violent stomach aches, rambling speech and foaming of the mouth. Unsure how to treat him, his court physicians eventually decided to call in an "expert" in mental illness, the Rev. Francis Willis, who ran a private lunatic asylum in Lincolnshire as a sideline. The reverend arrived at Windsor Castle armed with his cutting-edge psychiatric equipment — a straitjacket, iron clamps, a chair and some rope — and proceeded to brutalise his patient into a state of manageable docility, if not actual recovery. For his effects in effecting this so-called cure Willis and his son were granted a lifetime pension.

5. Elizabeth II (1926–)

Has long relied on homeopathic doctors to treat her chronic sinusitis. Among the more unusual remedies that they've prescribed are diluted arsenic (to prevent sneezing) and pills containing deadly night-shade (for sore throat).

Princess Diana (a month before her death).

6. Diana, Princess of Wales (1961–97)

According to no less an expert than pioneering heart transplant surgeon the late Dr. Christiaan Barnard, the princess would most likely have survived her 1997 car accident had she been taken to a hospital immediately. Emergency workers instead spent over an hour in a misguided attempt to stabilise her on the scene, resulting in her eventual death from internal bleeding.

EIGHT ROYALS WHO HAD SYPHILIS

In former centuries syphilis was the most feared of all venereal diseases, lying dormant in the victim's system for decades before ultimately destroying them both physically and mentally.

1. Henry VIII (1491–1547)
2. Edward VI (1537–53)
3. Mary I (1516–58)
4. Elizabeth I (1533–1603)
5. James II (1633–1701)
6. George of Denmark (1653–1708)

7. *GEORGE I (1660–1727)*
8. *ALBERT VICTOR, DUKE OF CLARENCE (1864–92)*

THREE ROYALS WHO HAD GONORRHOEA

This dread disease was formerly known as the "Preventer of Life," owing to the fact that it frequently left its victims sterile.

1. *EDWARD III (1312–77)*
Infected by his mistress, Alice Perrers, the disease would ultimately contribute to his death at age 65.

2. *GEORGE I (1660–1727)*
Some historians have suggested that the real reason George was so vindictive towards his ex-wife, Sophia Dorothea of Celle, was that it was she who gave him this disease.

3. *WILLIAM IV (1765–1837)*
A frequent sufferer.

11 ROYALS WHO HAD MISCARRIAGES OR STILLBIRTHS

1. *KATHERINE OF ARAGON (1485–1536)*
2. *ANNE BOLEYN (C. 1500–36)*
3. *ANNE OF DENMARK (1574–1619)*
4. *KATHERINE HENRIETTA OF BRAGANZA (1638–1705)*
5. *MARY OF MODENA (1658–1718)*
6. *MARY II (1662–94)*
7. *ANNE (1665–1714)*
8. *CAROLINE OF BRANDENBURG-ANSBACH (1683–1737)*
9. *CHARLOTTE OF MECKLENBURG-STRELITZ (1744–1818)*
10. *PRINCESS CHARLOTTE (1796–1817)*
11. *ADELAIDE OF SAXE-MEININGEN (1792–1849)*

THREE ROYALS WHO MAY HAVE HAD PORPHRYIA

Porphyria is a rare and as yet incurable hereditary disease that affects the central nervous system. It is characterized by myriad unpleasant symptoms, including hallucinations, severe abdominal pain, dizziness, swelling of the glands, and bluish urine.

1. ANNE (1665–1714)

Porphyry or syphilis would seem to be the two most likely root causes of the queen's unending health problems.

2. GEORGE III (1738–1820)

During the late twentieth century it was fashionable among medical historians to ascribe George's periods of mental illness to this disease. More recent investigation, however, has cast serious doubts upon the diagnosis, though to date no one has yet come forward with a convincing alternative. The official royal family line, incidentally, is that the king suffered from lead poisoning.

3. MARGARET, COUNTESS OF SNOWDON (1930–)

It has been suggested by some authors that the real reason for Princess Margaret's lifelong migraine headaches (and, in more recent years, her minor strokes) is actually hereditary porphyria.

FOUR ROYALS WHO WERE TOTALLY (OR PARTIALLY) DEAF

1. EDWARD VI (1547–53)

Among his many physical shortcomings, the boy king was said to have been rather deaf.

2. ALEXANDRA OF DENMARK (1844–1925)

The long-suffering Danish wife of Edward VII had a hearing problem that grew steadily worse with age. Many people, unaware of the condition, came away after meeting her in the belief that she was stupid, her deafness having made it difficult for her to follow conversations.

3. ALBERT VICTOR, DUKE OF CLARENCE (1864–92)

Like his mother Queen Alexandra the prince could only hear at one particular pitch — a fact that, incredibly, wasn't recognised until he was an adult. Unfortunately for the troubled prince, hearing loss would prove to be among the least of his problems, mental or physical.

4. PRINCESS ALICE OF BATTENBERG (1885–1969)

Stone deaf from birth, Prince Philip's mother ultimately became quite adept at lip-reading.

THREE FLATULENT MONARCHS

1. GEORGE II (1683–1760)

According to his German *valet de chamber*, the king was "a loud and garrulous farter." He would ultimately die of a stroke while straining on his toilet.

2. GEORGE IV (1762–1830)

Often depicted passing wind by the bawdy cartoonists of the day.

3. VICTORIA (1819–1901)

The queen always ate too quickly and often mixed malt whisky with claret, resulting in persistent flatulence.

NINE ROYALS WHO SUFFERED FROM GOUT

1. HENRY VII (1457–1509)
2. HENRY VIII (1491–1547)
3. CHARLES II (1630–85)
4. ANNE (1665–1714)
5. GEORGE I (1660–1727)
6. GEORGE II (1683–1760)
7. GEORGE III (1738–1820)
8. GEORGE IV (1762–1830)
9. VICTORIA (1819–1901)

SIX ROYALS WHO HAD RHEUMATISM OR ARTHRITIS

1. ANNE (1665–1714)

By the time she was in her mid-thirties the fat queen was so debilitated by rheumatism that she was only able to walk short distances with the aid of a stick.

2. CAROLINE OF BRANDENBURG-ANSBACH (1683–1737)
Used to treat her rheumatic legs by dipping them in freezing mud.

3. GEORGE IV (1762–1830)
Severely crippled in his later years by rheumatism, gout and dropsy.

4. VICTORIA (1819–1901)
First developed rheumatism after falling down some stairs at Windsor in 1883. The condition gradually worsened, and by the final decade of her life the queen was confined to a wheelchair.

5. EDWARD VII (1841–1910)
Customarily shook hands with his elbow kept stiffly in at his side, owing to painful rheumatism in his arm. The practice was later widely emulated.

6. ALEXANDRA OF DENMARK (1844–1925)
Left with a pronounced limp as a result of rheumatic fever. Amazingly, it afterwards became fashionable among upper-class women to imitate the queen's hobbled walk.

TEN ROYALS INVOLVED IN ACCIDENTS

1. EDWARD I (1239–1307)
Fell from his horse the night before the Battle of Falkirk in 1298, resulting in two broken ribs. He chose to hide his painful injury and was able to lead his men to victory over the forces of William Wallace.

2. ANNE OF DENMARK (1574–1619)
Wife of James I. In 1615 gases from the queen's mineral bath momentarily ignited, causing much consternation but no injury.

3. GEORGE IV (1762–1830)
Once sprained his ankle badly while teaching his daughter to dance the "highland fling."

4. VICTORIA (1819–1901)
In 1863, a drunken coachman later described as "utterly confused and bewildered" managed to overturn the queen's carriage. She sus-

tained a black eye and a broken thumb.

5. MARY OF TECK (1867–1955)

In May 1939 the queen's Daimler crashed into a heavy lorry, causing the car to overturn in a ditch. Miraculously, she was able to emerge from the wreckage with nothing more than a broken umbrella.

6. EDWARD VIII (1894–1972)

During a tour of western Australia in 1920, the train that the prince had been riding in was derailed on some washed-out track. He managed to escape from the carriage completely unhurt.

7. ELIZABETH, THE QUEEN MOTHER (1900–)

Had to undergo emergency surgery in 1982 to remove a fish-bone that had become lodged in her throat.

8. PHILIP, DUKE OF EDINBURGH (1921–)

In 1957 the prince broadsided another car while on the way home from delivering a luncheon speech on road safety.

9. CHARLES, PRINCE OF WALES (1948–)

In March 1988, while skiing at the alpine resort of Klosters in Switzerland, the prince and several of his companions were caught in a sudden avalanche that had been set off when they entered a restricted area. Though Charles had managed to get out of the way in time, his close friend Major Hugh Lindsay was buried alive and another was seriously injured.

10. PRINCE WILLIAM (1982–)

In 1991 the prince was accidentally hit in the head with a golf club wielded by a school friend, resulting in a slightly fractured skull.

FOUR ROYALS WHO SUFFERED FROM HEMORRHOIDS

1. *GEORGE II (1683–1760)*
2. *VICTORIA (1819–1901)*
3. *EDWARD VII (1841–1910)*
4. *EDWARD VIII (1894–1972)*

Madness
and
Eccentricity

REX NOSTER INSANIT: FIVE MAD BRITISH KINGS

> "History seems to show that hereditary royal families gather from the repeated influence of their corrupting situation some dark taint in the blood."
>
> Walter Bagehot, 1867

1. JOHN (1166–1216)
A deeply disturbed, perhaps even psychotic individual, King John was said to have been "sent mad by sorcery and witchcraft." When in a rage (as he frequently was) he would bite and gnaw things or set fire to houses in which he had been entertained.

2. RICHARD II (1367–1400)
Showed definite signs of mental instability consistent with schizophrenia.

3. HENRY VI (1421–71)
In August 1453 the king suffered a complete mental breakdown, during which he remained in a catatonic state and was quite unable to recognise even his closest associates. Seventeen months later he recovered just as suddenly as he had become stricken, though he was to succumb to a second, briefer attack shortly thereafter.

4. HENRY VIII (1491–1547)
The victim of a severe and progressive personality disorder, the result of brain damage brought on either from a head injury or from the latter stage of syphilis.

5. George III (1738–1820)

The best-known "mad" British monarch. Today, historians are still debating the precise cause of George III's mental illness, which in any event seems to have been confined to around four relatively brief (if admittedly intense) periods during his sixty-year reign, each characterised by fits of uncontrollable violence. The king first showed signs of this instability in 1788–89, then again in 1801 and 1804, though by 1810 he was quite irretrievably insane.

TWO SHY ROYALS

1. George VI (1895–1952)

The king was so neurotically shy as a child that, on one occasion, he sat in a darkened room rather than ask a servant to light the gas.

2. Diana, Princess of Wales (1961–97)

Originally dubbed "Shy Di" by the press for her habit of dropping her head while being photographed. One of the main reasons (apart from her alleged virginity) that Diana was chosen by the Queen Mother as a suitable match for Prince Charles was the belief that she would be easily intimidated and controlled. In actual fact she proved to be far tougher than she looked, and would easily hold her own during her later public relations battles with the "Royal Firm."

FOUR EXAMPLES OF QUEEN VICTORIA'S MORBID OBSESSION WITH DEATH

1. Dead Flowers

The queen collected dead flowers from royal gravesites (in fairness it should be noted that this was not an uncommon hobby during the nineteenth century).

2. Death-bed Photos

Victoria had a disturbing habit of requesting photographs and sketches of friends and acquaintances on their deathbeds. She also kept a photo or portrait of her dead husband Albert in every room in every one of her houses.

3. PRINCE ALBERT'S BEDROOM

During the almost forty years of her widowhood Victoria decreed that her husband's suite at Windsor be kept precisely as he had left it at the time of his death. Each morning, hot water for shaving was dutifully brought in by the servants, his empty chamber pot was scoured, fresh towels and bed linen were laid out, and clean pyjamas were placed upon the bed.

4. BURIAL OBJECTS

Among the many unusual items that Victoria insisted be placed in her coffin after her death was one of her husband's dressing gowns, along with a plaster cast of his hand.

FIVE ROYALS WHO WENT SENILE

1. EDWARD III (1312–77)

Became prematurely senile, with affairs of state consequently devolving upon his son the Black Prince.

2. HENRY VIII (1491–1547)

Towards the end of his life the king became ever more absent-minded, frequently issuing conflicting rulings on succeeding days.

3. GEORGE III (1738–1820)

As if his madness wasn't enough to contend with, in his later years the king would become increasingly senile as well as deaf and blind. Largely abandoned by his wife and family into the care of servants, he spent the last decade of his life alone in his apartments on the north side of Windsor Castle, a sad, Lear-like figure with a long white beard. There, his days would be spent alternately raving to himself (or to his long-dead friends) and pounding away tunelessly on his harpsichord.

4. ALEXANDRA OF DENMARK (1844–1925)

In her old age the queen took to giving away priceless family heirlooms, which would then have to be surreptitiously retrieved by a courtier.

5. WALLIS, DUCHESS OF WINDSOR (C. 1896–1986)

Despite warnings about the possible risks associated with surgery owing to her advanced age, when she was in her seventies the duchess insisted on going ahead with one last facelift. Unfortunately, during the procedure there was indeed some difficulty with the anesthesia and the oxygen to her brain was temporarily cut off, resulting in massive brain damage. She spent the remaining years of her life completely bedridden.

EIGHT ROYALS WHO SUFFERED FROM DEPRESSION

1. MARY I (1516–58)
More or less permanently depressed.

2. ANNE (1665–1714)
Worn out by ill-health and gynecological problems, Anne was subject to powerful fits of "melancholia."

3. GEORGE III (1738–1820)
On two separate occasions as a young man the king became so depressed that he considered abdicating.

4. CHARLOTTE OF MECKLENBURG-STRELITZ (1744–1818)
Suffered terribly from post-natal depression (a particularly devastating affliction in light of her fifteen pregnancies).

5. VICTORIA (1819–1901)
Devastated by the death of her beloved husband Albert, for the remainder of her life the queen never again attended any social gatherings and is said to have slept each night with his bedclothes in her arms. Indeed, her behaviour during her widowhood was so odd that many became convinced that she was suffering from a much more serious, manic-depressive disorder.

6. GEORGE VI (1895–1952)
In his later years the king was prone to fits of depression.

7. MARGARET, COUNTESS OF SNOWDON (1930–)
Fell into a deep depression in 1999 after badly scalding her feet in very hot bathwater. The incident had left her in almost continuous pain.

8. DIANA, PRINCESS OF WALES (1961–97)
Despondent over her failing marriage, during the 1980's Princess Diana made numerous half-hearted attempts at ending her life. Her first

"cry for help" occurred while she was still pregnant with Prince William, when she threw herself down a flight of stairs at Sandringham. Her only injuries, however, were some severe bruising around the stomach, and the fetus was fortunately unharmed. The princess was subsequently known to have slashed her wrists at least twice, the first time with a razor and the second with the serrated edge of a lemon slicer. On another occasion, during a particularly heated argument with her husband, she grabbed a penknife and began cutting herself in the chest and thighs.

FIVE ROYALS WHO SUFFERED FROM PHOBIAS

1. Elizabeth I (1533–1603)
Suffered from anthophobia (the fear of roses).

2. James I (1566–1625)
The king had such a fear of being stabbed that he made a point of wearing heavily padded clothing for protection, which unfortunately made him waddle like a duck.

3. Elizabeth II (1926–)
Like her predecessors Edward VII and Edward VIII, Elizabeth is said to suffer from triskaidekaphobia (fear of the number 13).

4. Margaret, Countess of Snowdon (1930–)
Has had a lifelong fear of the dark.

5. Diana, Princess of Wales (1961–97)
When she was ten years old, the future Princess of Wales fell off her horse and broke her arm. She later confessed that the incident had caused her to lose her riding nerve, which she was only able to regain years later thanks to the efforts of riding instructor Captain James Hewitt, with whom she had an affair.

SEVEN ROYALS WHO WERE ABUSED AS CHILDREN

"You English are none of you well bred because you were not whipped when young!!"

George II

1. MARY I (1516–58)

Mary's governess was once instructed by Anne Boleyn to beat the girl from time to time, "for the cursed bastard she is."

2. ELIZABETH I (1533–1603)

Sexually abused as a young teenager by her guardian Thomas Seymour (the brother of Henry VIII's third wife Jane Seymour, and husband of his sixth wife Katherine Parr). Some believe that she even became pregnant by him, but later miscarried.

3. FREDERICK, PRINCE OF WALES (1707–51)

Nourished largely on goat's milk by his mother (who incidentally despised him), in a bizarre effort to curb his sexual precocity.

4. GEORGE IV (1762–1820)

Treated as an errant child for most of his life by his father, George was actually kept in the royal nursery (and made to wear outsized baby clothes) until he was almost a teenager.

5. VICTORIA (1819–1901)

Hoping to make the future queen weak and subservient so that he could become the real power behind the throne, Sir John Conroy, the comptroller of her mother's household mercilessly browbeat Victoria. Under his so-called "Kensington system" she was isolated from others and made utterly dependant upon him, never being allowed, for instance, to hold a conversation unless he was present or to climb the stairs without holding someone's hand. She was also forced to endure gruelling tours of the British Isles in an attempt to make her more popular, which often left her exhausted or ill.

6. EDWARD VIII (1894–1972)

All but abandoned by his parents George V and Queen Mary, the future king was left in the care of a psychotic nanny who physically abused him and did her best to turn the boy against his parents. The abuse went on for three years, and left the future king an emotional cripple. George V once reportedly summed up his approach to child-rearing to a friend: "My father was frightened of his mother, I was frightened of my father, and I am damned well going to see to it that my children are frightened of me."

George V with three of his children (including the future kings George VI and Edward VIII).

7. GEORGE VI (1895–1952)

Largely raised, like his older brother, by a harsh, mentally unstable nanny who frequently beat him with a rod (when she wasn't ignoring him altogether). This, combined with his tutor's punitive attempts to "cure" the boy of his left-handedness, ultimately left him with a torturous stammer and nervous stomach that plagued him throughout his life.

ECCENTRICITIES OF 22 ROYALS

1. HENRY II (1133–89)

The king was so hyperactive that he could barely sit still long enough to eat (and in fact often ate while standing up).

2. MARY I (1516–58)

The ageing queen was so desperate to produce a Catholic heir that, in 1554 and again four years later, she talked herself into phantom pregnancies.

3. CHARLES II (1630–85)

Known to gather up powder from the mummies of Egyptian pharaohs and rub it on himself, in the belief that he would acquire "ancient greatness."

4. GEORGE I (1660–1727)

Insisted on personally giving his son's fiancée a physical examination before consenting to the match, in order to confirm that she was a virgin.

5. GEORGE II (1683–1760)

Exploded in a rage at the sight of anyone reading a book.

6. GEORGE III (1738–1820)

Despite having had the second longest reign in British history, George never once left England and indeed never went any further from London than Worcester.

7. GEORGE IV (1762–1830)

The king often insisted to those around him that he had fought at the Battle of Waterloo, in spite of the well-known fact that he had actually spent the entire war against Napoleon at home in England. Another of his favourite fantasies involved the time he supposedly helped the Germans win the Battle of Salamanca in 1812, by leading a charge of dragoons while disguised as General Bock. When he once asked the Duke of Wellington to corroborate his story for the benefit of some guests, the latter replied, diplomatically: "I have often heard Your Majesty say so."

8. CAROLINE OF BRUNSWICK-WOLFENBÜTTEL (1768–1821)

Though not normally known for her personal hygiene, in later years Caroline had an open-air bath installed in the middle of her garden.

9. WILLIAM IV (1765–1837)

Had the unnerving habit of nodding off during conversations.

10. ALBERT, PRINCE CONSORT (1819–61)

As an adult, the prince customarily slept in baby-type sleeper pyjamas that entirely covered his feet.

11. EDWARD VII (1841–1910)

Established the custom of keeping all the clocks at Sandringham set half an hour fast, ostensibly to allow his guests more time for shooting. In 1936, when his son George V lay dying there, mistakes were made as to the precise timing of his death owing to the discrepancy between real time and "Sandringham time." The new king, Edward VIII, was so enraged at this that, in his first official act, he ordered the clocks to be set back at once. Among Edward's other, more interesting eccentricities was his lifelong habit of weighing everyone who visited his country estate. He also refused to allow anyone in his presence to carry loose change, because the slightest jingling of coins unnerved him.

12. GEORGE V (1865–1936)

The king always went to bed at precisely 11:10 p.m.

13. MARY OF TECK (1867–1953)

A kleptomaniac. Mary was an obsessive collector of royalty-related knick-knacks, and whenever she saw an object that she didn't already have she would immediately attempt to talk the owners into freely handing it over. If this tactic failed to achieve results, however, she would simply pocket the item as soon as no one was looking. When her victims (among them a few antique stores) began to complain to the palace her ladies-in-waiting were subsequently instructed to keep an eye on her, and to quietly return any stolen goods with a covering letter apologising for the "mistake."

14. EDWARD VIII (1894–1972)

A dog lover, Edward had special steps built beside his bed so that his rheumatic cairn terrier could get on to it easier. He would also frequently dress his pugs in little wing collars and bow ties.

15. GEORGE VI (1895–1952)

The king's favourite pastime was to watch home movies run backwards.

16. WALLIS, DUCHESS OF WINDSOR (C. 1896–1986)

After the death of her husband, the duchess reportedly took to sleeping with a loaded pistol at her bedside.

17. HENRY, DUKE OF GLOUCESTER (1900–74)

One of the mentally deficient younger sons of George V, Henry alternated between spontaneous fits of giggling and crying and spent much of his life watching cartoons on television.

18. Elizabeth, The Queen Mother (1900–)
Keeps a pair of stone angels astride her bed at Clarence House, each clad in a frilly white dress that must be regularly laundered and ironed.

19. Philip, Duke of Edinburgh (1921–)
Not all that enthusiastic about horse racing, the prince consort has been known to visit Ascot with a portable radio hidden in his top hat — in order to listen to the cricket coverage.

20. Margaret, Countess of Snowdon (1930–)
As a child the princess developed an intense dislike of Lewis Carroll's *Alice in Wonderland*, and to this day finds the work highly disturbing.

21. Diana, Princess of Wales (1961–97)
Allegedly inundated a married former lover, over an 18-month period in the early 1990s, with anonymous crank phone calls.

22. Charles, Prince of Wales (1948–)
Often dismissed as a moralizing crank who talks to plants.

SEVEN MONARCHS WHO KEPT EXOTIC ANIMALS

1. Henry I (1068–1135)
Kept such unusual creatures as lions, leopards and camels in the walled grounds of Woodstock Palace.

2. Richard I, "The Lionheart" (1157–99)
The king brought a crocodile home with him from the crusades, which unfortunately slipped into the Thames and was never to be seen again.

3. Henry III (1207–72)
After receiving an elephant as a gift from Louis IX of France, Henry had a special house built for it at the Tower of London.

4. James I (1566–1625)
Enjoyed baiting the bears that lived in the royal menagerie.

5. CHARLES II (1630–85)

Owned a tame fox, which frequently frightened his wife by jumping up onto her bed. He also build an aviary in St James's Park.

6. GEORGE IV (1762–1830)

Kept his own private zoo near Royal Lodge in Windsor Great Park, which included such curiosities as a giraffe given to him by the Pasha of Egypt.

7. ELIZABETH II (1926–)

The flamingoes that live in the pond behind Buckingham Palace are the personal property of the queen.

Fashion

EIGHT REMARKABLY UGLY ROYALS

"You can get used to anyone's face in a week."
Charles II

1. ANNE OF CLEVES (1515–57)
Pasty, bony, and scarred by smallpox.

2. MARY I (1516–58)
Aside from her sheer repulsiveness, the queen's husband was often heard to complain of the horrid stench that emanated from her nose.

3. CHARLOTTE OF MECKLENBURG-STRELITZ (1744–1818)
George III's wife was so unattractive that, on first arriving in England to take her throne, Londoners greeted her with cries of "pug-face" (when the queen asked for a translation, she was told that it meant, "God bless Your Royal Highness"). Years later, after having been involved in a carriage accident, the resulting broken nose that she sustained was said to have greatly improved her appearance.

4. CAROLINE OF BRUNSWICK-WOLFENBÜTTEL (1768–1821)
Much has been made of the plainness of George IV's wife, which in many ways was a typical Hanoverian trait brought about by excessive inbreeding.

5. ADELAIDE OF SAXE-MEININGEN (1792–1849)
The tiny, German-born wife of William IV was once described by a contemporary as "frightful...very ugly with a horrid complexion" (the latter evidently having been caused by scurvy).

6. EDWARD VII (1841–1910)

An unattractive man who nevertheless had little trouble getting women. Edward's mother, Queen Victoria, perhaps summed up his appearance best in one of her diary entries: "Handsome I cannot think him, with that painfully small and narrow head, those immense features and total want of chin."

7. WALLIS, DUCHESS OF WINDSOR (C. 1896–1986)

The royal photographer, Cecil Beaton, famously described the duchess as "attractively ugly, *une belle laide*." It is perhaps worth noting that, although the latter was always stated to have been two years younger than her husband, common sense would seem to suggest that the opposite is true.

8. ANNE, THE PRINCESS ROYAL (1950–)

Though not exactly homely, Anne nevertheless remains the archetypal horse-faced royal.

SEVEN FAT ROYALS

1. WILLIAM I, "THE CONQUEROR" (C. 1027–87)

Enormously fat, particularly as he grew older.

2. HENRY VIII (1491–1547)

In later life the king became grotesquely obese, having put on over forty centimetres to his waist in one five-year period alone. This (combined with a badly ulcerated leg that refused to heal) made it necessary for him to be hauled about in a specially padded sedan chair and, on occasion, by means of pulleys.

3. ANNE (1665–1714)

The queen was short and so fat that she actually had to be carried through her coronation ceremony in a chair. She was ultimately buried in a square coffin.

4. GEORGE IV (1762–1830)

By the time he reached middle age the king had become so corpulent that, in order to squeeze himself into the splendid clothing he favoured, it was necessary for him to wear a series of corsets and stays.

Journalist William Cobbett once speculated that George weighed "perhaps a quarter of a ton."

5. VICTORIA (1819–1901)

Although thin and reasonably attractive as a teenager (with the exception of her large, puffy face, weak chin and bulbous eyes), by the time Victoria was in her twenties she had already begun to balloon up considerably.

6. EDWARD VII (1841–1910)

Customarily ate five large meals per day, with dinner usually being an exhausting, ten-course or more affair. Weighing in excess of 135 kilograms, the king had an iron constitution when it came to rich or unusual foods and could easily down dozens of oysters in a matter of minutes.

7. SARAH, DUCHESS OF YORK (1959–)

Although her weight has been more or less under control in recent years, in the late 1980s Fergie was widely referred to in the press as "The Duchess of Pork." She has since become a highly paid television spokesperson for "Weight Watchers," with whom she wrote the book *Dieting With the Duchess* in 1998.

THREE ROYAL ANOREXICS AND BULEMICS

1. EDWARD IV (1442–83)

A big eater, Edward was known to take an emetic after large meals so that he might have the pleasure of gorging himself all over again.

2. ANNE BOLEYN (C. 1500–36)

Had a habit of purposely vomiting during meals. Not wishing to offend the other guests at public dinners, however, the queen would always be sure to bring along a special noblewoman, whose job it was to hold aloft a sheet for privacy whenever the urge to throw up came upon her.

3. DIANA, PRINCESS OF WALES (1961–97)

Suffered from bulimia throughout much of the 1980s, during which time her weight occasionally dropped to life-threatening levels. The princess's preferred "binge food" was said to have been massive amounts of frosted flakes and heavy cream, after which she would forcibly regurgitate the sticky mass. Diana would later make a point of publicly discussing her battle with the illness at every opportunity, much to the consternation of the royal family.

TEN ROYAL FASHION VICTIMS

1. ELIZABETH I (1533–1603)
The queen's breasts were always heavily powdered with ceruse (a potentially deadly lead-based whitener) and her veins carefully highlighted with blue dye in order to achieve a more consumptive, translucent look. She was said to own over 2,000 dresses.

2. GEORGE IV (1762–1830)
Unhappy with his too-ruddy complexion, the king often had himself bled to a more suitable shade for important engagements. He also spent vast amounts of money on cosmetics and perfumes, and routinely coloured his greying hair with vegetable dye.

3. VICTORIA (1819–1901)
Wore nothing but basic black during the forty years of her widowhood (the only exception to this rule was an inexplicable fondness for wearing aprons and white bonnets).

4. GEORGE V (1865–1936)
As a 16-year-old naval cadet, the future king had a Tokyo practitioner tattoo a large blue and red dragon on his right arm.

5. MARY OF TECK (1867–1953)
To augment the queen's arrested, Victorian-retro style she characteristically wore vast amounts of gaudy jewellery, which often included as many as half a dozen heavy diamond necklaces at once.

6. GEORGE VI (1895–1952)
In later life the king often applied tan makeup for official occasions to hide his pale complexion. He was also a consummate clotheshorse.

7. PRINCE MICHAEL OF KENT (1942–)
Bears a striking physical resemblance to his grandfather George V.

It is for this reason alone that, uniquely among the modern royals, he has been allowed by the present queen to sport a beard.

8. ELIZABETH II (1926–)

Has often been criticised for her frumpy clothing and unflattering head scarves (not to mention the fact that she has never once changed her hairstyle, ever). Indeed, one of the few occasions when she did actually cut loose with her wardrobe was, unfortunately, on the day she learned of her accession, when she happened to be wearing russet-coloured bush slacks with a canary yellow shirt and cardigan.

9. SARAH, DUCHESS OF YORK (1959–)

For her wedding to Prince Andrew in 1986 (which was reported to have had a worldwide audience of 800 million), Sarah wore a ghastly puff-shouldered satin gown with a five-metre-long train, the latter gaudily beaded with her family's coat of arms.

10. DIANA, PRINCESS OF WALES (1961–97)

The ultra-glamorous princess went to exhaustive lengths to maintain her famous beauty, including streaking her normally dark-brown hair blond, dyeing her eyelashes, wearing coloured contact lenses, and (reportedly) undergoing a nose-job and breast-implantation procedure.

FIVE ROYAL FASHION TIPS

1. VICTORIA (1819–1901)

"Rings on each finger improve an ugly hand." (*The queen wore them on her thumbs as well*).

2. WALLIS, DUCHESS OF WINDSOR (C. 1896–1986)

"A woman can never be too rich, or too thin." (*Ironically, the precise cause of the duchess's death was malnutrition*)

3. CHARLES, PRINCE OF WALES (1948–)

"I don't believe in fashion, full stop." (*In the wake of this remark, several leading Savile Row shops sent the prince angry letters of protest*)

4. ANNE, THE PRINCESS ROYAL (1950–)

"A good suit goes on forever." (*The princess, incidentally, has often been criticised for her matronly style of dress*)

5. DIANA, PRINCESS OF WALES (1961–97)

(*To a young punk rocker*) "You should wear what you like."

14 ROYAL FASHION INNOVATORS

1. EDWARD II (1284–1327)

The first king to wear buttons on his garments (specifically, on his boots).

2. RICHARD II (1367–1400)

Although originally invented by the Romans, the handkerchief is said to have been first popularised by Richard II.

3. HENRY VIII (1491–1547)

Started a trend for wearing hand-knitted stockings.

4. ELIZABETH I (1533–1603)

Popularised among the nobility the wearing of whalebone corsets and neck ruffs stiffened with starch; commoners were expressly forbidden by royal decree, incidentally, to wear the latter. The queen was also known to affect a large black (fake) spider on her shawl.

5. CHARLES II (1630–85)

Started a fashion among gentlemen for wearing full-length wigs.

6. GEORGE III (1738–1820)

Designed the so-called Windsor family uniform, consisting of a dark blue tail-coat with red collar and cuffs and white breeches. His equally conservative distant successor George V insisted on wearing the outfit at every meal.

7. GEORGE IV (1762–1830)

Always a flamboyant dresser, one of the king's favourite outfits included a black coat with pink spangles and shoes with high scarlet heels.

8. VICTORIA (1819–1901)

Well aware of her power to influence fashion, in 1840 the queen wore Honiton lace for her wedding veil in the hopes of encouraging the waning Devon lace industry (she would later be buried wearing it). Victoria was also the first to dress her children in sailor's suits, thereby launching a trend among the upper classes that would continue well into the twentieth century.

9. EDWARD VII (1841–1910)

The most influential fashion trendsetter of his day, introducing as he did to Britain the dinner jacket (to replace tails on informal occasions), double-breasted suits, the homburg hat and knickerbockers. It is to him as well that we owe the sideways trouser crease, along with the ongoing tradition of leaving the bottom button of a waistcoat undone.

*Edward VIII,
as Prince of Wales.*

10. EDWARD VIII (1894–1972)

Popularised "plus fours" (baggy golf pants) and loud tweeds while still a student at Oxford, along with Fair Isle sweaters, suede shoes, and the revolutionary Windsor knot for ties. He would also introduce the bowler hat to America and bring about the convention of wearing a grey top hat instead of the traditional black silk one.

11. EARL LOUIS MOUNTBATTEN OF BURMA (1900–79)

Believed to have been the first man to wear trousers with a zipper.

12. ELIZABETH, THE QUEEN MOTHER (1900–)

Rarely seen without her strands of pearls, even when fishing.

13. SARAH, DUCHESS OF YORK (1959–)

The duchess's onetime penchant for wearing a large, flat bow in her hair led to an inexplicable proliferation of "Fergie bows" in the 1980's.

14. DIANA, PRINCESS OF WALES (1961–97)

Hands-down the most photographed woman in history, during the 1980s and '90s the strikingly beautiful Princess of Wales served as an unofficial fashion ambassador for Britain. Among the more tangible fashion trends that she personally initiated was the piecrust dress collar and a shortened hairstyle (the latter soon copied by millions of women around the world).

SIX ROYALS WHO EMPLOYED COSMETIC AIDS

1. ELIZABETH I (1533–1603)

Constantly ate sugared candies to mask her bad breath, and when she finally lost all her teeth as a consequence took to stuffing wads of cotton beside her gums to fill out her face. In later life, after her hair had thinned, the queen took to wearing an enormous, spangled red wig.

2. GEORGE IV (1762–1830)

Wore high neck cloths to disguise the swollen glands in his throat.

3. ALEXANDRA OF DENMARK (1844–1925)

Customarily wore high collars or several rows of pearls in order to conceal a scar on her neck.

4. MARY OF TECK (1867–1955)

Wore a small hairpiece on her forehead.

5. GEORGE VI (1895–1952)

Forced to wear iron braces on his legs at night as a boy, in an effort to correct his knock-knees.

6. ELIZABETH, THE QUEEN MOTHER (1900–)

Known for wearing clouds of "sweet pea" coloured chiffons (with matching hats and feather boas), to disguise both her stout figure as well as her colostomy bag.

TWO FASHION-RELATED ROYAL AUCTIONS

1. THE DUCHESS OF WINDSOR'S JEWELLERY AUCTION

In April 1987 Sotheby's held an auction of jewellery that had formerly belonged to the late Duchess of Windsor. Afterwards called "The Sale of the Century," for several weeks prior to the auction the collection of mainly tacky yet no less valuable relics were on public display in London and New York, with interest steadily building among rich celebrities throughout the world. The actual event was an enormous success, bringing in some £31 million for charity.

2. PRINCESS DIANA'S CLOTHING AUCTION

At the suggestion of her son Prince William, shortly before her death Diana agreed to sell off many of her old gowns for charity. The resulting auction took place at Christie's in June 1997, and raised millions for charity.

FOUR KILT-RELATED FASHION *FAUX PAS*

Whenever a member of the royal family makes a public appearance in Scotland they generally wear a kilt, either in their own Balmoral tartan (designed by Prince Albert in black, red and lavender on a grey background) or in the more formal Royal Stuart. Despite the fact that the garments are specially weighted to help keep things in place, embarrassing mishaps have occurred over the years.

1. GEORGE IV (1762–1830)

During the king's official visit to Scotland in 1822 he was unwisely advised to wear a kilt around his ample waist, in addition to a pair of flesh-coloured tights for modesty's sake.

2. GEORGE VI (1895–1952)

Owned a tartan dinner jacket, which he occasionally combined with a kilt.

3. PHILIP, DUKE OF EDINBURGH (1921–)

Although he generally wears his kilt proudly, on one occasion as a young man Philip was forced to curtsey to his father-in-law George VI (rather than bow) because the one he was wearing was too short.

4. ANDREW, DUKE OF YORK (1960–)

At the 1986 Braemar Games, the prince inadvertently revealed to the entire world what was worn beneath that particular item of Scottish national costume.

FOUR FASHION RULES FOR THE WORKING QUEEN-REGNANT

First introduced by Elizabeth II during a tour of Australia in 1970, the "walkabout" among the crowd has since become an important — and expected — royal ritual. Despite its apparent informality, proper dress is of the utmost importance.

1. *Always Wear Bright, Clear Colours*
So that you will stand out better and therefore be more easily seen.

2. *Never Wear Black*
The only exceptions to this rule are during periods of mourning, the Remembrance Sunday ceremony and when meeting with the pope.

3. *Never Notice What Other People are Wearing*
It is absolutely vital (for the sake of colour coordination) to know in advance what others will be wearing on formal occasions, though of course one must never admit to making such inquiries.

Elizabeth II on walkabout.

4. CLOTHING MUST BE COMFORTABLE AND PRACTICAL

Owing to the need for mobility, skirts must not be either too short or too long, and sleeves not too tight. Similarly, all clothing must be easy to get in and out of in a hurry. Even handbags are customised for convenience, each coming equipped with a special clip that allows it to be secured on to tables.

Leisure

SEVEN INDEFATIGABLE ROYAL SPORTSMEN

1. CHARLES II (1630–85)
Won the Newmarket Plate twice on his own horse.

2. EDWARD VII (1841–1910)
Had a bowling alley installed at Sandringham.

3. GEORGE VI (1895–1952)
The best cricket player in his family; in his youth "Bertie" once had the unique distinction of bowling out King Edward VII and the future George V and Edward VIII in quick succession.

4. ELIZABETH, THE QUEEN MOTHER (1900–)
Was still salmon fishing hip-deep in icy Scottish rivers until well into her '80's.

5. PHILIP, DUKE OF EDINBURGH (1921–)
Once used a Royal Navy destroyer and an aircraft to get him home from a state visit in time to play in a polo playoff.

6. ANNE, THE PRINCESS ROYAL (1950–)
During her equestrian career the princess suffered a number of horse-related injuries, from a broken nose to a cracked vertebrae. Her most famous tumble, however, occurred at the 1976 Olympics in Montreal as a member of the British riding team. During the early rounds she fell and suffered a mild concussion, in the process losing too many points to be a medal-contender.

7. CHARLES, PRINCE OF WALES (1948–)

An avid polo player, the prince has fallen from his ponies on numerous occasions and often broken bones in the process. His most serious polo-related accident, however, occurred in 1980, when he collapsed after a particularly exhausting match upon drinking some ice-cold champagne; medics who attended him reported that, for a brief period, he was without a pulse.

SEVEN ROYAL GAMBLERS

1. ELIZABETH I (1533–1603)

Held the country's first national lottery.

2. GEORGE II (1683–1760)

Having learned that bookmakers were betting 10 to 1 that he would die within a year, the king overcame his uneasiness long enough to place a bet of 50 guineas that said he wouldn't. A year later he was heard to remark that he'd never won 500 guineas with greater pleasure.

3. GEORGE IV (1762–1830)

After losing a four-in-hand race with his coachman, the king made good his debt by knighting him.

4. VICTORIA (1819–1901)

The queen loved to play cards for money, and required that all who lost to her pay-up in newly minted coins.

5. EDWARD VII (1841–1910)

Edward's favourite pastime was baccarat, an illegal card game for which he had his own ivory chips created with the Prince of Wales feathers on them. After his involvement in the notorious Tranby Croft scandal (in which a close friend of his was accused of cheating at the game), his mother Queen Victoria demanded that he give it up. His subsequent refusal to do so is one of the few instances where he successfully defied her.

6. GEORGE V (1865–1936)

A sizeable portion of the king's famed philatelic collection was the product of his skill at betting on the ponies.

7. ELIZABETH, THE QUEEN MOTHER (1900–)

An avid racing fan, in 1965 the Queen Mother ordered a bookie-wire (known informally as "the blower") to be installed in Clarence House so that she could follow the progress of her horses. In recent years it has been replaced with closed-circuit television.

13 BIBULOUS ROYALS

"He that's drunk is as great as a king."

Charles II

1. HENRY VIII (1491–1547)

A violent drunkard.

2. ANNE (1665–1714)

A notoriously heavy drinker with a particular fondness for brandy. The queen's statue in St Paul's Churchyard (which faced a liquor store) was once defaced with the lines:

Brandy Nan, left in the lurch,
Her face to the gin-shop,
Her back to the church.

George IV as a young man.

3. GEORGE IV (1762–1830)

Justly remembered as a rakish alcoholic who would drink virtually anything. During the course of an average dinner George would customarily consume three entire bottles of wine, chased by various liqueurs (in particular cherry brandy) for dessert, generally ending up each evening either with a bout of brawling or by passing out stone cold, or both. Once, during a party for the politician Charles Fox, he fell flat on his face during a rather intricate quadrille and vomited all over the dance floor. On numerous occasions he was observed, clearly the worse for drink, riding his horse like a maniac through Hyde Park. Charles Lamb wrote a poem about the then prince regent that gives a good indication of the kind of esteem in which his contemporaries held him:

> Not a fatter fish than he
> Flounders round the polar sea.
> See his blubbers — at his gills
> What a world of drink he swills…
> Every fish of generous kind
> Scuds aside or shrinks behind;
> But about his presence keep
> All the monsters of the deep…
> Name or title what has he?
> Is he Regent of the sea?
> By his bulk and by his size,
> By his oily qualities,
> This (or else my eyesight fails),
> This should be the Prince of Whales.

4. FREDERICK, DUKE OF YORK (1763–1827)

A favourite crony of his brother George IV in the pursuit of drinking and whoring, Frederick began his career of debauchery as soon as he was able to hold a glass and never looked back.

5. WILLIAM IV (1765–1837)

Like his brothers George and Frederick, the king drank himself to death.

6. VICTORIA (1819–1901)

Had a weakness for Scotch whisky.

7. EDWARD VII (1841–1910)

A social drinker, the king once invented a special cocktail of his own. It consisted of rye whisky, crushed ice, pineapple and lemon peel, a dash of maraschino, champagne, and powdered sugar.

8. & 9. GEORGE V (1865–1936) AND MARY OF TECK (1867–1953)

Closet alcoholics both.

10. EDWARD VIII (1894–1972)

A moody, bad-tempered drunk. Throughout the 1920s there were numerous public sightings of the then Prince of Wales "three sheets to the wind," although thanks to a deferential press none were ever widely reported. Later, during the period of his abdication, the king was said to drink vast quantities of brandy and soda and on at least one occasion had to be administered to with a stomach pump.

11. GEORGE VI (1895–1952)

A secret boozer whose reliance on whisky increased steadily with the passing years.

12. ELIZABETH, THE QUEEN MOTHER (1900–)

Despite her advanced age the Queen Mother still manages to down a bottle of gin a day.

13. ANDREW, DUKE OF YORK (1960–)

During celebrations marking his mother's Silver Jubilee, the prince got so wasted that he had to be carried home to bed by his friends.

FOUR ROYALS WHO USED DRUGS

1. GEORGE IV (1762–1830)

Relied heavily on laudanum (a mixture of opium in alcohol) as a hangover remedy, in doses of up to a hundred drops at a time.

2. VICTORIA (1819–1901)

The queen took Mariani wine (a beverage made from the coca plant, from which cocaine is extracted) "for medicinal purposes."

3. ALBERT VICTOR, DUKE OF CLARENCE (1864–92)

An alcoholic and drug-addict from his teens, the heir to the throne is known to have used opium, cocaine and marijuana on numerous occasions.

4. GEORGE, DUKE OF KENT (1902–42)

During the late 1920s and early 1930s this younger son of George V became seriously addicted to cocaine and, to a lesser extent, morphine. After an attempt to kick both habits on his own resulted in a nervous breakdown, his older brother the Prince of Wales ultimately placed him under house arrest and forced him to quit cold turkey.

SIX ROYALS WHO WERE HEAVY SMOKERS

"A custom loathsome to the eye, hateful to the nose, harmful to the brain, dangerous to the lungs, and in the black, stinking fume thereof, nearest resembling the horrible Stygian smoke of the pit that is bottomless."

James I

1. EDWARD VII (1841–1910)

Helped to popularise the smoking of cigarettes (rather than cigars) after dinner, accompanied by brandy. Edward was said to smoke over twenty unfiltered cigarettes a day, along with at least a dozen enormous cigars. Died from chronic bronchitis.

2. GEORGE V (1865–1936)

A chain-smoker despite his chronic bronchitis.

3. EDWARD VIII (1894–1972)

A lifelong, heavy smoker of both cigarettes and cigars. Died of throat cancer.

4. GEORGE VI (1895–1952)

Smoked as many as eighty cigarettes each day. Died of chronic arteriosclerosis and lung cancer.

5. MARGARET, COUNTESS OF SNOWDON (1930–)

Despite an operation in 1985 to have part of a lung removed, up until quite recently the queen's sister still clung stubbornly to her unhealthy habit. She continued to use long cigarette holders as well — a misplaced emblem of glamour left over from the 1950s.

6. PRINCE WILLIAM (1982–)
A regular smoker.

FOUR ROYAL SWIMMERS

1. GEORGE III (1738–1820)
It was the king's belief in the power of sea bathing to improve his erratic health that actually launched the modern concept of seaside holiday resorts. Whenever George went for a dip (dressed, suitably, in his blue serge costume) he would invariably be accompanied by a coterie of young ladies draped in patriotic colours and fiddlers playing out "God Save the King."

2. GEORGE IV (1762–1830)
Began his long relationship with the resort town of Brighton in the 1780s, after a doctor recommended a course of sea bathing to treat his swollen neck-glands.

3. VICTORIA (1819–1901)
Went swimming using a special "bathing hut" — a little horse-drawn cabin for privacy that could be rolled in and out of the sea — while wearing a voluminous swimming costume that covered most of her body. Although she enjoyed the activity the queen did reportedly have an aversion to getting her head wet.

4. DIANA, PRINCESS OF WALES (1961–97)
Won a school prize for swimming as a teenager. Later she would often travel to the Caribbean for beach holidays, where she would invariably be photographed in the skimpiest of bikinis (once, while heavily pregnant with Prince William).

FOUR ROYAL GARDENERS

1. CAROLINE OF BRANDENBURG-ANSBACH (1683–1737)
The queen, with the assistance of her daughter-in-law Princess

Augusta, created a wild, gothic-inspired garden at Kew Palace that would later become the basis for the Royal Botanical Gardens. The former included such landscaping curiosities as a hermitage (complete with real hermit) and something called Merlin's cave, which contained Caroline's library along with a set of unintentionally eerie waxwork effigies.

2. MARY OF TECK (1867–1953)
The queen had an intense dislike for ivy, and was known to supervise its removal from the walls of buildings even when she was only staying there as a guest.

3. GEORGE VI (1895–1952)
Created, with the help of his wife, the grandest display of rhododendrons to be seen in Britain, in the garden at Royal Lodge.

4. CHARLES, PRINCE OF WALES (1948–)
Inordinately proud of his organic gardens at Highgrove, with their waist-high grasses and spectacular array of wildflowers.

12 ROYAL HUNTERS

A mandatory pastime activity for British royals, many of who have become so obsessed with the "sport" that they have actually taken up residence in Gloucestershire — the heart of Beaufort fox-hunting country. The term "shooting," incidentally, is preferred over "hunting."

1. WILLIAM I, "THE CONQUEROR" (C. 1027–87)
Created the vast New Forest in southern England in 1079 as an exclusive royal hunting preserve, which he protected by way of highly punitive anti-poaching laws.

2. HENRY VIII (1491–1547)
The young Henry was said to throw a spear well and could draw a bow "with greater strength than any man in England." When not actually killing animals he was often to be found shooting at small targets with his handgun at Windsor.

3. JAMES I (1566–1625)
One of the king's greatest passions was hunting at his country retreat,

Theobalds, in Hertfordshire. After each kill he would personally disembowel the stag and then thrust his hands and feet into the entrails, in the belief that it "strengthened the sinews." Lastly he would daub the faces of his courtiers with blood in recognition of their sportsmanship (modern royals continue the latter ritual to this very day).

4. ARTHUR, DUKE OF CONNAUGHT (1850–1942)

In 1892 the duke, one of Queen Victoria's younger sons, accidentally shot out the eye of a visiting Danish prince at Sandringham (*thus proving the old adage: "it's only fun until…"*).

5. EDWARD VII (1841–1910)

In order to accommodate the estimated 30,000 game birds that he and his guests were killing annually at Sandringham, the king ordered to be constructed there the world's biggest larder.

6. GEORGE V (1865–1936)

George was doubtless the most enthusiastic hunter of all the royals, and in his day arguably the best shot in Europe. Although he generally preferred to blast away at half-tame pheasants on his estate at Sandringham (he once killed 1,000 of them in a single day), during a brief visit to Nepal in 1911 he personally slaughtered 39 tigers, 18 rhino and four bears. It is worth noting that, in spite of the king's subsequent boasting about his "record bag," this particular hunt had been carefully stage managed so that none of the animals actually had any chance to escape.

7. & 8. GEORGE VI (1895–1952) AND ELIZABETH, THE QUEEN MOTHER (1900–)

In 1924 the future king and his wife went on an extended shooting holiday in East Africa, during which the latter gleefully blew away rhinoceros, water buffalo and various species of antelope. For his part, George killed an elephant whose tusks weighed 40 kilograms apiece.

9. & 10. ELIZABETH II (1926–) AND PHILIP, DUKE OF EDINBURGH (1921–)

Both the queen and her husband were reported to have shot and killed some endangered tigers during a visit to India in 1961. Philip's participation in the hunt was particularly shocking, given his position as president of the World Wildlife Fund.

11. CHARLES, PRINCE OF WALES (1948–)
Named "Hooligan of the Year" for 1978 by the RSPCA, for his hunting of boar in Liechtenstein.

12. PRINCE WILLIAM (1982–)
An unapologetic "gun-freak."

THREE ROYAL JOUSTERS

Considered to be one of the most important "noble arts" for any young medieval prince to learn, jousting originated during the chivalric age of the Hundred Years' War. The tournaments themselves (which were usually associated with much feasting and entertainment) consisted of two armour-clad knights on horseback charging each other with long blunted lances across a barrier known as a tilt, the object being to knock the other one from his mount.

1. EDWARD I (1239–1307)
Known in his time as "the best lance in all the world."

2. EDWARD, PRINCE OF WALES (1330–76)
It was the Black Prince's habit of wearing three ostrich feathers in his helmet during tournaments that originated the motif for future Prince's of Wales.

3. HENRY VIII (1491–1547)
Once accidentally broke the arm of the man who was in the process of teaching him the sport; on another occasion, he had a heavily armoured horse fall on him.

FOUR ROYAL GOLFERS

1. JAMES I (1566–1625)
It was James who first introduced this Scottish sport into England.

2. CHARLES II (1630–85)
Said to have worked off his sumptuous coronation feast in Scotland by playing a round of golf.

3. EDWARD VII (1841–1910)

Owned a golf bag made from an elephant's penis.

4. EDWARD VIII (1894–1972)

Scored a total of three holes-in-one during the course of his golfing career.

MONTHLY HIGHLIGHTS FROM THE VICTORIAN SOCIAL CALENDAR

Victorian upper-class society was organised by an unchanging calendar of social and sporting activities. Its 1500 or so privileged members lived by a rigid moral code; to transgress this (for example to divorce) was to risk ostracism from the calendar. At the apex of this social hierarchy was the Prince of Wales (the future Edward VII), his various mistresses and, marginally, his wife Alexandra; Queen Victoria never participated in these activities. It was Edward who first opened up this society to deserving, non-titled individuals as well as aristocrats, the main criteria for inclusion being enormous wealth. The following outline of events continues, incidentally (and with only slight variations) to this very day.

JANUARY — FEBRUARY:

Sandringham season. The home that the Prince and Princess of Wales loved more than any other, mainly because it was the one place where they could be truly alone.

MARCH:

The Prince of Wales made his annual five-week visit to some French seaside resort (usually Biarritz) beginning in mid-March, stopping off at Paris at either end to call on old friends and *demi-mondaines*.

APRIL — JUNE:

Marlborough House and the beginning of the London season. The beginning of three solid months of lavish dinners, operas and society balls, punctuated with special weekends at palatial country homes.

JUNE:

Royal Ascot Races (always the third week in June, from Tuesday to

Saturday). Although ostensibly about "the sport of kings," the Ascot horse races were (and are) really more about snobbery. Seating is divided into several "classes," the most important of course being the royal enclosure, and the dress code is rigid and highly formal, with hats mandatory for both sexes. It was Queen Anne herself, incidentally, who originally selected the site for the track and organised the first race in 1711.

JULY — AUGUST:

Summers were usually spent on or near the water, the season being highlighted to two major social events. The first of these was the Henley Royal Regatta, which generally took place in the last week of June or the first week of July at Henley-on-Thames. The most prestigious event in rowing competition, its main purpose was to serve as an opportunity for well-dressed high society mavens to watch each other as they gathered in one gigantic, riverbank lawn party. Even more important was Cowes Week in August. At the end of the nineteenth century this annual regatta off the Isle of Wight was the supreme yacht-racing event in the world, attended by czars, kaisers and American robber barons along with various members of the British royal family, many of whom actually participated in the races as well.

SEPTEMBER:

After Cowes the Prince of Wales generally proceeded to some health spa in Germany or Austria (often, though not always, Marienbad) to recover from the London season and prepare for Balmoral. The visit was frequently the occasion for informal talks with other European leaders.

SEPTEMBER — OCTOBER:

Balmoral season (roughly, mid-August to the end of October). Grouse-shooting and salmon-fishing, culminating in the annual Ghillies' Ball for the benefit of the staff; during the latter (which is still held to this day), male royals traditionally wear full Highland dress, females white ball gowns with tartan sashes.

NOVEMBER — DECEMBER:

Back to Sandringham. The prince always returned here to celebrate his wife's birthday in November and stayed on until the end of February.

The other members of the royal family, however, traditionally celebrated Christmas at Windsor Castle. It was actually Edward's father Prince Albert, incidentally, who first introduced many of the German customs now associated with the season into England, not the least of which being the Christmas tree. Indeed, it was a picture of the royal couple standing next to their candle-lit and ribbon-festooned *tannenbaum* on Christmas Eve, 1841, that subsequently inspired millions of their subjects to bring a fir tree into their own homes the following year.

*All
that
Glitters*

EIGHT ROYAL SPENDTHRIFTS

1. EDWARD III (1312–77)
After defaulting on a large personal loan in 1339, Edward became the first national leader in history to go bankrupt.

2. HENRY VIII (1491–1547)
Would almost certainly have bankrupted the country had he lived any longer.

3. JAMES I (1566–1625)
Years of wasteful extravagance ultimately rendered the king some £1 million in debt.

4. CHARLES II (1630–85)
Got himself out of a deep financial hole by accepting secret subsidies from France, in exchange for a disingenuous promise to re-introduce Catholicism to England.

5. GEORGE IV (1762–1830)
A scandalously extravagant spendthrift throughout his life, by 1795 the then Prince of Wales was some £630,000 in debt (equivalent to tens of millions of pounds in today's terms). Things became so bad in fact that the house where he and his mistress were staying was once surrounded by bailiffs, who gave him just 24 hours to pay a £2,000 bill. In the end he was forced to pawn the woman's jewellery to get rid of them.

6. EDWARD VII (1841–1910)

Despite the enormous financial resources available to him the king began his reign almost destitute, having already spent most of his fortune on travel, gambling, and entertaining.

7. ELIZABETH, THE QUEEN MOTHER (1900–)

A lavish spender who has long ignored an overdraft of several million pounds.

8. SARAH, DUCHESS OF YORK (1959–)

Ran up enormous debts during her married life. Commented one palace spokesman: "She lives beyond her means — and ours."

FIVE ROYAL TIGHTWADS

1. HENRY VII (1457–1509)

Although Henry acquired a reputation in his own day for stinginess, he did spend considerable sums on buying cloth of gold and silver, along with furs, fineries, and jewellery for himself and his consort — they being considered sound investments. Conscious of the need for pageantry, he nevertheless spent endless hours patiently auditing his court's ledgers.

2. GEORGE II (1883–1760)

A notorious miser.

3. GEORGE V (1865–1936)

Refused to throw anything away and filled Sandringham with cheap reproduction furniture. The ridiculously small amount that he paid to his estate workers — about 14 shillings a week — was the source of much contention in Norfolk.

4. EDWARD VIII (1894–1972)

In his later years the ex-king became extremely careful with his money, and was particularly notorious for sticking people with the dinner cheque.

5. ELIZABETH II (1926–)

Despite her enormous wealth Elizabeth has always been quite frugal. Perhaps the most well-known demonstration of this was the time her son, Prince Charles, took his dog out for a walk at Windsor and returned without its leash. When she learned of this, the billionaire queen made the boy march right back out to look for it, with the admonition, "Dog leads cost money."

SIX ROYAL COLLECTORS

1. GEORGE IV (1762–1830)
A compulsive hoarder; among the items that the king collected in particular were whips, canes and women's gloves.

2. VICTORIA (1819–1901)
Had marble models done of the hands of each of her children, along with one of her husband's "sweet little ear."

3. GEORGE V (1865–1936)
Built up a collection of 325 leather-bound stamp albums, now among the most valuable of its sort in the world.

4. EDWARD VIII (1894–1972)
Collected old snuff boxes, along with vast numbers of china Meissen pug dogs.

5. PHILIP, DUKE OF EDINBURGH (1921–)
Keeps his extensive collection of cartoons about himself hanging in the bathroom at Sandringham.

6. CHARLES, PRINCE OF WALES (1948–)
Said to have collected more than a hundred wooden toilet seats over the years, along with numerous hand-painted Victorian lavatories.

FIVE TYPES OF ROYAL CONVEYANCE

1. THE ROYAL COACHES
Originally built for George III in 1762 from a design by a Florentine artist living in London, the rococo-inspired coronation coach is gilded on the exterior and lined with crimson satin, and has been used for every coronation since 1831. For the annual state opening of parliament and other lesser occasions, however, Queen Victoria's

Irish state coach is normally used, while for royal weddings either the so-called glass coach or the state landau are preferred.

2. THE ROYAL YACHT BRITANNIA

A former hospital ship which was converted (at considerable expense) into an ocean-going palace for the royal family in 1953, in its heyday the *Britannia* had a crew of around 250 and included such amenities as a wine cellar, movie theatre, and a garage for a Rolls Royce. Over the next forty-five years it saw much service during the family's overseas visits, and when it was finally decommissioned as a public relations economy measure in 1997, the queen was seen to cry in public for the first time in her life. Today the ship is permanently moored at the port of Leith in Scotland, where it serves as a museum.

3. THE ROYAL AIRCRAFT

There are actually three jets currently being used for The Queen's Flight, along with several helicopters, the latter specially soundproofed to ensure passenger privacy. For security reasons whole sections of the sky leading up to the airports at London, Marsham (for Sandringham), Aberdeen (for Balmoral) and Caithness (for the Castle of Mey) are designated at "purple air ways." These areas must be avoided for one half hour before the royal family will pass through them.

4. THE ROYAL TRAINS

Up until the 1960s there were two private trains available to transport royals throughout Great Britain. Both have since been retired in favour of helicopters, though should a train be required for some special occasion British Rail will invariably provide one on demand.

5. AUTOMOBILES

The royal mews (which also house the state carriages and horses) contains a large collection of royal automobiles, primarily limousines and Rolls-Royces. It is worth noting that any car the queen travels in invariably bears her own, solid-silver mascot hood ornament. The latter represents St George on a horse, looking down upon a slain dragon.

TEN PRIVATE ROYAL RESIDENCES

The sovereign's personal standard invariably flies over wherever he or she is currently in residence.

1. FROGMORE HOUSE

Best-known as the site of the Royal Mausoleum built by Queen Victoria, Frogmore House first came into possession of the royal family during the reign of Henry VIII. The actual building is located on the grounds of Windsor Castle's Home Park, and though small is surrounded by many hectares of attractive gardens. It is still used today as a very exclusive private getaway by various members of the royal family.

2. BRIGHTON PAVILION

In 1786 the future George IV leased a pleasant farmhouse in Brighton that would later serve, during the years of his Regency, as the basis for an exotic, Oriental style pavilion by the sea. Designed largely by his architect John Nash, the Brighton Pavilion as it came to be known would be significantly enlarged and eventually boasted such curious additions as onion-shaped "Indian style" domes and elaborate Chinese interiors. George himself quickly grew tired of his Moghul confection, though his brother and successor William IV loved it. When Queen Victoria came to the throne in 1837, however, she so disapproved of the lavish pleasure palace that she stripped it of its furniture and planned to demolish it. Fortunately, she decided to sell it off instead in the 1850s to help pay for the enlargement of Buckingham Palace.

3. CLARENCE HOUSE

Located on The Mall near Buckingham Palace, Clarence House is the official London residence of the Queen Mother. In actual fact part of St James's Palace, its first resident was the future King William IV (when he was still known as the Duke of Clarence). The house was afterwards completely remodelled by William's wife, Princess Adelaide, under the direction of famed architect John Nash. Since that day it has seen a number of residents come and go, though it continues to be the place where royal brides traditionally stay on the eve of their wedding.

4. OSBORNE HOUSE

A creepy hilltop villa on the Isle of Wight, built by Victoria and Albert in the 1840s at their own personal expense. The house itself was designed in high Italian Renaissance style, incorporating as it did such engineering innovations as central heating. After the death of her husband the queen turned it into a shrine to his memory, and spent her final years there as a virtual recluse. Although she had specified in her will that the place be used in perpetuity by her heirs after her own death, it was soon handed over to the government for use as a combined naval training school and old sailor's home.

5. Sandringham Hall

"Dickens in a Cartier setting."
Edward VIII

Originally bought in 1862 for the Prince of Wales (the future Edward VII), and largely rebuilt, Sandringham in Norfolk is an ugly redbrick "Jacobethan" mansion set on 25 hectares of wooded grounds and over 8,000 hectares of estate. A favourite retreat for modern royals, it remains the destination of choice for family holidays and shooting weekends. Located nearby, incidentally, are a number of satellite royal residences, perhaps the most notable being the mock-Tudor York Cottage (the birthplace of George VI).

6. Marlborough House

Located near Buckingham Palace, Marlborough House has been a royal residence since the early nineteenth century but is probably best known as the elegant London home of Edward VII, during his years as Prince of Wales. After the death of George V in 1936 his widow Queen Mary took up residence there, and would continue to do so until her own death in 1953. Today the house is used for government conferences and entertainments.

7. Fort Belvedere

Originally built by one of George II's sons as a sort of fairytale castle, this smallish country house on the fringe of Windsor Great Park was a favourite weekend getaway for Edward VIII. After taking ownership of it in 1929 the latter had it furbished with all the comforts of modern life, including central heating, indoor plumbing, and even a swimming pool. The residence has since fallen out of royal possession.

8. ROYAL LODGE

Originally used as a love-nest by George IV, this smallish country residence near Windsor Castle was presented to the then Duke of York (later George VI) in 1931 by his father.

9. CASTLE OF MEY

The Queen Mother's beachfront retreat in northern Scotland. A virtual derelict when first purchased by her after the death of her husband, the ancient castle was chosen primarily because it was a place that wouldn't dredge up sad memories.

10. HIGHGROVE HOUSE

The country home of the Prince of Wales since 1980. This charming, nine-bedroomed Georgian home in the "royal triangle" of Gloucestershire is remarkably restrained compared to other royal residences, and has often been criticised as unbecoming the heir to the throne.

EIGHT ROYAL EXTRAVAGANCES

1. HENRY VI'S CORONATION BANQUET

The feline-themed menu included a large vat of red soup (containing whole white lions) and cooked golden leopards immersed in custard.

2. A QUEEN-SIZED BED

Elizabeth I's bed at Windsor was nearly four metres square.

3. AN INDOOR TENNIS COURT

Henry VIII installed the very first tennis court in England, at Hampton Court Palace. It is still used on occasion to this day.

4. VICTORIA'S BREAKFAST

The queen customarily breakfasted in the garden at Osborne House under a green-fringed parasol tent, waited on by turbaned Indian servants and with virtually every object on the table made from solid gold.

5. EDWARD VII'S FABERGÉ FARM ANIMALS

In 1907 the king commissioned Carl Fabergé (the famed jewelled-egg-maker to the czars) to model the farm animals at his beloved

Sandringham, including pigs, chickens, ducks, shire horses and his prize short-horn bull. Also requested were golden, jewel-encrusted sculptures of his dog, Caesar, his daughter-in-law Mary's Pekinese, and his Derby-winning horse Persimmon. Today, these priceless confections are stored away in the cavernous vaults that lie beneath Buckingham Palace, with the rest of the royal junk.

6. MARY OF TECK'S DOLLS' HOUSE

Designed and built between 1921 and 1924 by the great architect Sir Edwin Lutyens, and now on permanent display at Windsor Castle, Queen Mary's dolls' house is one of the most charming and ambitious miniatures ever created. Meticulous in its detail, among its countless Lilliputian-sized features are electric lights that actually work, key-locking doors, practical elevators, a tiny gramophone that plays such tunes as the national anthem and "Rule, Britannia!," famous paintings reproduced in 1/12 scale, and running water for each of its five bathrooms. There is even a library of little books by famous authors of the day, including a special Sherlock Holmes story written by Sir Arthur Conan Doyle himself.

7. THE DUCHESS OF WINDSOR'S BATHTUB

Among other things, Wallis Simpson's villa at Antibes, in the French Riviera, boasted a 22-carat, solid gold bathtub.

8. PRINCESS DIANA'S WARDROBE

During her fashion heyday in the mid-1980's Diana's closets expanded to six entire suites in Kensington Palace, with one entire room reserved merely for shoes.

THREE ROYAL SOUVENIRS

1. AN ASSASSIN'S BULLET

After an assassin narrowly missed shooting him in Brussels in 1900, Edward VII had one of the bullets dislodged from where it had struck and kept it in his pocket for good luck.

2. A UNION JACK

When India became independent in 1947, George VI requested that the last of the flags to be flown over the British Residency at Lucknow be, in the future, flown over Windsor Castle instead.

3. GEORGE VI'S DESK

Since the king's death in 1952 the Queen Mother has kept his desk at Royal Lodge, Windsor precisely as he left it. His daughter Elizabeth, meanwhile, still writes with the same pen that he always used.

SIX MEMORABLE EXAMPLES OF ROYAL GIFT-GIVING

1. A GOLDEN TOOTHPICK

Given by the about-to-be-executed Charles I to his gaoler.

2. A PALACE

Queen Anne gave Blenheim Palace to John Churchill, Duke of Marlborough, as a reward for his resounding victory over the French in 1704.

3. A BOOK

Queen Victoria gave a copy of one of her books to Charles Dickens, inscribed "To one of the greatest authors from one of the humblest."

4. A DEAD HORSE

When his beloved Derby-winning horse Persimmon died in 1908, Edward VII donated the body to the Natural History Museum in London for display.

Royal family portrait, taken on the occasion of Prince Charles's christening.

5. A SILVER GILT CUP

In honour of his christening, Mary of Teck presented Prince Charles with an antique cup that had once belonged to George III. As the queen later commented, "I gave a present from my great-grandfather to my great-grandson, 168 years later."

6. A CIGARETTE CASE

After twenty years of faithful (unpaid) service to Edward VIII, Walter Monckton was rewarded with a cigarette case on which the engraving of his name was misspelled.

FOUR MEMORABLE EXAMPLES OF ROYAL GIFT-GETTING

Unlike other monarchs and heads of state, the British royal family insists upon keeping all the gifts received on state occasions. Members have been known to make special visits to foreign countries for the express purpose of increasing their jewellery collection.

1. TENNIS BALLS

In 1414 the dauphin of France sent the unexpected and highly insulting gift of a box of tennis balls to the young Henry V — the message being that the English king should stick to childish frivolities and not get involved in international politics. Henry's reply to the dauphin was equally witty, he promising to " tosse him som tennis balles that perchance should shake the walles of the best court in France" (i.e. cannon balls).

2. A HUMAN LEG

Henry VII once received the mummified left leg of St George (the patron saint of England) as a gift.

3. AN ARCHITECTURAL MASTERPIECE

Inigo Jones' glorious Queen's House in Greenwich (now the National Maritime Museum) was originally commissioned by James I for his wife, Anne of Denmark.

4. MINIATURE SPORTS CARS

As a boy Prince Andrew once received a custom-made miniature James Bond car from his parents, complete with artificial machine guns and a smoke screen system. It cost an estimated £4000 to build. Years later, Prince William would be given a far more expensive miniature Jaguar, which he promptly set about destroying.

THE CIVIL LIST (AS OF 1993)

The infamous civil list specifies the annual allowances to be paid by the British treasury to members of the royal family, ostensibly to enable them to run their households and carry out their various public duties. Long a matter of controversy, in the mid-1990s Elizabeth II finally agreed to cut off everyone from the government teat with the exception of herself, her husband and her mother, and to fund them instead out of her own pocket.

1. *ELIZABETH II*   (£7,900,000)
2. *ELIZABETH, THE QUEEN MOTHER*   (£640,000)
3. *PHILIP, DUKE OF EDINBURGH*   (£360,000)
4. *ANDREW, DUKE OF YORK*   (£250,000)
5. *EDWARD, EARL OF WESSEX*   (£100,000)
6. *ANNE, THE PRINCESS ROYAL*   (£230,000)
7. *MARGARET, COUNTESS OF SNOWDON*   (£220,000)
8. *ALICE, DUCHESS OF GLOUCESTER*   (£90,000)

The Prince of Wales, incidentally, traditionally receives nothing from the treasury, supporting himself instead from the ample incomes of the Duchy of Cornwall. Among the latter's more unusual assets under this arrangement are Dartmoor Prison and the Oval Cricket Ground in London, not to mention an annual tribute of mainly fish-related products from his Cornish subjects.

The Arts
and
Architecture

SEVEN UNEXPECTEDLY CREATIVE ROYALS

1. *Alfred "The Great" (c. 849–c. 899)*
In 1693 a gold and enamel jewel bearing the Anglo-Saxon words "Alfred had me made" was found near the Isle of Athelney in Somerset. It is now to be seen in the Ashmolean Museum, Oxford.

2. *Elizabeth I (1533–1603)*
Created elaborately embroidered book covers.

3. *George III (1738–1820)*
Enjoyed making buttons for his clothes. He also designed an attractive little baroque clock that can still be seen at Windsor Castle.

4. *Victoria (1819–1901)*
An avid painter and drawer, the queen had the ability to render people and places from memory. Her sketchbooks of life at Osborne and Balmoral can still be seen in the Royal Library at Windsor.

5. *Mary of Teck (1867–1955)*
The queen spent eight years creating an enormous carpet measuring 32 by 24 metres, containing over a million stitches.

6. *George VI (1895–1952)*
Was quite adept at needlepoint.

7. *Charles, Prince of Wales (1948–)*
A talented watercolorist. Although primarily a means of relaxation for him, in 1987 the Prince managed (under an assumed name) to get

his painting *Farm Building in Norfolk* displayed at the Royal Academy's prestigious summer art show. In recent years he has exhibited his work to an even wider audience.

THREE ROYALS WHO APPEARED ON STAGE OR IN FILM

1. EDWARD VII (1841–1910)
One night in 1892 Edward played the part of the dead prince (over whom the actress Sarah Bernhardt was weeping) in a Paris production of Sardou's *Fedora*.

2. MARGARET, COUNTESS OF SNOWDON (1930–)
Played Queen Victoria in a 1965 movie-short produced by Peter Sellers. The film (which also featured Britt Ekland and Lord Snowdon in supporting roles) was presented to Elizabeth II on the occasion of her thirty-ninth birthday.

3. ANNE, THE PRINCESS ROYAL (1950–)
Once, in 1969, the princess got up on stage in London to dance in the finale of the hippy musical *Hair*. Although many in the cast were nude, she herself refrained from removing her purple pantsuit.

11 ROYAL PHILISTINES

1. JAMES I (1566–1625)
(*On the poetry of John Donne*) "Dr Donne's verses are like the peace of God; they pass all understanding."

2. GEORGE II (1683–1760)
(*On the arts in general*) "No more bainting, blays or boetry!"

3. GEORGE III (1738–1820)
"Was there ever such stuff as the great part of Shakespeare? Only it's Shakespeare, and nobody dare abuse him."

4. WILLIAM IV (1765–1837)
When presented with one of the splendid works from his predecessor George IV's art collection, the new king was recorded as saying,

"Aye — it seems pretty — I dare say it is. My brother was very fond of this Knickknackery. Damned expensive taste, though."

5. VICTORIA *(1819–1901)*

Victoria's views on art (as on everything else) had been formed by her husband Albert, who had a preference for Italian painting. She therefore had a tendency to turn up her nose at anything else.

6. GEORGE V *(1865–1936)*

Once famously declared that his favourite opera was *La Bohème* ("because it is the shortest.")

7. WALLIS, DUCHESS OF WINDSOR *(C. 1896–1986)*

"My approach to art, whether modern or traditional, is decorative. When I look at a picture I never see it by itself, I see it as part of a room."

8. GEORGE VI *(1895–1952)*

After an aide suggested he should attend the opera more often, the king threw a book at him.

9. ELIZABETH, THE QUEEN MOTHER *(1900–)*

Worried that her daughters Elizabeth and Margaret were not receiving a proper education owing to wartime privations, The Queen Mother once arranged for T.S. Eliot — one of the most respected literary figures of the twentieth century — to give a poetry evening at Windsor Castle. Unfortunately, soon after Eliot began reciting his masterpiece *The Waste Land*, the entire royal family got a serious case of the giggles. "Such a gloomy man," the queen was quoted as saying afterwards, "…looked as though he worked in a bank, and we didn't understand a word."

10. PHILIP, DUKE OF EDINBURGH *(1921–)*

(*On his reputation as a philistine*) "The art world thinks of me as an uncultured polo-playing clot." He once publicly referred to a Henry Moore sculpture as a "monkey's gallstone."

11. EDWARD, EARL OF WESSEX *(1964–)*

During his first visit to King's College Chapel, Cambridge, the prince said he found Rubens's enormous *Adoration of the Magi* "out of keeping with the rest of the chapel."

12 ROYAL ART PATRONS

1. HENRY III (1207–72)
Had Westminster Abbey rebuilt into the structure we see today.

2. RICHARD II (1377–99)
Aside from his support of such literary notables as Geoffrey Chaucer and William Langland, Richard II also opened the first art school in England.

3. HENRY VIII (1491–1547)
Lured many important artists and intellectuals to his magnificent court, among them the painter Hans Holbein and the Dutch humanist scholar Desiderius Erasmus.

4. ELIZABETH I (1533–1603)
Although the queen had little to do with the actual creation of the work, Edmund Spenser's epic romance *The Faerie Queen* was based largely upon episodes from her life; in 1589 the poet came to court to lay the first three books at her feet, where he was rewarded with a pension. Elizabeth was also responsible, indirectly, for the creation of Shakespeare's *The Merry Wives of Windsor*, having personally requested that he write a play for her.

5. JAMES I (1566–1625)
James's granting of a pension in 1616 to the dramatist Ben Jonson laid the foundation for the royal office of poet laureate. Years earlier he had helped an even more important poet / dramatist, however, by taking William Shakespeare's theatrical company under his protection as the "King's Men."

6. CHARLES I (1600–49)
A highly cultured man, Charles assembled one of the finest art-collections in Europe and was a personal patron of such masters as Rubens and Van Dyck. Sadly, much of it (including works by Dürer, Raphael, Titian and da Vinci) was sold off after his death.

7. CHARLES II (1630–85)
Like his father before him Charles was among the greatest of royal art patrons, having appointed such notables as Henry Purcell as court

musician and John Dryden as poet laureate. On a more prurient level, he once commissioned his official court painter and friend, Peter Lely, to do a nude portrait of his favourite mistress Nell Gwynne.

8. GEORGE I (1660–1727)

Though personally inartistic, George nevertheless founded the Royal Academy of Music and supported the exiled German composer George Frederick Handel. This love for the latter's work would be passed on to the king's son George II, who first instituted the custom of standing up for the "Hallelujah Chorus" of the *Messiah*. Handel's music, incidentally, is still an integral part of each Coronation ceremony.

9. GEORGE III (1738–1820)

Despite his efforts to encourage the arts in Britain (he founded the Royal Academy in 1768) and his personal financial support of the colonial American painter Benjamin West, when the king was shown the latter's historical masterpiece *The Death of Wolfe* in 1770 he refused to purchase it for his collection. Instead of showing an ancient hero the artist had chosen to depict a recent one (in this case the general who had died while wresting Canada from the French during the Seven Years' War). Worse than this, West had shown his figures in contemporary costume rather than in classical garb, as was the practice. Yet when the painting was finally exhibited it proved to be an enormous success, and the king was persuaded to change his mind.

10. GEORGE IV (1738–1820)

Belying his rather absurd appearance and debauched lifestyle, George IV was an important patron of the arts. Among the more important individuals that he helped to encourage were the composer Joseph Haydn, the sculptor Antonio Canova and the novelists Jane Austin and Sir Walter Scott. He also spent lavishly on building pursuits, his commission of such noted architects as John Nash resulting in the so-called Regency style of architecture. It was George as well who supported Lord Elgin's removal to Britain of the Parthenon's marble friezes — a move much criticized at the time but one which doubtless saved them from destruction.

11. ALBERT, PRINCE CONSORT (1819–61)

A polymath who did much to further both science and the arts, it was Prince Albert as well who was responsible for rescuing the Egyptian obelisk known as Cleopatra's Needle and bringing it to London.

12. ELIZABETH II (1926–)

Elizabeth's private collection of artworks — as opposed to those merely held in trust by her for the state — is still rightly regarded as among the finest in the world. Though much of it remains inaccessible to the public, the Queen's Gallery at Buckingham Palace does display a small selection (on a rotating basis), while others may be seen in the state apartments at Windsor Castle. The queen personally owns important works by such old masters as Vermeer, Rubens, Rembrandt, and Canaletto.

EIGHT ROYAL MUSICIANS

1. RICHARD I (1157–99)

Wrote a well-known medieval ballad during his 14-month imprisonment in Austria.

2. HENRY VIII (1491–1547)

In addition to his proficiency on the lute and harpsichord the king also wrote at least two motets and two masses, and was probably the author of the ballad "Greensleeves."

3. CHARLOTTE OF MECKLENBURG-STRELITZ (1744–1818)

Played the harpsichord, and once accompanied the young Mozart in an aria during a royal audience.

4. GEORGE IV (1762–1830)

A decent cellist and pianist.

5. ALBERT, PRINCE CONSORT (1819–61)

Composed a *Te Deum* that was later used at his wife's Golden Jubilee service at Westminster Abbey.

6. VICTORIA (1819–1901)

The queen had a beautiful singing voice, which the actress Ellen Terry once compared to "a silver stream flowing over golden stones." In later life she enjoyed singing the role of Buttercup from the Gilbert & Sullivan operetta *HMS Pinafore*, accompanied by her daughter Princess Louise on piano.

7. *Edward VIII (1894–1972)*

A competent player of the bagpipes, Edward even went so far as to write a tune for them called "Majorca." His father George V was not impressed with the young man's talent, however, once reprimanding him after a performance: "Don't do it again. My advice to you is to leave this art to the Highlanders. They know what they're doing."

8. *Diana, Princess of Wales (1961–97)*

An accomplished musician (who was also blessed with perfect pitch), Diana once showed up her husband during a joint-appearance at a music school in Melbourne in 1988. While he plucked away ineptly at a cello on the urging of his hosts, the princess sat down at a piano and proceeded to play a difficult piece by Rachmaninov.

SEVEN REMARKABLE ROYAL PALACES

A royal family gathering on the balcony at Buckingham Palace,
on the occasion of George VI's coronation.

1. BUCKINGHAM PALACE

"A sepulchre."
Edward VII

The official London residence of the royal family since 1837, this enormous grey expanse at the end of Pall Mall started off as a small, ordinary looking redbrick building known as Buckingham House. First purchased in 1762 by George III, in 1824 it was largely rebuilt and enlarged by his son George IV under the direction of architect Nash at considerable cost. Queen Victoria made major improvements as well, though it wasn't until 1913 that the characteristic Portland stone façade (with its famous royal balcony overlooking the forecourt) was constructed. Today, Buckingham Palace boasts some 10,000 windows, five kilometres of red-carpeted corridors, 1,000 clocks, 10,000 pieces of furniture, over 600 rooms, a staff of 230 servants, and an 18-hectare backyard.

2. THE PALACE OF HOLYROODHOUSE

Located at the end of Edinburgh's historic Royal Mile, Holyrood's best-known former resident was Mary, Queen of Scots; today, it is the British sovereign's official residence in Scotland. First founded as a monastery in 1128, after Charles II assumed the throne he ordered the palace rebuilt on a much grander scale in the architectural style of France's Louis XIV.

3. THE PALACE OF WESTMINISTER

There has been a palace standing on the bank of the Thames in London, not far from Westminster Abbey, in one form or another for a thousand years. Although still theoretically the monarch's principle residence in the city, it hasn't been occupied as such since the reign of Henry VIII and is now the home of Britain's Houses of Parliament. The present complex of structures (including the clock tower with its famous bell, Big Ben) was constructed in a mock-medieval "gothic revival" style after a devastating fire in 1834.

4. ST JAMES'S PALACE

Known as the "senior palace" of the sovereign (in spite of it having been superseded by Buckingham Palace as an official residence), St. James' is still the official court to which foreign ambassadors are accredited. Built in the mid-sixteenth century and inhabited thereafter by kings and queens for over 300 years; today it serves primarily as the London base for the Prince of Wales.

5. KENSINGTON PALACE

A Jacobean mansion originally purchased by William III in 1689, and later extended and improved by the classical architect Christopher Wren. The palace itself (and indeed the whole district of Kensington) actually owes its rise to the king's asthma; it seems the latter, "much incommoded by the Smoak of the Coal Fires of London," decided to abandon drafty Whitehall and relocate to this area, which in the seventeenth century was but a small village on the outskirts of the city. Kensington Palace presently serves as the London residence for a number of minor royals such as Princess Margaret, and was the home of Princess Diana until her death in 1997.

6. HAMPTON COURT PALACE

Located on the banks of the Thames between London and Windsor, the enormous, red-bricked Hampton Court Palace was the centre of English court life for almost two centuries. Originally begun in 1514 by the powerful Lord Chancellor Cardinal Wolsey, who obsequiously donated it to Henry VIII, the palace was later greatly enlarged under the commission of William and Mary by their preferred architect, Christopher Wren (who would also work on Kensington Palace). No longer a home for British monarchs, part of the structure was long ago divided up into so-called "grace and favour" apartments for retirees who had served the royal family well.

7. KEW PALACE

The smallest and least-known royal palace, Kew is a modest, four-storey brick manor house that was originally designed as the country retreat of a wealthy Dutch merchant. Built in 1631, "the Dutch House" (as it is commonly known) was purchased by the crown the following century and would see much royal service, being a particular favourite of George III and his family. Today it primarily serves as a museum to their memory.

FOUR REMARKABLE ROYAL CASTLES

Though admittedly remarkable, Edinburgh Castle has few actual associations with English royalty.

1. BALMORAL CASTLE

"The Highland Barn of a thousand draughts."

Edward VII

The place where the royal family traditionally spends its summers, Balmoral is located in the wild Scottish highlands of Aberdeenshire, on the banks of the River Dee. Designed as a sort of fantasy retreat by Queen Victoria's husband Prince Albert in the 1850s, to this day it retains much of his imprint, particularly in its gaudy tartan wallpaper and carpets. Set on some 7,000 hectares of grounds, it features 67 fire-places, towers with turrets, and even a cozy separate hideaway nearby (known as Birkhall) for those who require additional privacy. Construction of this grey granite baronial edifice was first made possible, incidentally, after an eccentric miser, John Neild, inexplicably left the queen £250,000 in his will.

2. WINDSOR CASTLE

It was William the Conqueror who first chose the site for Windsor Castle on a bluff overlooking the Thames, the intention being to guard the western approaches to London. Since that time it has been continuously occupied and improved upon by English sovereigns, though it was George IV who really made it into what it is today, adding as he did the magnificent Waterloo chamber and giving the formerly austere structure a sense of gothic-inspired unity. During the twentieth century the castle became the royals' preferred home-away-from-home, with each branch of the family — the Wales's, the Yorks, the Kents — taking up residence in their own separate towers.

3. THE TOWER OF LONDON

First begun under William the Conqueror, the Tower is still officially counted among the royal palaces despite the fact that no monarch since the sixteenthth-century has actually lived there. Today its main function (aside from being a major tourist attraction) is to provide a secure home for the crown jewels.

4. CAERNARVON CASTLE

Europe's finest surviving example of medieval military building, Caernarvon Castle was begun by Edward I in 1283 as a symbol of his determination to subdue the Welsh. With its 2-metre-thick walls, the actual, moated design was based on the Roman walls at

Constantinople, though perhaps the most notable feature is the colossal trio of eagles that originally crowned its tallest tower (only one still exists). The inside of the castle, long in ruins, has in recent years undergone some restoration.

SEVEN ROYAL RESIDENCES THAT NO LONGER EXIST

In addition to those royal residences that have been destroyed outright, a considerable number have also been converted over for nonroyal purposes. Examples include Greenwich Palace (now the Royal Naval College); Elton Palace (now part of the University of London); Leeds Castle (now privately owned) and White Lodge (now the Royal Ballet School).

1. WINCHESTER PALACE
Winchester in Hampshire was once the capital of the Anglo-Saxon kingdom of Wessex. The royal palace used there by certain medieval English kings was ultimately destroyed by fire in 1302, although Henry III's great hall still stands.

2. & 3. SHEEN PALACE AND RICHMOND PALACE
After his beloved wife Anne of Bohemia died at Sheen in 1394, Richard II was so tormented with grief that he had the palace levelled. It was later rebuilt under the Tudors as Richmond Palace, though little of it still survives.

4. NUNSUCH PALACE
So-named because "none such" like it had ever existed before, this magnificent palace in Surry was originally constructed by Henry VIII. Sadly, its ownership later fell into dispute and today barely a trace of it remains.

5. THEOBALD'S PARK
Pronounced "Tibbalds"; James I's beloved hunting lodge in Hertfordshire has long since disappeared.

6. WHITEHALL PALACE
This enormous central London palace (aptly described as "two thousand rooms badly arranged and no doors") was largely destroyed

by fire in 1698. Fortunately, the famous Banqueting House survived virtually unscathed.

7. THE NEW PALACE AT KEW

In 1802 George III ordered construction of an immense gothic palace on the site of the old White House at Kew (the place where he was often confined during his first bouts of mental illness). Unfortunately, it would remain unfinished in his lifetime, and his son George IV — who considered it a white elephant — had it blown up in 1827. All that remains is the staircase, which was later used at Buckingham Palace.

FIVE ROYAL POETS

1. CANUTE (C. 995–1035)

Wrote a song to commemorate a visit to the abbey on the island of Ely, one verse of which still survives:

Merrily sung the monks in Ely,
When Canute the king rowed thereby;
Rowed knights near the land,
And hear we these monks sing.

Henry VI

2. HENRY VI *(1421–71)*

Written in the Tower of London:

> Kingdoms are but cares,
> State is devoid of stay;
> Riches are ready snares,
> And hasten to decay.

3. HENRY VIII *(1491–1547)*

The king wrote the following for Anne Boleyn:

> Now unto my lady
> Promise to her I make
> From all other only
> To her I me betake

4. ELIZABETH I *(1533–1603)*

The following stanza was said to have been written by Elizabeth in response to a question from her Catholic half-sister, Queen Mary I:

> *Hoc est corpus meum*
> As Christ willed it and spake it
> And thankfully blessed and brake it
> And as the sacred word doth make it
> So I believe in it and take it
> My life to give therefore
> In earth to live no more.

5. CHARLES, PRINCE OF WALES *(1948–)*

The prince wrote (and later sang) this clever bit of doggerel while on a tour of Canada:

> Insistent, persistent, the press never end,
> One day they will drive me right round the bend;
> Recording, re-phrasing every word that I say:
> It's got to be news at the end of the day.
>
> Disgraceful, most dangerous, to share the same plane,
> Denies me the chance to scratch and complain;
> Oh where, may I ask you, is the monarchy going

When princes and pressmen are in the same Boeing?

FIVE ATTACKS ON MODERN ARCHITECTURE BY PRINCE CHARLES

The present Prince of Wales is staunchly conservative when it comes to the environment in which he lives, and has been a harsh critic of excessive modernism in architecture. Such an attitude, it should be noted, is hardly surprising in a country that suffered far more than others from ill-conceived post-war "development."

1. ON THE PROPOSED EXTENSION TO THE NATIONAL GALLERY, LONDON
"…it looks as if we may be presented with a kind of vast municipal fire station — complete with the sort of tower that contains the siren. I would better understand this type of 'high-tech' approach if you demolished the whole of Trafalgar Square and started again with a single architect responsible for the entire layout. But what is proposed is like a monstrous carbuncle on the face of a much-loved and elegant friend."

2. ON A NEW BUILDING BY MIES VAN DER ROHE IN MANCHESTER SQUARE
"…a giant glass stump, better suited to downtown Chicago than to the City of London."

3. ON THE NEW BRITISH LIBRARY IN LONDON
"Looks like an academy for the secret police."

4. ON THE PROPOSED RE-DEVELOPMENT OF PATERNOSTER SQUARE, NEAR ST PAUL'S CATHEDRAL
"What *have we done* to St Paul's since the bombing (of the Blitz)? In the space of a mere fifteen years (city planners, architects and developers) wrecked the London skyline and desecrated the dome of St Paul's. Not only did they wreck the London skyline in general; they also did their best to lose the great dome in a jostling scrum of office buildings, so mediocre that the only way you ever remember them is by the frustration they induce — like a basketball team standing shoulder-to-shoulder between you and the Mona Lisa…Can you imagine the Italians walling in St Mark's in Venice or St Peter's in Rome?…You

have, ladies and gentlemen, to give this much to the *Luftwaffe*: when it knocked down our buildings, it didn't replace them with anything more offensive than rubble. *We* did that"

5. ON THE NEW CENTRAL LIBRARY IN BIRMINGHAM
  "Looks like a place where books are incinerated."

Science
and
Learning

SEVEN THINGS DESIGNED OR INVENTED BY ROYALS

1. A Clock
In order to be more precise in attending to his religious duties, Alfred the Great had a clock created consisting of specially designed wax candles which, when lit at a set time, showed the exact hour by a series of markers on their side. The latter was also protected from winds by a lantern cover made of ox-horn.

2. Imperial Measurements
In 1305 Edward I defined the yard (a unit of measurement roughly equal to a metre, still in use in America) as consisting of three, 12-inch feet; he further decreed that an inch should be equal to "three grains of dry barley laid end to end." He was also the first to standardize the area of an acre.

3. Cast-Iron Execution Weights
Henry IV's most lasting contribution to mankind was the idea of using specially designed weights, resembling bodybuilding plates, for use in pressing people to death. Prior to this innovation large stones had been the norm.

4. An All-Weather Chair
Elizabeth I designed a special outdoor chair for her visits to Windsor Castle, which consisted of a swivelling seat with a hood that could be turned away from the wind or sun.

5. A Title
James I created the title of baronet in order to raise money (he sold them for the sum of £1,095). He also coined the name "Great Britain."

6. FUNERAL TRAPPINGS

Prince Albert personally designed the Duke of Wellington's enormous bronze funeral car and coffin, for his state funeral in 1852.

7. PLEXIGLASS BUBBLE TOP

Designed by Prince Philip for his wife's motorcade during a 1951 tour of Canada. Originally intended merely as a cover for her open car during times of bad weather, the idea would later be taken up by virtually every head of state from then on, though more for reasons of security than accessibility.

FIVE ROYAL REPORT CARDS

1. EDWARD VI (1537–53)

"Every day," ran one of Edward's tutor reports, "(he) readeth a portion of Solomon's Proverbs, wherein he delighteth much; and learneth there…to beware of strange and wanton women." Whenever the prince did badly at his lessons, incidentally, it was his whipping boy Barnaby Fitzpatrick who would be punished.

2. ALBERT VICTOR, DUKE OF CLARENCE (1864–92)

The heir to the throne; during Prince Eddy's brief lifetime the royal family went to enormous lengths to conceal the fact that he was an imbecile. In recognition that he could not be kept under wraps forever, though, the best tutors in the land were eventually called upon to help him through Cambridge. Unfortunately, they quickly concluded that university life was not for him, and ended their report to his parents with the observation: "He hardly knows the meaning of the words 'to read.'" He was subsequently sent off to the army, though not without first being awarded an honorary degree in law.

3. EDWARD VIII (1894–1972)

"Bookish he will never be." (*Oxford report*).

4. GEORGE VI (1895–1952)

In 1910 "Bertie" graduated dead last in his class of 68 at Dartmouth Naval College.

5. DIANA, PRINCESS OF WALES (1961–97)

No scholar by her own admission, Diana's highest academic achievement was said to have been a class prize awarded for "best guinea-pig."

13 LESS INTELLECTUALLY GIFTED ROYALS

1. STEPHEN (C. 1097–1154)

A contemporary, Walter Map, recorded that the king was "adept at the martial arts but in other respects little more than a simpleton."

2. JOHN (1166–1216)

Since he was unable to write his own name, the king never actually signed the *Magna Carta* in 1215. He placed his seal on it instead.

3. CHARLES I (1600–49)

Backward as a child, as king Charles was utterly out of his depth.

4. GEORGE OF DENMARK (1653–1708)

The husband of Queen Anne (herself not renowned for her mental powers) was notoriously unintelligent, his life revolving entirely around his twin interests of model ship building and drinking. Charles II summed him up best with his oft-repeated quote: "I've tried him drunk and I've tried him sober, but there's nothing in him."

5. ANNE (1665–1714)

Lazy, bovine and dreary; when the queen wasn't busy having miscarriages she was usually to be found playing cards in the company of her lesbian lover.

6. GEORGE III (1738–1820)

Didn't learn to read until age 11, and at twenty still wrote like a child.

7. WILLIAM IV (1765–1837)

Brainless and reactionary.

8. EDWARD VII (1841–1910)

"He knows everything except what is in books."

William Gladstone

Although not strictly speaking unintelligent, the king was always more of a man of action than of learning. As his father, Prince Albert, once said of him: "His intellect is of no more use than a pistol packed in the bottom of a trunk if one were attacked in the robber-infested Apennines!" His mother Queen Victoria was rather more direct in her assessment, dismissing him as "dull and ignorant."

9. ALBERT VICTOR, DUKE OF CLARENCE (1864–92)
An illiterate dyslexic.

10. GEORGE V (1865–1936)
As his official biographer himself admitted, the king "was neither a wit nor a brilliant raconteur, neither well-read nor well-educated, and he made no great contribution to enlightened social converse." He was also notable for being the only major European royal who could not speak a second language.

11. GEORGE VI (1895–1952)
Once described by Edouard Daladier, the future premier of France, as "a moron." The king is said to have read very little, preferring gossip sheets to serious newspapers.

12. DIANA, PRINCESS OF WALES (1961–97)
Not the brightest diamond in the tiara. Once, while visiting a hospital in Surrey, the princess entered a ward where some patients were playing *Trivial Pursuit*. When one of the latter picked out a question for her to answer, she declined to even try, admitting with admirable candour: "No thanks, I'm as thick as a plank."

13. PRINCE WILLIAM (1982–)
Inherited his mother's intellect, as well as her good looks.

FOUR GREAT DOCUMENTS SPONSORED BY ROYALTY

1. THE ANGLO-SAXON CHRONICLE
Begun by monks in the reign of Alfred the Great (who made such literary efforts possible), this historically important series of annals serves as a record of life in England from the Roman invasion until the mid-twelfth century.

2. *The* Doomsday Book

In 1080 William the Conqueror ordered a detailed inventory to be made of his new lands for purposes of taxation. The resulting work (known as the *Doomsday Book* because, as a contemporary explained, "it spared no man but judged all men indifferently, as the Lord in the great day will do") appeared six years later, and remains a classic example of Norman organization. It is now housed in the Public Records Office, London.

3. *The* Magna Carta

After provoking his barons into rebellion with his numerous abuses, in 1215 King John was forced to agree to the terms of the *Magna Carta* — a list of the nobles' rights and privileges — as a way of redressing their grievances. Although somewhat overrated in its effect (it merely serving to entrench the feudal way of life), later generations took it as an important statement of civil liberties and the document would go on to form the basis of English common law.

4. *An* English-Language Bible

James I was responsible for commissioning (and supervising the creation of) the first authorised, English-language bible — the celebrated "King James" version. First published in 1611, its purpose was the make the word of God accessible to all of his subjects.

SEVEN ROYALS WHO ATTENDED ETON

Perhaps the most famous of Britain's exclusive "public" (i.e. private) boys' schools, Eton has produced generations of the country's ruling class. The college itself was founded in 1440 by that great royal patron of academia, Henry VI. Students here still wear the distinctive pin-stripe trousers, swallow-tailed coats and stiff collars that have long been associated with the school, though top hats have not been worn since the 1940s.

1. *Edward, Duke of Kent (1935–)*
2. *Prince Michael of Kent (1942–)*
3. *Richard, Duke of Gloucester (1944–)*
4. *George, Earl of St Andrews (1962–)*
5. *Lord Frederick Windsor (1979–)*

6. *PRINCE WILLIAM (1982–)*
7. *PRINCE HENRY (1984–)*

EIGHT ROYALS WHO ATTENDED CAMBRIDGE

One of the two great medieval universities in England (the other of course being Oxford); it is thought that the scattered colleges that make up Cambridge first began to appear sometime during the thirteenth century. It was Henry VI who personally founded the magnificent, late-Gothic King's College there in 1441, thus beginning a longstanding tradition of royal patronage. Lady Margaret Beaufort (the mother of Henry VII) founded Christ's College in 1505, and her grandson Henry VIII would establish the famed Trinity College in 1546.

1. *ALBERT VICTOR, DUKE OF CLARENCE (1864–92)*
2. *EDWARD VII (1841–1910)*
3. *GEORGE VI (1895–1952)*
4. *HENRY, DUKE OF GLOUCESTER (1900–74)*
5. *EARL LOUIS MOUNTBATTEN OF BURMA (1900–79)*
6. *RICHARD, DUKE OF GLOUCESTER (1944–)*
7. *CHARLES, PRINCE OF WALES (1948–)*
8. *EDWARD, EARL OF WESSEX (1964–)*

FOUR ROYALS WHO ATTENDED OXFORD

A leading centre of learning since the twelfth century, Oxford was England's first university and remains among its most cherished historic places. The majority of Britain's foremost literary, scientific and political figures have been educated here over the centuries, though (it must be admitted) relatively few members of the royal family. Up until the second part of the twentieth century those of the latter were never required to sit for exams or attend lectures.

1. *EDWARD VII (1841–1910)*
2. *LEOPOLD, DUKE OF ALBANY (1853–84)**
3. *MARY OF TECK (1867–1955)**
4. *EDWARD VIII (1894–1972)*

* *Honorary degree*

FOUR FAMOUS TUTORS OF ROYALTY

1. JOHN SKELTON (c. 1460–1529)

This cynical poet served as tutor of classics to the young Henry VIII and wrote for him the *Speculum Principis*, a little manual on how royalty should behave.

2. FELIX MENDELSSOHN (1809–47)

The German composer gave Queen Victoria lessons in singing.

3. DAVID LLOYD GEORGE (1863–1945)

The former prime minister taught Edward VIII enough Welsh to get him through his Investiture as Prince of Wales in 1911. Years later, Winston Churchill helped the king write his abdication speech.

4. SIR LAURENS VAN DER POST (1906–96)

The mystical South African philosopher / filmmaker was a major influence on the present Prince of Wales' thinking, as well as the godfather of Prince William. During his honeymoon in 1981 Charles is said to have treated his new bride to readings of Van der Post's work as she lay beside him in the Balmoral heather.

NINE ROYAL AUTHORS

"People who write books ought to be shut up."

George V

1. ALFRED THE GREAT (c. 849–899)

Translated Bede and Boethius into English from Latin, creating the concept of popular literature in the process.

2. HENRY VIII (1491–1547)

Wrote (with the help of Thomas Cranmer) *Necessary Doctrine and Evolution for any Christian Man*, which emphasised the Royal Supremacy.

3. EDWARD VI (1537–53)

Wrote *A Tract Against the Pope* at the age of twelve (not to mention over a hundred essays in Latin before the age of ten).

4. JAMES I (1566–1625)

Best known for the early anti-smoking booklet *A Counterblaste on the Use of Tobacco*, the king also wrote works on the bible, sports and demonology.

5. VICTORIA (1819–1901)

Wrote (and illustrated) *Leaves from the Journal of Our Life in the Highlands*, along with a sequel entitled, rather unimaginatively, *More Leaves from a Journal of Our Life in the Highlands*. The queen also wrote *A Biography of John Brown*, about her beloved male companion (and possible lover), which her friends dissuaded her from publishing.

Queen Victoria with one of her Indian servants.

6. EDWARD VIII (1894–1972)

The only British sovereign ever to write an autobiography (the fact that it was largely ghost-written notwithstanding), Edward published his historically worthless *A King's Story* in 1951. His wife also wrote a memoir, entitled *The Heart Has Its Reasons*.

7. PHILIP, DUKE OF EDINBURGH (1921–)

Has written extensively on the subjects of wildlife preservation and identification, often accompanied by his own photographs. In 1982 he also published a manual entitled *Competition Carriage Driving*, which is widely considered to be the definitive book on this sport.

8. CHARLES, PRINCE OF WALES (1948–)

Published *The Old Man of Lochnagar* in 1980, an illustrated children's book that he had originally written for his brothers; the story was about an old man who leaves his comfortable cave to explore the Scottish countryside. In more recent years the prince has published works on various subjects close to his heart, as for instance his 1989 look at modern architecture entitled *A Vision of Britain*. One book of his that never did see the light of day was a manual for the men of the Royal Regiment of Wales, *A Guide to the Chatting Up of Girls*.

9. SARAH, DUCHESS OF YORK (1959–)

The duchess's *Budgie the Helicopter* books have earned her a small fortune since their introduction back in the 1980s. This success comes, incidentally, despite the revelation that they bear more than a passing similarity to a children's book published by an early 1960s author.

EIGHT ROYALS WHO HELPED TO FURTHER SCIENCE AND LEARNING

1. ALFRED THE GREAT (C. 849–C. 899)

Although the king didn't actually learn to read until he was in his teens, in later life he acquired a reputation both for his own scholarship as well as for his (often enforced) promotion of learning among his nobles.

2. EDWARD I (1239–1307)

Commissioned the first national land survey in Britain, complete with maps.

3. HENRY VII (1457–1509)

Among the many enterprises the king sponsored was the voyage from Bristol by John Cabot in 1497, which led to the discovery of the

North American mainland. After reporting to his patron that the royal flag had been planted on a land far across the Atlantic Ocean, the Italian-born explorer was rewarded with a gift of £10.

4. ELIZABETH I (1533–1603)

Though several great explorers were associated with her reign (not the least of which being Sir Francis Drake and Sir Walter Raleigh), the queen actually had very little to do with their expeditions other than providing some financial backing.

5. CHARLES II (1630–85)

Granted a charter for the establishment of the Royal Society in 1662, in an effort to bring together the leading scientists of the day, as well as founding the Royal Observatory at Greenwich. Such was the king's zeal for learning, in fact, that he even went so far as to install his own laboratory in the palace at Whitehall.

6. GEORGE III (1738–1820)

Although the king had little grasp of science himself, he was nevertheless a generous scientific patron. Among his many contributions was the personal financial backing of William Herschel, the Hanoverian astronomer who discovered the planet Uranus.

7. GEORGE IV (1762–1830)

Largely responsible for bringing the first street lighting to England. He also helped to support such important scientists as Sir Humphrey Davy (the discoverer of laughing gas and inventor of the miners' safety lamp) and William Congreve, who invented a ballistic missile known as the Congreve rocket.

8. ALBERT, PRINCE CONSORT (1819–61)

It was Queen Victoria's husband Prince Albert who, through his initiative and enthusiasm, brought about the epoch-making Great Exhibition of 1851 in Hyde Park. Intended to celebrate the achievements of the Industrial Revolution, the six-month-long international event was considered by many to be "the grandest spectacle the world has ever witnessed." Housed inside a specially constructed, multi-level structure of iron and glass known as the "Crystal Palace," more than six million visitors were able to view over 100 000 exhibits, including such nineteenth century technological wonders as Nasmyth's steam hammer and a giant hydraulic press that was used to form the Menai Bridge supports. Much of the collection was later transferred to the new Victoria & Albert Museum, at which Victoria herself laid the foundation stone in her final public London appearance in 1899. The vast Crystal Palace itself (which, among other things, was the first large building to contain public wash-rooms) was later moved to South London, where it was damaged by fire in 1936. It was finally demolished in 1941 to prevent its being used by Nazi bombers as a ground guide.

Communication

NINE EXAMPLES OF ROYAL HUMOUR

It would appear that most British royals would do better to leave the comedy to their jesters.

1. ARTHUR, PRINCE OF WALES (1486–1502)
On the morning after his marriage to Katherine of Aragon in 1501, the prince was heard to joke: "I have been deep into Spain this night." (For her part, Katherine later claimed that the marriage was *never* consummated, owing to Arthur's youth and premature death).

2. ANNE BOLEYN (C. 1500–36)
(*On her impending execution*) "The people will have no difficulty in finding a nickname for me; I shall be Queen Anne Lack-Head."

3. JAMES I (1566–1625)
Once placed live frogs down the earl of Pembroke's neck. The earl retaliated by letting loose a pig in the king's bedroom.

4. GEORGE II (1683–1760)
(*To someone who claimed that General Wolfe was mad*) "Then I wish he would bite some other of my generals!"

5. EDWARD VII (1841–1910)
(*On his lifelong wait for the throne*) "I don't mind praying to the eternal Father, but I must be the only man in the country afflicted with an eternal mother." A lifelong practical joker, even while king Edward enjoyed placing dead birds (and on one memorable occasion, a live lobster) in the beds of his houseguests.

6. GEORGE VI (1895–1952)

While bestowing a knighthood upon his surgeon in 1949, the king remarked wittily, "You used a knife on me, now I'm going to use one on you."

7. ELIZABETH, THE QUEEN MOTHER (1900–)

Caught up in a crowd that was pressing much too close, the Queen Mother was once heard to exclaim (with some irritation), "Please don't touch the exhibits."

8. PHILIP, DUKE OF EDINBURGH (1921–)

Once chased the queen around the royal train while wearing a pair of vampire fangs.

9. CHARLES, PRINCE OF WALES (1948–)

In his younger days the prince was known to hand out exploding cigars to his friends, and once placed a whoopee-cushion on bishop of Norwich's chair.

FOUR ROYAL REBUKES TO MEMBERS OF THE PRESS

1. PHILIP, DUKE OF EDINBURGH (1921–)

When simultaneously confronted with both a free-living colony of monkeys and a coterie of photographers during a visit to the Rock of Gibraltar, Prince Philip was heard to ask archly, "Which are the monkeys?" He also once described the *Daily Express* as, "A bloody awful newspaper...full of lies, scandal and imagination...a vicious newspaper."

2. ANNE, THE PRINCESS ROYAL (1950–)

(*To photographers at the Badminton Horse Trials in 1982*) "Why don't you just naff off?"

3. ANDREW, DUKE OF YORK (1960–)

During his first official visit to America in 1984 the prince turned a paint-sprayer on a group of astonished photographers. He later claimed it was an accident.

4. DIANA, PRINCESS OF WALES (1961–97)

(*To someone who had addressed her as "Di"*) "My name's *Diana*."

SEVEN MULTILINGUAL ROYALS

1. EDWARD VI (1537–53)
Something of a child prodigy, at twelve Edward was translating the Latin of Cicero's philosophy into Greek. He was also fully conversant in French.

2. JANE (1537–54)
Well taught in Greek, Latin and Hebrew.

3. ELIZABETH I (1533–1603)
Highly educated, among her many attributes the queen could speak five languages.

4. VICTORIA (1819–1901)
Spoke German, French and a bit of Hindustani.

5. EDWARD VII (1841–1910)
Fluent in French and German.

6. ELIZABETH II (1926–)
Spoke fluent French by the age of ten.

7. DIANA, PRINCESS OF WALES (1961–97)
Was fully conversant in sign language for the deaf.

TEN ROYALS WHO SPOKE WITH A REAL (OR AFFECTED) GERMAN ACCENT

"Every drop of blood in my veins is German"
Edward VIII

Since the days of the first Hanoverian kings until the present generation, all British royals (to varying degrees) have had at least a hint of a German accent. Indeed, this accent has been so effectively assimilated into the dialect of the royal family that it has long been considered the proper manner of pronunciation among the upper classes as well. This would seem to account for the present queen's peculiar vocal stylings, as for example, "I now pronounce the Commonwealth Games *euw-pin*."

*A flattering portrait of Queen Adelaide (wife of William IV),
by Sir William Beechey.*

1. GEORGE I (1660–1727)

Although the popular assertion that George spoke no English is untrue, his facility with the language was nevertheless extremely limited. The question is however rather a moot one, as the king invariably preferred to speak French whenever communication with his ministers was necessary.

2. GEORGE II (1683–1760)

(*Addressing parliament*) "I have not one drop of blood in my veins dat is not English."

3. AUGUSTA, PRINCESS OF WALES (1719–72)

When George III's mother first arrived in England she didn't speak a single word of English. Her own mother had assured her however that this wouldn't be a problem, as the House of Hanover had already ruled there for twenty years and therefore all the inhabitants would certainly have learned German.

4. GEORGE III (1738–1820)

In an effort to assert his pro-British sympathies, during his first speech before parliament the king proclaimed the memorable phrase: "Born unt educated in zis country, I glory in ze name of Briton." Nevertheless, German remained the language used when conversing with his wife.

5. ADELAIDE OF SAXE-MEININGEN (1792–1849)

Wife of William IV. At the time of her wedding Adelaide could not speak any English whatsoever.

6. ALBERT, PRINCE CONSORT (1819–61)

Utterly German.

7. VICTORIA (1819–1901)

Despite having been born in England Victoria's family spoke only German in the home, and the queen herself would never entirely master the English language. Interestingly, she wrote many of her personal letters in French.

8. EDWARD VII (1841–1910)

Spoke English with a slight German accent, which became much more pronounced in times of anger. He was also fond of using tender German endearments with his wife.

9. GEORGE V (1865–1936)

Both he and his English-born wife Mary of Teck spoke with a noticeable trace of German. It is perhaps worth noting that he couldn't actually *speak* German, however.

10. PHILIP, DUKE OF EDINBURGH (1921–)

Speaks fluent German (though French is his true second language).

FOUR MEMORABLE PHRASES COINED BY ROYALS

1. "LET THE BOY WIN HIS SPURS"
Said by Edward III of his son (Edward, the Black Prince) at the Battle of Crécy in 1345.

2. "TELL IT TO THE MARINES"
Charles II first used this phrase after a colonel of marines claimed to have seen a flying fish; the king was essentially saying that, though he considered this to be merely a tall-tale, he would be prepared to believe it if his well-travelled marines did so.

3. "WE ARE NOT INTERESTED IN THE POSSIBILITIES OF DEFEAT"
Said by Queen Victoria to Prime Minister Arthur Balfour, after hearing news of a "black week" of British losses during the Boer War.

4. "THIS IS A PRETTY KETTLE OF FISH"
Said by Queen Mary to Prime Minister Baldwin, in regards to her son Edward VIII's Abdication Crisis.

FIVE PECULIARITIES IN QUEEN VICTORIA'S USE OF LANGUAGE

1. PLURALITY
Victoria's famous use of the royal "We" when referring to herself stemmed from a reluctance to separate her own wishes from those of Prince Albert — even long after his death. This plurality carried over inexplicably into other areas as well (e.g. "these news from Khartoum are frightful.")

2. MIMICRY
The queen often spoke with an affected Scottish accent when in the Highlands.

3. GERMANICISMS
Owing to her strict Hanoverian background Victoria's English notations on state papers always had a decidedly Teutonic flavour.

4. MALAPROPISMS
Examples of this are numerous. Perhaps typical was the time she

asked Lord Salisbury to "do all you can to pour oil on the flames" after hearing of some unusually bellicose statements by her grandson, the German Kaiser.

5. EUPHEMISMS

Victoria was often remarkably pretentious, and would never use just one word when ten would do. Thus the phrase "there was applause," for instance, would be written as "the efforts elicited the approbation of the Royal circle," while the queen's birthday was described as "an auspicious return of her natal day."

NINE ROYALS WHO WERE PUBLICLY RIDICULED OR LIBELED

1. HENRY III (1207–72)

The Italian poet Dante, in his *Divine Comedy*, placed Henry III in the limbo of ineffectual souls — a region of purgatory normally reserved for simpletons and children.

2. CHARLES II (1630–85)

John Wilmot, Earl of Rochester wrote the following famous lines in honour of the king:

> We have a pretty witty king,
> Whose word no man relies on;
> Who never said a foolish thing
> Nor ever did a wise one.

3. GEORGE III (1738–1820)

Much of the American Declaration of Independence consists of a detailed catalogue of the king's alleged crimes and failures.

4. GEORGE IV (1762–1830)

In 1813 the poet Leigh Hunt was imprisoned for two years and fined £500 for referring to the then Prince Regent, in his radical journal the *Examiner*, as "a corpulent gentleman of fifty" and "...a man who has just closed half a century without one single claim on the gratitude of his country or the respect of posterity." The prince was not averse to dishing it out a little on occasion, however: one of his favourite gags was to read out the American Declaration of Independence while impersonating his father, George III, as a raving madman.

5. WILLIAM IV (1765–1837)

The victim of rumours that he was mad, which had been promulgated by his own brother Ernest, Duke of Cumberland.

6. GEORGE V (1865–1936)

Author H. G. Wells once famously condemned George and his court as "alien and uninspiring." On hearing this, the outraged king is said to have responded, "I may be uninspiring, but I'll be damned if I'm an alien."

7. WALLIS, DUCHESS OF WINDSOR (C. 1896–1986)

In an effort to discredit the duchess, MI5 put together the notorious "China Report," a dossier detailing her supposed "deviant" sexual practices in high-class Hong Kong brothels.

8. ELIZABETH II (1926–)

In 1957 a young peer, Lord Altrincham, shocked royalists across Britain with his much-publicized (and highly astute) attacks on the monarchy. He had taken particular aim at the queen's overly rehearsed and lifeless formal appearances, claiming that the image she created was one of "a priggish schoolgirl (and) captain of the hockey team" who was evidently "unable to string even a few sentences together without a written text." Altrincham's criticisms brought him widespread unpopularity at the time, but have since been acknowledged as justified even by some monarchists.

9. CHARLES, PRINCE OF WALES (1948–)

During a state visit to Swaziland in 1987 the prince was entertained by rows of bare-breasted young tribal women, who sang a song that translated as, "Prince Charles, why are you so confident? You don't even own a cow."

SEVEN MONARCHS WITH A SPEECH IMPEDIMENT

1. WILLIAM II, "RUFUS" (C. 1056–1100)

The son of William the Conqueror stammered so badly in public that when he was excited or angry he was almost incoherent.

2. EDWARD I *(1239–1307)*

The king had a slight lisp but was nevertheless said to be quite eloquent.

3. RICHARD II *(1367–1400)*

Said to have been rather abrupt and stammering of speech.

4. JAMES I *(1566–1625)*

The king had a tongue that was much too large for his mouth, resulting in a mild speech impediment.

5. CHARLES I *(1600–49)*

A lifelong stutterer, Charles' only words during his first address before parliament were, "I am unfit for speaking," He then promptly sat down.

6. EDWARD VII *(1841–1910)*

A childhood stammerer.

7. GEORGE VI *(1895–1952)*

In his youth the future king was almost incomprehensible. The problem would be considerably reduced in the late 1920s, however, with the help of an Australian voice therapist, though thereafter his speeches would still be routinely pruned to eliminate difficult words and film footage of him edited to play down his constant facial twitching.

TWO INFAMOUS CELL-PHONE INTERCEPTIONS

1. "SQUIDGYGATE"

On December 31, 1989, a steamy phone-sex conversation between Princess Diana and her lover James Gilbey was randomly intercepted by a scanning device and tape-recorded. When transcripts (which also showed "Squidgy" complaining bitterly — and profanely — about her treatment by the royal family) were later made available to the public, her reputation was all but destroyed.

2. "CAMILLAGATE"

Not to be outdone by his adulterous wife, in January 1993 a transcript was released of a six-minute taped telephone conversation between Prince Charles and Camilla Parker-Bowles, which had been secretly made in 1989. In it, he revealed a desire to be reincarnated as his middle-aged mistress's sanitary napkin.

THREE ROYALS WHO HAD TO BUY BACK INCRIMINATING LETTERS

1. FREDERICK, DUKE OF YORK (1763–1827)

After she publicly admitted to having taken bribes from his military officers in the hopes of promotion, the duke quickly dumped his longstanding mistress Mary Anne Clark. In retaliation, the woman threatened to publish his embarrassingly effusive love letters to her, and was able to exact an enormous sum to prevent it.

2. EDWARD VII (1841–1910)

After the death of Edward's Italian mistress Giulia Barucci (a woman who once described herself as "the greatest whore in the world") in 1871, the latter's brother wrote to the then Prince of Wales demanding £1,500 for the return of his love letters to her. After much negotiation, the blackmailer eventually agreed to sell the letters back for a fraction of the price.

3. GEORGE, DUKE OF KENT (1902–42)

During the 1930s the duke was forced to buy back some love letters that he had earlier written to a young Parisian man.

THREE DAMNING ROYAL OBITUARIES (AND ONE POSTHUMOUS JUDGMENT)

1. STEPHEN (C. 1097–1154)

The *Anglo-Saxon Chronicle* summed up the king's reign of continuous anarchy as, "nineteen long winters when God and his saints slept."

2. GEORGE IV (1762–1830)

(*Written by a journalist for The Times*) "There never was an individual less regretted by his fellow-creatures than this deceased King."

3. WILLIAM IV (1765–1837)

(*Written by a journalist for The Spectator*) "His late Majesty, though at times a jovial and, for a king, an honest man, was a weak, ignorant, commonplace sort of person."

AND ONE POSTHUMOUS JUDGMENT ...

ANNE (1665–1714)

On the news of the queen's death the total value of the British stock market immediately rose by three per cent.

Religion

THREE EXCOMMUNICATED MONARCHS

1. JOHN (1166–1216)

Greatly antagonized Pope Innocent III by refusing to accept his papal nominee as archbishop of Canterbury, Stephen Langton. The country was promptly laid under an interdict (no church services were allowed), with John himself being excommunicated in 1209. He would later be fully absolved after repenting of his "illegal acts."

2. HENRY VIII (1491–1547)

Although he had earlier dissolved the monasteries and confiscated their property, it was actually for his attempts at divorcing his first wife Katherine of Aragon that Henry was excommunicated by Pope Paul III. Ironically, as a young man the king had earned the title *Defensor Fidei* ("Defender of the Faith") from Pope Leo X for his pamphlet attacking Martin Luther. The title is still held by British sovereigns today.

3. ELIZABETH I (1533–1603)

Pope Pius V did everything he could to turn Elizabeth's Catholic subjects against her, including the issuing of a papal bull in 1570 excommunicating her from the church.

TWO MONARCHS WHO BECAME SAINTS (AND ONE WHO MIGHT SOMEDAY)

1. ELGIVA (D. 944)

First wife of Edmund I. Popularly worshipped as St. Elgiva after her death.

2. EDWARD THE CONFESSOR (C. 1004–66)

The only king of England thus far ever to be made a saint, Edward was canonised (after a suitable bribe was paid) by Pope Alexander III in 1161.

AND ONE WHO MIGHT SOMEDAY...

HENRY VI (1421–71)

Efforts to have poor, murdered Henry canonised have been in the works for some time. Interestingly, the hapless king may have been present (at the age of eight) during the trial of another future Catholic saint, John of Arc.

RELIGIOUS INCLINATIONS OF 14 ROYALS

1. EDWARD THE CONFESSOR (C. 1004–66)

Scrupulously pious, Edward could not even be persuaded to consummate his own marriage; the consequent lack of a direct heir would result in bloody dynastic conflict after his death.

2. MATILDA OF SCOTLAND (1080–1118)

The first wife of Henry I, Matilda was known to wash and even kiss the feet of beggars in order to prove her humility. Her courtiers understandably thought this a deplorable practice, and begged her "for Godde's love" to desist.

3. HENRY III (1207–72)

So devout was Henry that, while travelling once to see his brother-in-law Louis IX of France, he insisted upon hearing mass every time he met a priest. This is said to have delayed his arrival to such an extent that, for a future visit, the French king actually had all the priests in Henry's route temporarily banished.

4. HENRY VII (1457–1509)

Not one to take chances, before his death the king arranged for no less than 10,000 masses to be performed for the repose of his soul.

5. MARY I (1516–58)

In 1555 the zealot queen banned any version of the bible in English translation, and further commanded that, "no manner of persons presume to bring into this realm any manuscripts…containing false doctrines against the Catholic faith."

6. JAMES I (1566–1625)

James was once famously described by the French statesman Maximilien, duc de Sully as "the most learned fool in Christendom." Indeed, he enjoyed nothing better than to formulate elaborate disputations over the most abstruse points of theology.

7. HENRIETTA MARIA OF FRANCE (1609–69)

Catholic wife of Charles I. Known to disrupt Anglican services in the royal household by bursting in suddenly with her pack of beagles and making hunting noises.

8. CHARLES II (1630–85)

Converted to Catholicism on his deathbed. During his lifetime the king was known to receive Holy Communion with three bishops on one side of him and three illegitimate sons (by three different mistresses) on the other.

9. GEORGE III (1738–1820)

The king obliterated the words "our most religious and gracious king" in his private prayer book, and substituted "a most miserable sinner" in their place.

10. CAROLINE OF BRUNSWICK-WOLFENBÜTTEL (1768–1821)

During a visit to Jerusalem in 1819 the Princess of Wales had herself led, Christ-like, into the city on a donkey. It was there that she afterwards founded the Order of St Caroline, setting her Italian lover Bartolomeo Pergami up as its first grand master.

11. VICTORIA (1819–1901)

Had an intense aversion to bishops.

12. EDWARD VII (1841–1910)

Forced the archbishop of York to ban the wearing of moustaches among his clergymen.

13. PRINCESS ALICE OF BATTENBERG *(1885–1969)*

After being deserted by her husband, Prince Philip's mother spent the remainder of her life as Russian Orthodox nun.

14. ELIZABETH II *(1926–)*

In 1985 the queen refused to allow the Prince and Princess of Wales to attend a private mass with the pope at the Vatican.

NINE (POST-REFORMATION) CATHOLIC ROYALS

Since the passing of the Act of Settlement in 1701 all British sovereigns have been legally required to be a member of the Church of England, and must promise to uphold it. Already forbidden to be Catholics themselves, under the terms of the Royal Marriages Act of 1772 it also became illegal for British monarchs to marry Catholics.

1. KATHERINE HOWARD (C. 1522–42)
2. MARY I (1516–58)
3. ANNE OF DENMARK (1574–1619)*
4. CHARLES II (1630–85)*
5. JAMES II (1633–1701)*
6. HENRIETTA MARIA OF FRANCE (1609–69)
7. KATHERINE HENRIETTA OF BRAGANZA (1638–1705)
8. MARY OF MODENA (1658–1718)
9. PRINCESS MICHAEL OF KENT (1945–)

* Converted to Catholicism later in life

FIVE ROYAL RESPONSES TO MEN OF THE CLOTH

1. RICHARD I *(1157–99)*

When a prominent churchman once accused Richard of begetting three shameless daughters — Pride, Avarice, and Sensuality — the king promptly responded with the following pithy rejoinder: "I give my daughter Pride to the Knights Templar, my daughter Avarice to the Cistercians, and my daughter Sensuality to the Princes of the Church."

2. ELIZABETH I (1533–1603)

The extravagantly dressed queen once commanded a bishop to change the subject after he began sermonizing on vanity. On another occasion she ordered the right hand of extreme puritan John Stubbs be cut off, after he dared to suggest that she was too old to marry.

3. JAMES I (1566–1625)

Once interrupted a Presbyterian minister in mid-sermon by shouting out, "I give not a turd for your preaching!"

4. VICTORIA (1819–1901)

In an effort to console the queen after the death of her husband, a clergyman unwisely suggested that she should perhaps regard herself as married to Christ instead. "That is what I call twaddle," Victoria replied angrily.

5. CHARLES, PRINCE OF WALES (1948–)

After Princess Michael of Kent was refused a church wedding by the pope, Charles made a public speech condemning "the needless distress" that resulted from inflexible religious doctrines.

NINE GREAT ROYAL RELIGIOUS GESTURES

1. CANUTE (C. 995–1035)

This Danish-born king is best known today for something that probably never even happened. According to legend, in order to demonstrate to his toadying courtiers that the power of the monarchy could not overcome nature, he once had his throne placed on the seashore in front of the incoming tide. When his verbal commands for the waters to turn back resulted only in soaked feet, he at last got up and exclaimed that nobody was worthy of the name king except "He whom heaven, earth and sea obey by eternal laws." Afterwards Canute is said to have never worn his crown again, hanging it instead on a crucifix in Winchester cathedral as a sign of respect.

2. EDWARD THE CONFESSOR (C. 1004–66)

This holiest of English kings devoted the final years of his life to building Westminster Abbey, which he intended to be larger and grander than any church in England or Normandy. Modelled on the Norman abbey at Jumièges, craftsmen spent fifteen years constructing it on marshy land beside the River Thames. Just eight days after it was finally consecrated, Edward died and was buried behind the high altar.

3. WILLIAM I, "THE CONQUEROR" (C. 1027–87)

Founded an enormous Benedictine abbey to commemorate the site of the most momentous event in English history — the Battle of Hastings in 1066. It is said that the high altar (its place now marked by a memorial stone) stood on the exact spot where Harold II was killed. The abbey itself fell victim to Henry VIII's destructive binge in 1539.

4. HENRY II (1133–1189)

Henry's guilt over his unintentional complicity in the death of his onetime friend, Archbishop Thomas à Becket, was both genuine and intense. For three days after the event the king refused to eat or to see anyone, even going so far as to exchange his royal robes for sackcloth and ashes. But it was perhaps his public penance that was most impressive. After travelling to Canterbury the king entered the cathedral

Henry II

barefoot and prostrate, where he remained overnight in prayer before finally requesting absolution from the bishops. Then, by way of punishment, he allowed each of the 70-odd monks there assembled to give him a few lashes across his naked back with rods.

5. JOHN (1166–1216)

In an effort to patch things up with Pope Innocent III, with whom he had been quarrelling, the king resigned his crown to the papal legate, Pandulf, in 1213. The latter kept it for four days, before finally giving it back as a sign that he held John's kingdom as a papal fief.

6. ELIZABETH I (1533–1603)

It was the queen's authorisation of a Welsh translation of the bible in 1588 that not only brought those subjects easier access to religion, but helped to preserve their language in the process.

7. WILLIAM IV (1765–1837)

Personally rammed through the Catholic Emancipation Bill in 1829, over the fanatical opposition of his own brother Ernest, Duke of Cumberland.

8. GEORGE V (1865–1936)

Once refused to deliver the Parliamentary Declaration until its rabidly anti-Catholic rhetoric was toned down.

9. CHARLES, PRINCE OF WALES (1948–)

Revealed in a recent television documentary that, as king, he would like to see the title "Defender of the Faith" replaced by the more inclusive "Defender of Faith."

THREE RENOWNED RELIGIOUS LEADERS EXECUTED BY ROYALS

1. THOMAS À BECKET (C. 1118–70)

Not so much a planned execution as a case of unintended wish fulfillment, Thomas Becket, archbishop of Canterbury was murdered in 1170 by four loyal if slow-witted knights who mistakenly believed that they were carrying out the king's orders. It seems that the men had overheard Henry II call out in frustration "Will no one rid me of this turbulent priest?," after the stubborn Becket had once again defied him regarding the legal jurisdiction of clergyman. The archbishop was subsequently murdered in the very heart of Canterbury Cathedral itself, where an extravagant shrine was later built in his honour. He was canonised in 1173, his tomb becoming an important place of pilgrimage for English Catholics (not to mention the characters in Geoffrey Chaucer's *Canterbury Tales*).

Becket's story doesn't end there, however. During the Reformation some 350 years later, Henry VIII not only had Becket's shrine destroyed but actually put the martyr-rebel himself on trial as well, the charge being that of usurping papal authority. The skeleton was, perhaps inevitably, convicted of treason and publicly burned "to admonish the living of their duty" to the crown.

2. SIR THOMAS MORE (1478–1535)

Henry VIII's one-time mentor, More was a learned but morally inflexible man who was ultimately beheaded for refusing to go along with the king's break with Rome. The 1966 film *A Man for All Seasons* was based on his life.

3. THOMAS CRANMER (1489–1556)

Archbishop of Canterbury during the reign of Henry VIII (and a willing participant in all the king's religious turnabouts), Cranmer was burnt at the stake by Queen Mary in 1556. He would afterwards be considered a martyr for the brave way he faced his terrible fate, deliberately placing his right hand first into the flames to make up for having signed his earlier recantations of his Protestant beliefs.

THREE ACCOMPLISHED ROYAL BLASPHEMERS OR DESECRATERS

1. HENRY II (1133–89)

In 1189, the king's beloved city of Le Mans was accidentally razed to the ground. Enraged at God for doing such a thing, he declared that he would "retaliate as best I can by damaging that part of me in which you take most delight" (i.e. his soul).

2. JOHN (1166–1216)

Once while out hunting a magnificent stag was brought down in the presence of the king, prompting him to observe mockingly, "Oh what a good life that beast has led…and yet it has never heard holy Mass!"

3. HENRY VIII (1491–1547)

Terrible as it was, the king's dissolution (and, frequently, destruction) of the monasteries in the mid sixteenth-century helped to curb the power of the Roman Catholic Church in England and thus paved the way for the Reformation. That he significantly increased his own power in the process was of course quite beside the point.

FOUR ROYAL ANTI-SEMITES

1. RICHARD I, "THE LIONHEART" (1157–99)

Prior to his coronation day in 1189, Richard had issued a public notice banning Jews from attending the celebration. Unfortunately, a few Jewish leaders did try to crash the coronation banquet anyway, resulting in their torture and murder at the hands of courtiers. The people of London quickly followed suit, and before long a sizeable number of the city's Jews were massacred.

2. HENRY III (1207–72)

Extorted vast amounts of gold and silver from the Jews of England.

3. EDWARD I (1239–1307)

In 1290, the king expelled all Jews from England.

4. MARGARET, COUNTESS OF SNOWDON (1930–)

According to a recent book on the House of Windsor, when the princess was introduced to the famed American advice columnist Ann Landers, Margaret looked her over closely. "Are you a Jew?…are you a Jew?" she demanded. When the columnist admitted that she was, the princess quickly moved on.

FIVE ROYAL VIEWS ON RELIGION

1. *Elizabeth I (1533–1603)*

"There is only one Jesus Christ and all the rest is a dispute over trifles."

2. *James I (1566–1625)*

(*On his determined support of church government*) "No bishop, no king!"

3. *Charles I (1600–49)*

"Presbytery is not a religion for gentlemen."

4. *Edward VII (1841–1910)*

"I do not mind what religion a man professes, but I distrust him who has none."

5. *Diana, Princess of Wales (1961–97)*

(*On the afterlife*) "My idea of heaven is shopping at Harrods."

DIEU ET MON DROIT: THREE KINGS WHO ENJOYED DIVINE PROTECTION

1. *Edmund I (c. 921–946)*

The king once had a narrow escape from death when, out hunting a stag near Cheddar Gorge, his quarry suddenly ran over the edge of the cliff along with his baying hounds. It appeared that Edmund's horse could not be restrained from following suit either, and the story goes that it was only by offering up a quick vow to make amends for past sins that he was able to stop in time.

2. *Edward I (1239–1307)*

Once, as a boy, Edward had been playing a game of chess with one of his knights in a vaulted room when he inexplicably got up and walked away. Just then a massive stone crashed from the roof on to the very spot he had vacated, which would easily have killed him had he remained. In later life the king, throughout his numerous battles, had an uncanny knack of remaining uninjured while those around him fell like flies.

3. EDWARD IV (1442–83)

After being deposed in 1471 Edward is said to have gone to a little parish church in Daventry and kneeled before an alabaster image of St Anne, requesting her help. According to one account, the statue gave very definite signs that it had heard his plea, and a short time later the king had regained his throne.

The
Great
Beyond

EIGHT ROYALS WHO BELIEVED IN THE SUPERNATURAL (AND ONE WHO DID NOT)

1. JOAN OF NAVARRE (1370–1437)

Henry IV's second wife was for years rumoured to be involved in necromancy. In 1419 she was finally accused of seeking the death of her stepson, Henry V, by witchcraft and quietly confined to do penance.

2. RICHARD II (1367–1400)

The king relied heavily on a specially prepared book of astrological divinations to help guide his decisions.

3. JAMES I (1566–1625)

Published an essay on demonology in 1597, in which he outlined the various supernatural abilities of witches. According to the king (who did admit to having a few doubts), the latter can fly if they hold their breath, raise storms, and cause insanity, impotence, and urgent sexual desire.

4. EDWARD VII (1841–1910)

Had a strong belief in the power of goodluck charms, and hung them in festoons from his bed in each of his royal residences.

5. ALEXANDRA OF DENMARK (1844–1925)

Believed herself to be both clairvoyant and clairaudient.

6. GEORGE V (1865–1936)

On July 11, 1881, while serving as a naval officer in the South Atlantic, the future King George V was convinced that he had sighted the fabled *Flying Dutchman*, and entered full details of the experience into the ship's log. According to legend the phantom ship's captain, a Dutchman named Hendrik Vanderdecken, had shouted such fearful curses as he sailed around the Cape of Good Hope in a storm that, by some supernatural means, he was condemned to sail the seas for eternity. Sightings of the ship are said to bring bad luck.

7. ELIZABETH, THE QUEEN MOTHER (1900–)

Remained firmly convinced throughout her life that fairies inhabit the woods near her childhood home.

8. CHARLES, PRINCE OF WALES (1948–)

Reportedly made attempts to contact his murdered mentor, Earl Louis Mountbatten of Burma, by means of a ouija board (he denies this).

AND ONE WHO DID NOT…

HENRY VII (1457–1509)

Irritated by word that an astrologer had prophesied his early death, the king had the man brought before him for an audience in the hopes of exposing him for a fraud. At first Henry feigned interest in his abilities, until the point when the man admitted he couldn't predict where he himself would be at Christmastime. "Then I am a better astrologer than you!," exclaimed the king in triumph. "…I can tell where you will be — in the Tower of London!"

THREE ROYALS WHO HAD PERSONAL PSYCHICS

1. ELIZABETH I (1533–1603)

Had as her personal psychic the famous crystal ball-using seer Dr. John Dee. The queen later rewarded the doctor for his services by installing him as chancellor of St. Paul's.

2. VICTORIA (1819–1901)

During the 1860s the widowed queen made repeated attempts to contact her dead husband Albert, reputedly by holding séances under the guidance of a teenage medium named Robert James Lee.

3. DIANA, PRINCESS OF WALES (1961–97)

Spent tens of thousands of pounds each year on assorted psychics, astrologers, numerologists and holistic counsellors.

FIVE ROYAL SUPERSTITIONS

1. CAROLINE OF BRUNSWICK-WOLFENBÜTTEL (1768–1821)

Used to make wax figures of her hated husband George IV (complete with devil horns), then stick pins in them and throw them on the fire.

2. VICTORIA (1819–1901)

In keeping with an old Scottish tradition, the queen wouldn't allow any of her children to marry in the month of May.

3. EDWARD VII (1841–1910)

Horrified at the sight of a crossed knife and fork.

4. WALLIS, DUCHESS OF WINDSOR (C. 1896–1986)

A firm believer in the adage that blondes brought luck, the duchess would only ever employ fair-haired servants.

5. ELIZABETH, THE QUEEN MOTHER (1900–)

Refused to wear black or green during the Second World War.

SIX SIGNIFICANT ROYAL PREDICTIONS

1. DEATH IN JERUSALEM

Henry IV was once warned by a soothsayer that he was destined to "depart this life in Jerusalem." Years later, while preparing to embark on a crusade, the king was taken ill at Westminster Abbey and found himself recovering in a small anteroom known as the "Jerusalem Chamber." When informed of the name, the king immediately cried out: "Lauds be given to the Father of Heaven, for now I know I shall die here in this chamber, according to the prophecy of me beforesaid." And indeed he would.

2. THE VISIONS OF NOSTRADAMUS

In the mid-sixteenth century a French mystic, known to history as Nostradamus, laid down a series of prophecies (in verse form) that have proven at times to be eerily accurate. Though rather vague, a few of them could be said to concern the fate of British monarchs, as for instance this passage regarding Charles I and his opponents, the parliamentary "roundheads":

The Parliament of London will put their King to death…
He will die because of the shaven heads in council.

Another prophecy would seem to apply to Edward VIII and his successor, the woefully unprepared George VI:

For not wanting to consent to the divorce,
Which afterwards will be recognised as unworthy,
The King of the islands will be forced to flee
And one put in his place who has no sign of kingship

3. A FUTURE QUEEN

While stationed in Gibraltar George III's son Edward, Duke of Kent, went to see a gypsy and was informed that his "only child would be a great Queen." Although the prospect seemed remote at the time (given the fact that he had three older brothers), many years later he would indeed father the future Queen Victoria.

4. THE EDWARDIAN STYLE

The magazine *Punch* made a peculiar (if startlingly accurate) prediction on the birth of the future Edward VII: "The time of the Prince will be glorified by good cooking and good cheer. His drumstick will be the drumsticks of turkeys, his cannon the popping of corks." Edward would in due course grow up to be one of history's greatest gourmands.

5. THE ABDICATION OF EDWARD VIII

Before the future king's relationship with Wallis Simpson was widely known, an astrologer who called himself "Cheiro" wrote: "The Prince of Wales' chart shows influences that point to changes greatly affecting the Throne of England…He is determined not to settle down until he feels a *grande passion*, but it is well within the range of possibility that he will fall victim to a devastating love affair. If he does, I predict that (he) will give up everything… rather than lose the object of his affection."

6. ELIZABETH II'S MARRIAGE TO PRINCE PHILIP

When the present queen was still a teenager, the noted court diarist Sir Henry "Chips" Channon wrote the following passage, dated January 21, 1941: "An enjoyable Greek cocktail party. Prince Philip of Greece was there…he is to be our Prince Consort, and that is why he is serving in the Navy."

FOUR ROYALS BELIEVED TO POSSESS HEALING POWERS

For centuries British monarchs would ceremonially lay hands on victims of scrofula (the so-called "King's Evil"), a tubercular condition that enlarges the lymph glands and also affects the skin. The belief that kings and queens could heal the disease by a mere touch would persist intermittently up to the eighteenth century, until George I finally discontinued the practice for good.

1. EDWARD THE CONFESSOR (C. 1005–66)
During his lifetime Edward was believed to be able to heal sores and ulcers merely by touch, and as a consequence many people flocked to him for cures.

2. ELIZABETH I (1533–1603)
Elizabeth was a firm believer in her own healing powers, and followed a set ritual. After kneeling in prayer she would proceed to "press" the sores and ulcers of the sufferers, "boldly and without disgust."

3. CHARLES II (1630–85)
Said to have ceremonially touched 90,000 of his subjects over the course of his lifetime.

4. ANNE (1665–1714)
The last monarch to touch for the "King's Evil," Anne revived the practice after William III had abandoned it. It is believed that over 100,000 afflicted people sought out a cure from the queen during the course of her career.

SIX ROYAL OMENS

1. THE COMET OF 1066
In earlier centuries comets were invariably considered to be bad omens. During the fateful year 1066 Halley's Comet coincidentally made its appearance, and was dutifully depicted above the Battle of Hastings in the Bayeux Tapestry.

2. THE MYSTERIOUS LIGHTNING BOLT
During a visit to France in 1287 lighting struck the room that

Edward I and his wife, Queen Eleanor, were sitting in, killing two people but leaving the royal couple unhurt. Many took the incident as an omen of trouble to come in the king's French lands.

3. *Elizabeth I's Coronation Ring*

Throughout her long reign the queen refused to remove her coronation ring. Unfortunately, by 1603 it had grown so deeply into the flesh of her finger that her doctor had no choice but to cut it away. Within a week she was dead.

A typically stylized portrait of Elizabeth I.

4. *Charles I's Marble Bust*

At the very moment that Charles first unveiled a bust of himself by Bernini in his garden at Whitehall Palace, a hawk flew overhead with a bird in its beak and dropped some blood on the effigy's throat. In 1649, the king would be beheaded by the forces of Oliver Cromwell.

5. *Edward VII's Broken Ritual*

The king had an endless number of superstitions, but perhaps the most deep-rooted was the one concerning New Years' Eve. Each year he would invariably kick everyone out of Sandringham a few minutes before midnight; then, as twelve o'clock struck he would escort Queen Alexandra back in through the front door. On New Year's 1910, however, the young man who would one day be Edward VIII was late in getting out of the house, and the ritual was ruined. "We shall have very bad luck this year," the king predicted afterwards. Five months later he was dead.

6. *A Doomed Marriage*

When Prince Charles and Lady Diana were asked, during an interview following their engagement, if they were in love, their replies was telling. To Diana's immediate "Of course," the prince added the ominous addendum "Whatever 'in love' means."

12 TERRIFYING ROYAL HAUNTINGS

1. MARGARET OF ANJOU (1430–82)

Henry VI's queen is said to haunt Owlpen Manor in the Cotswolds.

2. & 3. EDWARD V (1470–C. 1483) AND RICHARD, DUKE OF YORK (1473–C. 1483)

The ghosts of two boys — that of King Edward V and his brother Richard — are said to haunt the Tower of London.

4. KATHERINE OF ARAGON (1485–1536)

Said to haunt Kimbolton Castle in Cambridgeshire.

5. ANNE BOLEYN (1507–36)

The queen's ghost is said to return to the site of her childhood home, Blickling Hall in Norfolk, every year on May 19, the anniversary of her execution. She sits (with her severed head in her lap) in a phantom coach drawn by four headless horses, the latter driven by a headless horseman, that drives slowly up the avenue to the mansion and vanishes at the front door.

Other locations allegedly haunted by Anne Boleyn's spirit include Windsor Castle and the Tower of London). It has also been said that the queen's ghost wanders in the oak panelled chamber of her one-time home Hever Castle each December 24th, singing sad songs in a low voice.

6. JANE SEYMOUR (C. 1508–37)

Visitors to Hampton Court Palace have occasionally spotted an apparition resembling Henry VIII's third wife, who died in childbirth.

7. KATHERINE HOWARD (C. 1525–42)

Hampton Court Palace also supposedly echoes with the shrieks of Katherine Howard, the fifth wife of Henry VIII. Imprisoned here in 1541 for adultery, on one occasion she escaped from her guards and ran to the chapel to beg the king for mercy, who merely ignored her as she pounded away on the locked doors. The queen was then dragged away shrieking and was executed soon after. To this day her ghost is said to rush along the gallery and pass through the door at the end, which leads into the chapel, loudly pleading her innocence. Some believe that the beheaded queen also haunts Eythorne Manor, in Hollingbourne, Kent.

8. KATHERINE PARR (c. 1513–48)

Henry VIII's sixth wife is said to haunt Sudeley Castle in Gloustershire, her ancestral home and burial place. Witnesses say she is a rather melancholy spirit, dressed in green, who tends to keep to herself.

9. ELIZABETH I (1533–1603)

The ghost of "Good Queen Bess" is said to haunt both Windsor Castle and, formerly, Richmond Palace.

10. CHARLES I (1600–49)

Has allegedly been sighted at Windsor Castle (with his head on).

11. GEORGE II (1683–1760)

At Kensington Palace, so the story goes, the ghost of George II has often been seen gazing out of his bedroom window.

12. GEORGE III (1738–1820)

Locked away in Windsor Castle near the end of his life, the now wholly deranged George III would occasionally be seen at his window saluting the guards as they passed below. It is said that a certain ensign, when so confronted by His Majesty, would always give the "Eyes right!" command in response. Legend has it that, a week after the king's death, the ensign saw him once more at the window. Overcoming his initial shock, he shouted out, "Eyes right!" just as he always had. George III's ghost is also said to sit in the castle library, where he repeatedly mutters his catchphrase "What? What? What?"

THREE DECEASED ROYALS ON PUBLIC DISPLAY

1. RICHARD II (1367–1400)

In 1413 Henry V had his hapless predecessor's body exhumed from the little church where he had originally been buried, embalmed and then put on public display (in full royal regalia) in Westminster Abbey. There it remained for three days, before finally being interred once more.

2. KATHERINE OF VALOIS (1401–37)

Wife of Henry V. At the beginning of the sixteenth century the queen's grandson, Henry VII, made major alterations to Westminster Abbey that involved moving her mummified body. As a "temporary" measure the latter was placed in a crude wooden coffin and left above ground, where it remained, a public spectacle, for over 250 years. Among the royal corpse's countless visitors during this time was Samuel Pepys. On his thirty-sixth birthday in 1668 the celebrated diarist went to the abbey with his family and later wrote about the experience: "Here we did see…the body of Queen Katherine of Valois, and (I took the) upper part…in my hands. And I did kiss her mouth, reflecting upon it that …I did first kiss a Queen." The body was finally removed from public view in 1776.

3. CHARLES I (1600–49)

After the king's execution soldiers charged a fee to allow gawkers to see him in his coffin.

THE AUTHOR'S SIX PREDICTIONS REGARDING THE MONARCHY'S FUTURE

1. ELIZABETH II will remain on the throne until her death sometime around 2020, thus making her the longest-reigning British monarch in history.

2. PRINCE CHARLES will marry his longtime mistress, Camilla Parker-Bowles, in a private ceremony in Scotland before 2005.

3. THE PRINCE will become King Charles III on the death of his mother. Well into his early 70s by this point, he will therefore be the oldest person ever to ascend the throne.

4. HIS WIFE will be accepted by the people as Queen Camilla.

5. CHARLES III (and later, his son) will make drastic changes to the monarchy, leaving it more in tune with those of the Scandinavian countries. In the process, support for a British republic will increase considerably.

6. PRINCE WILLIAM will, by 2030, succeed his father as King William V (despite his oft-expressed reluctance to do so). Though personally popular, he will nevertheless be the last constitutional monarch.

Crowning Glory

FOUR ONGOING ROYAL CEREMONIES AND TRADITIONS

1. SWAN-UPPING

Each year during the third week of July, the Dyers and Vintners livery companies etch their respective "upping" marks on the bills of their swans, ostensibly to prevent the sovereign (who traditionally owns all *unmarked* mute swans on the Thames) from laying claim to them. The swan-obsessed royal family also employs its own scarlet-clad keeper of the royal swans, to handle all swan-related responsibilities. It is still a crown offence to steal or kill a swan in Britain.

2. ROYAL MAUNDY (PART I)

Dating from Saxon times, each Maundy Thursday (the Thursday before Easter) the sovereign personally distributes specially minted silver coins, enclosed in a white purse, to a select group of elderly recipients. This somewhat eccentric tradition was abandoned by James II, only to be revived by George V in 1932.

3. THE OFFERING AT EPIPHANY

Each January 6th, the present queen's representatives make a token offering of gold, frankincense and myrrh on her behalf at a communion service in St James's Palace. Afterwards, £30 is deposited in the alms dish for the poor of the parish.

4. BREAKING THE SEAL

At the beginning of each new reign, the incoming sovereign purposely damages the Great Seal of his or her predecessor with a hammer. A new one is then created, which is only used on the most important of state documents.

FIVE ROYAL TRADITIONS THAT HAVE BEEN ABANDONED

1. THE TRIPLET BOUNTY

The Queen Victoria-initiated tradition of sending £3 to each set of triplets born in Great Britain was abandoned in 1957, as was the replacement idea of sending £4 to quadruplets.

2. ROYAL MAUNDY (PART 2)

As part of the ancient tradition of "Maundy Service," up until the time of George III the sovereign was required to ceremonially wash the feet of a select group of old people. Elizabeth I, incidentally, was said to be particularly enthusiastic about kissing the big toes of the recipients.

3. HAIR POWDERING

Prince Philip was responsible for finally putting a stop to the "unmanly" practice, among footmen, of powdering their hair white.

4. THE WITNESSING OF THE BIRTH

Beginning with the reign of Queen Anne all royal births had been officially witnessed by the secretary of state. The tradition was discontinued after the birth of Princess Margaret in 1930.

5. STOPPING AT TEMPLE BAR

Up until fairly recently, whenever the sovereign made a ceremonial visit to the City of London he or she had to stop first at Temple Bar (the original city gates) and receive permission to enter from the lord mayor.

THREE IMPORTANT ANNUAL EVENTS RELATED TO ROYALTY

1. THE QUEEN'S BIRTHDAYS

The queen, unlike lesser mortals, celebrates two birthdays each year. The actual date of her birth (April 21) is marked by a 41-gun salute in Hyde Park, while her official British ceremonial birthday is celebrated in London by the famed Trooping of the Colour at Horse Guards Parade on the second Saturday in June, during which she takes the Royal Salute (her official birthday gift). This is followed by a spectacular RAF flyover of Buckingham Palace.

2. CHARLES I COMMEMORATION

Each year on January 31 — the anniversary of the king's execution in 1649 — large numbers of Londoners turn out (dressed in seventeenth century garb) for a march tracing his last walk from St. James's Palace to the Banqueting House in Whitehall.

3. STATE OPENING OF PARLIAMENT

One of the best opportunities for the average person to see the queen, the state opening of parliament occurs each year in late October or early November. The actual ceremony consists of having the sovereign ride by horse-drawn coach from Buckingham Palace to Westminster, escorted by mounted officers of her household cavalry. Once inside the House of Lords she takes her place on the throne and summons the members of the House of Commons to join them. This being done, she then reads out a speech outlining the government's upcoming legislative agenda.

THREE UNUSUAL ROYALTY-RELATED JOB-DESCRIPTIONS

1. THE CHAMPION OF ENGLAND

As originally conceived, the primary duty of the holder of this hereditary title was to ride in full armour into Westminster Hall at the start of the coronation banquet and challenge to mortal combat (by "throwing down the gauntlet") anyone who dared dispute the monarch's right to the crown. In more recent years the champion has been relegated to carrying the royal standard during coronation ceremonies.

2. THE EARL MARSHAL

The original holder of this title, William Marshal, Earl of Pembroke was one of the most important servants of the Angevin dynasty, eventually rising to the position of regent for the young Henry III. The office of marshal (essentially, army commander under the king) became hereditary under William's descendants, the dukes of Norfolk. Though the title itself survives in the military rank of "field marshal," the Earl Marshal's main responsibilities now are in organising various ceremonial occasions, the most notable being coronations.

3. GROOM OF THE STOOL

First employed by Henry VIII and thereafter used by subsequent monarchs, the job essentially entailed wiping the royal anus.

FIVE ROYAL ORDERS

1. THE ORDER OF THE GARTER

Founded in 1348 by Edward III, in fulfilment of a vow to restore King Arthur's Round Table. Edward's original intention was to have a band of three hundred knights assembled in a huge round feasting hall; eventually, this number was reduced to just twenty-four special knights, along with himself and his son Edward "the Black Prince." There have been just twenty-four knights companion ever since (in addition to certain miscellaneous "stranger knights"), with a new one chosen each time one dies. Each of these knights, in turn, has his or her own stall in St. George's Chapel, Windsor, and wears a special blue velvet robe and plumed cap during the yearly garter ceremony in June, along with a garter of blue on their right leg. The chivalric order's commanding French motto, *Honi soit qui mal y pense* ("Evil be to him who evil thinks") has been historically attributed to the king himself, reputedly after he stooped to pick up a lady's blue undergarment. The Order of the Garter is the oldest and still one of the most desirable of all the honours to be bestowed.

2. THE ORDER OF THE BATH

Instituted by Henry IV in 1399, his four sons being among its first members. Today there are several thousand military and civilian members of the order; women were first admitted in 1971.

3. THE ROYAL VICTORIAN ORDER

Bestowed in recognition of service to the crown (as distinct from service to the state), and based at the Savoy Chapel, London.

4. THE ORDER OF MERIT

Despite carrying no actual social rank the "OM" is the most prestigious Order of them all, for the simple reason that it is the sovereign's own gift. Granted for outstanding service to the nation, it was instituted by Edward VII in 1902.

5. ORDERS OF THE BRITISH EMPIRE

Beginning with George V the monarch has bestowed six types of Orders of the British Empire. Ostensibly a reward for those subjects deemed to have served their country well, in recent years it has been used more as a subtle but effective way of keeping critics in line. In descending order of importance they are: Knight or Dame Cross of the British Empire (GBE), Knight Commander of the British Empire (KBE), Dame Commander of the British Empire (DBE), Commander of the British Empire (CBE), Officer of the British Empire (OBE), and Member of the British Empire (MBE).

THREE MEMORABLE PRINCELY INVESTITURES

The actual investiture ceremony for a Prince of Wales is not itself ancient; rather, it was largely invented by then chancellor of the exchequer (and future prime minister) David Lloyd George in 1911 as a public relations exercise. Prior to that time, such investitures were carried out by the sovereign from the throne in parliament.

1. RICHARD II (1367–1400)

In 1376 the exhausted, nine-year old prince had to be carried out of Westminster Abbey after collapsing during his investiture. It seems that the long ceremonial, following as it did a period of fasting, had taken a toll on the boy.

2. EDWARD VIII (1894–1972)

Invested as Prince of Wales at Caernarvon Castle in Wales on July 13, 1911, in what was his first public duty. The 17-year-old prince found the proceedings to be highly embarrassing (primarily owing to the "preposterous rig" of satin and velvet that he was forced to wear) and was particularly worried about making a fool out of himself in front of his naval college classmates. The occasion also marked, incidentally, the first time that a reigning sovereign (George V) had visited the great Welsh castle since Henry IV led his army there in 1400.

3. CHARLES, PRINCE OF WALES (1948–)

Although Charles had been created Prince of Wales when he was nine, it was not until he came of age that he was formally invested with the title. The resulting ceremony, which took place at Caernarvon Castle on July 1, 1969, was intended as a major, worldwide television event, with Princess Margaret's photographer husband Lord Snowdon having been placed in charge of the setting. After accepting his specially made crown, amethyst ring, and silver-handled sword from his mother the prince then swore a loyalty oath to her, before finishing things up with a passable speech in the Welsh language.

SEVEN ROYAL CROWNS

The British crown jewels are among the most famous — and valuable — artifacts in existence. Long housed, rather inadequately, in the Tower of London's central Keep (known as the White Tower), today they are to be seen in their own separate, ultra-modern "jewel house," amid laser lighting and impenetrable security.

1. THE MEDIEVAL CROWN

The original English crown probably dated back to the time of Edward the Confessor, and is believed to have been broken up or melted down (along with the rest of the royal regalia) at the time of Charles I's execution, although this is not entirely certain. Indeed, the possibility exists that the priests of Westminster Abbey preserved parts of it, or that Cromwell did, while the present St Edward's Crown may contain elements that stretch back a thousand years. Medieval kings, incidentally, often had several "spare" crowns; Edward II was known to have had at least ten, which he occasionally pawned as the need arose.

2. ST EDWARD'S CROWN

Despite its name, the coronation crown in use today was actually made for Charles II in 1661, as a replacement for the original. Weighing nearly 2.3 kgs, it is made of solid gold with pearl-studded arches and is embellished with hundreds of other precious stones. It is said that Elizabeth II, in order to get used to balancing it on her head for her upcoming coronation ceremony in 1953, took to wearing the crown for a time while doing such mundane activities as feeding her corgis.

3. THE IMPERIAL STATE CROWN

Originally made for the coronation of Queen Victoria in 1838, and now worn at state openings of parliament. Unquestionably the single most valuable item of jewellery in the world, this silver-arched crown with ermine fringe contains, among other things, the oldest of the crown jewels — a sapphire from the coronation ring of Edward the Confessor. In addition, it also boasts a ruby that belonged to Edward the Black Prince (and which was known to have been worn by Henry V at Agincourt); vast pearls that Elizabeth I used for earrings; an enormous, a 317-carat diamond known as Cullinan II; and another huge sapphire that was owned by the Stuart kings. Not surprisingly it is also quite heavy, with at least one of its wearers (George V) complaining that it gave him a headache.

4. THE IMPERIAL CROWN OF INDIA

Originally made for George V's coronation at Delhi in 1911, at a cost of some £60,000. Although the people of India paid for the crown (which, incidentally, is studded with some 6,000 gems) most never got the chance to see it. Worn only on that one occasion, it has been kept locked up in the Tower of London ever since.

5. THE QUEEN MOTHER'S CROWN

Notable for containing the priceless, 106-carat Koh-i-noor ("mountain of light") diamond as its centerpiece. Legend has it that the Koh-i-noor is cursed, and that any *man* who wears it is doomed to death. Since 1850, this mainly platinum crown is worn only by queens-regnant and consorts.

6. THE CROWN OF SCOTLAND

Said to have been made originally for King Robert the Bruce, and still worn by British sovereigns during their separate Scottish coronation. Along with the other so-called "Honours of Scotland" it is kept at Edinburgh Castle.

7. THE GEORGE IV DIADEM

A personal favourite of Queen Victoria's, this lightweight, diamond and pearl-encrusted band continues to see much service with Elizabeth II as well. Worn by the latter at her 1953 coronation, it is also the diadem that she is seen wearing in her portraits on stamps and banknotes.

EIGHT EXAMPLES OF ROYAL REGALIA

Most of the regalia used today was first made for the coronation of Charles II in 1660, as replacements for those lost during the Interregnum.

1. THE GOLDEN ORB

Traditionally held in the sovereign's left hand. Perhaps the most sacred of all the coronation regalia, the orb symbolises the dominion of the Christian religion over the world. Essentially a hollow gold ball, it is decorated with 365 diamonds, emeralds, sapphires, and rubies, as well as some 368 pearls.

2. THE CORONATION SCEPTRE

The symbol of regal power and justice, the royal sceptre is traditionally held in the sovereign's right hand. The one in current use is noted for containing the largest cut diamond in the world (the 530-carat Star of Africa) below the cross, which enfolds an exceptionally fine amethyst.

3. THE AMPULLA AND ANOINTING SPOON

Used in containing and applying the specially prepared holy oil with which the sovereign is anointed — the oldest and most important rite of the coronation ceremony. Both objects were among the few to escape dispersion during the Interregnum, with the ampulla probably having been made for the coronation of Henry IV in 1399. The spoon dates from over a century earlier, while the oil itself continues to be made from a formula devised by Charles I.

4. THE CORONATION RING

Also known as "The wedding ring of England," the royal ring is made up of sapphires and rubies.

5. THE ARMILLAS

Golden bracelets have been worn at coronation ceremonies since the Middle Ages. Those in use today were made for Elizabeth II's coronation.

6. ST GEORGE'S SPURS

The golden spurs have remained essentially unchanged since they were first made in 1661. The actual *buckling on* of the spurs to the sovereign's ankles, however — once an important part of the coronation ceremony — was abandoned at the time of Queen Anne, owing to the fact that her ankles were too fat to hold them.

7. THE SWORD OF STATE

A symbol of authority, the sword of state is carried before the monarch at each coronation. There are actually five swords among the English regalia.

8. CORONATION ROBES

The gold *supertunica* worn by Elizabeth II at her coronation was a copy of a Roman consul's dress uniform, originally made for George V.

13 MONARCHS WHO WERE NEVER CROWNED

1. SWEYN, "FORKBEARD" (C. 960–1014)

Claimed the English throne by right of conquest, having no dynastic right to it, and deposed before he could be crowned.

2. MATILDA, "THE EMPRESS" (1102–67)

Daughter of Henry I. Proclaimed "Lady of the English" on April 7, 1141, but never crowned.

3. EDWARD V (1470–83)

Reigned for less than three months in 1483, before being deposed and (probably) murdered by his uncle Richard III.

4. JANE SEYMOUR (C. 1508–37)

Third wife of Henry VIII. Her coronation was postponed because of plague and she died in childbirth before it could be rescheduled.

5.–7. ANNE OF CLEVES (1515–57), KATHERINE HOWARD (C. 1525–42) AND KATHERINE PARR (C. 1513–48)

Henry VIII's later wives.

8. JANE (1537–54)

Proclaimed queen on July 10, 1553, and deposed nine days later.

9. HENRIETTA MARIA OF FRANCE (1609–69)

Wife of Charles I. A devout Roman Catholic, she would not allow herself to participate in the Anglican coronation ritual.

10. KATHERINE HENRIETTA OF BRAGANZA (1638–1705)

Wife of Charles II. Never crowned because of the religious difficulties involved.

11. SOPHIA DOROTHEA OF CELLE (1666–1726)

Wife of George I. Never acknowledged as queen, and had in fact been divorced from him in Germany before his accession.

12. CAROLINE OF BRUNSWICK-WOLFENBÜTTEL (1768–1821)

The estranged wife of George IV. In 1821 she was forcibly excluded from his coronation and denied the right to be crowned separately.

13. EDWARD VIII (1894–1972)

Abdicated before his scheduled coronation could take place.

EIGHT ROYALS WHO WERE ALSO EMPEROR (OR EMPRESS) OF INDIA

"India should belong to me."
Queen Victoria

It was Queen Victoria's favourite prime minister, the oily Benjamin Disraeli, who first dreamed up the title "Empress of India" and had it officially bestowed upon her by parliament in 1876. The queen herself never actually visited India but, like all Victorians, considered the subcontinent to be the "jewel in the crown" of her vast British Empire. The tradition would be maintained until 1947, when India officially declared independence.

1. VICTORIA (1819–1901)
2. EDWARD VII (1841–1910)
3. ALEXANDRA OF DENMARK (1844–1925)
4. GEORGE V (1865–1936)
5. MARY OF TECK (1867–1953)
6. EDWARD VIII (1894–1972)
7. GEORGE VI (1895–1952)
8. ELIZABETH, THE QUEEN MOTHER (1900–)

11 UNFORGETTABLE CORONATIONS

The ancient ceremony of coronation consists of five main stages: the shout of recognition, the oath to the people, the unction / anointment, the investiture, and the homage.

The coronation of William the Conqueror.

1. WILLIAM I, "THE CONQUEROR" (C. 1027–87)

When cheers began to emanate from inside Westminster Abbey on Christmas Day, 1066, as William was crowned king, his nervous French-speaking guards mistakenly thought that a riot had broken out. Their somewhat excessive response was to immediately set fire to all the buildings in the vicinity. The ceremony continued on without interruption however, even though the king himself was said to be "trembling from head to foot."

2. HENRY IV (1366–1413)

During the course of the procession one of the king's shoes dropped off, shortly followed by a spur from the other leg. Later, at the coronation banquet, a sudden gust of wind was said to have carried the crown from his head.

3. MARY I (1516–58)

The Catholic queen refused to sit in the coronation chair since it had previously been sat in by her Protestant predecessor Edward VI, whom she considered to be a heretic. The consecrating oil was rejected for the same reason.

4. CHARLES II (1630–85)

The originally intended date for the ceremony had to be postponed when it was learned that Oliver Cromwell had sold off all the necessary regalia.

5. GEORGE III (1738–1820)

Just before the ceremonies were slated to begin it was discovered that both the coronation chair and the sword of state had somehow been lost. Later, during the actual service, the presiding bishop rambled on interminably, at one point referring to the extraordinary number of years the king had already sat on the throne.

6. GEORGE IV (1762–1830)

The king chose prize fighters to be his pages, for the express purpose of preventing his hated estranged wife, Caroline of Brunswick-Wolfenbüttel, from crashing the proceedings. In the event the would-be queen did try to force her way into the ceremony by banging her fists on the doors of the abbey, a disturbance that she further punctuated with high-pitched wailing.

7. VICTORIA (1819–1901)

Several small mishaps conspired to slightly tarnish Victoria's coronation in 1838. Among the most notable concerned the coronation ring; originally created for her little finger, during the ceremony it had been rammed down the queen's fourth finger instead by the archbishop and got stuck there, resulting in considerable pain.

8. EDWARD VII (1841–1910)

After one postponement (when the king suddenly had to have his appendix removed) the rescheduled ceremony went relatively smoothly, aside from a few minor procedural mistakes on the part of the alarmingly frail, octogenarian archbishop.

9. GEORGE V (1865–1936) AND MARY OF TECK (1867–1955)

On December 12, 1911, the king and queen were respectively crowned emperor and empress of India in an exotic ceremony known to history as the Delhi Durbar. Aside from the creation of an expensive new crown for the occasion the royal couple was also showered with gems by Indian princes, the value and extent of which has still yet to be fully disclosed.

10. GEORGE VI (1895–1952)

Although admittedly quite a spectacle, George VI's coronation on May 12, 1937 was unfortunately marred by a series of minor misfortunes. During the ceremony a bishop who had been charged with holding the oath for the king to read unfortunately obscured a key section of it with his thumb; later, the lord chamberlain accidentally struck the new sovereign with the hilt of the sword of state and someone clumsily trod on his royal train as he was leaving the throne, thereby pulling him up short in a most undignified manner. This was, incidentally, the first coronation to be televised.

11. ELIZABETH II (1926–)

Much of this flawless 1953 ceremony (by far the most extravagant — not to mention expensive — ever staged) was arranged with the help of director Sir Alexander Korda, who employed a number of carriages from his film studios as props.

War
and
Disaster

NINE ROYALS WHO SERVED IN THE NAVY

It was Henry VIII who was primarily responsible for creating the Royal Navy as a unified fighting force, building as he did the first man-of-wars with funds stolen from the church. Prior to that time, the nation was forced to rely on the haphazard merchant ship fleet of the English Channel *Cinque Ports* for its maritime defence.

1. EDWARD III (1312–77)
During the naval battle of Sluys in 1340, Edward personally commanded a company of archers and marines on board ship and helped to inspire an important English victory over the French.

2. JAMES II (1633–1701)
James had been in command at the battle of Lowestoft, aboard the *Royal Charles*, during the Dutch naval invasion of 1665. He conducted himself courageously and led his forces to victory. Later, as lord high admiral of the fleet, he devised one of the earliest known sets of naval semaphore.

3. WILLIAM IV (1765–1837)
Sent off as an ordinary able-seaman at the age of fourteen by his father George III, in an effort to boost public pride in the Royal Navy. Despite captaining two ships during his more than half a century at sea (a period encompassing the entire Napoleonic Wars), the man who would later be known as the "sailor-king" nevertheless managed somehow to avoid active service. He ended his career as lord high admiral.

4. GEORGE V (1865–1936)

The youngest cadet ever admitted to Dartmouth Naval College, George had joined the navy in 1877 at the age of twelve along with his older brother, Prince Albert Victor. Unable to pass the entrance exam as written, the navy actually lowered the standards considerably to allow him to succeed.

5. EDWARD VIII (1894–1972)

Entered naval college at the age of thirteen (in lieu of a more fitting education for an heir to the throne), and later served briefly on board ship.

6. GEORGE VI (1895–1952)

Despite a proneness to seasickness, during the First World War the then Prince Albert was assigned to the battleship HMS *Collingwood* as a midshipman, which later saw action in the Battle of Jutland. Unfortunately for him he had little chance to experience this history-making event (a Pyrrhic victory for the Germans), having been confined to the sickbay by an ulcer.

7. PHILIP, DUKE OF EDINBURGH (1921–)

A career naval officer until the accession of his wife in 1952, the Duke of Edinburgh served with distinction throughout World War II, achieving the rank of lieutenant. After taking part in the ill-fated defence of Crete and the later invasion of Sicily he subsequently saw action in the Pacific War as well, where he was on hand for the Japanese surrender ceremonies in Tokyo Bay. During the post-war years he was eventually given command of his own frigate by his uncle Louis Mountbatten, who was then in charge of the Mediterranean fleet. As a captain Philip was said to have been respected (if not actually loved) by his crew, who referred to him behind his back as "Dukey."

8. CHARLES, PRINCE OF WALES (1948–)

Commanded the coastal minesweeper HMS *Bronington* in 1976, at the end of his Royal Navy career. The Prince of Wales had previously served in the RAF (where he qualified for both fighter jets and helicopters) as well as in the army.

9. Andrew, Duke of York (1960–)

Served aboard the aircraft carrier HMS *Invincible* during the Falklands War in 1982, where he distinguished himself as a helicopter pilot. The prince had the dangerous job of flying decoy missions against possible Exocet missiles, in addition to performing anti-submarine patrols, and was reportedly in the thick of some heavy action at times.

FIVE NOTABLE ROYAL REGIMENTS

The various household regiments officially charged with guarding the royal family have long since abandoned their former military roles, in favour of more ceremonial ones. Perhaps the best known of these is the famous Changing of the Guard that culminates in front of Buckingham Palace, though far more spectacular is the annual Trooping of the Colour at Horse Guards Parade, during which one is selected each year to bestow an official birthday salute to the sovereign and to show its regimental flag. Each unit has its own distinctive style of bearskin busby hat and tunic.

1. The Beefeaters

More properly known as the Yeomen Warders of the Tower, these privileged ex-servicemen in their resplendent (if impractical) Tudor uniforms are officially responsible for guarding the Tower of London and the crown jewels contained within. The unit was first established by Henry VII in 1485, and since that time its members have become one of Britain's most recognisable and beloved icons. Their peculiar nickname, incidentally, originated in 1669 during a visit to England by one Cosimo, Grand Duke of Tuscany, who wrote: "This magnificent body of men are great eaters of beef, of which a very large ration is given them daily at the Court, and they might be called beef-eaters."

2. The Coldstream Guards

The oldest regiment of the household cavalry; it is for this reason that they have adopted the motto *nulli secundus* ("second to none").

3. The Grenadier Guards

First formed by Charles II during his exile. This was the regiment that the future Edward VIII served briefly in as a young officer during the First World War, and it is their uniform that the present queen is wearing on her Great Seal of England.

4. THE IRISH GUARDS

Formed by Queen Victoria in the year before her death, as a tribute to the courage of her Irish Troops. They are characterised by their blue feathers, and by the Irish wolfhound that always accompanies them as mascot while on parade.

5. THE KING'S TROOP

This mounted unit was largely the creation of George VI. In addition to Trooping the Colour its duties include firing royal salutes in Hyde Park on state occasions.

FOUR TRAGIC WARSHIPS NAMED FOR ROYALS

1. THE MARY ROSE

In July 1545 Henry VIII travelled to Portsmouth to watch his warships embark for an engagement with the French in The Solent. At the head of the English fleet, just behind the flagship the *Great Harry*, was his personal pride and joy the *Mary Rose* (named, ironically, after his sister Mary Tudor the queen of France), and from his vantage point on the top of a local castle he and his companions had a commanding view of the impending battle. There, before his very eyes, one of the greatest naval tragedies in history began to unfold. It seems that a strong wind, combined with too many open gun ports, caused the latter ship to capsize and sink within a matter of minutes, resulting in the loss of nearly 700 hands. More than four centuries later the wreck was finally located and raised, with Henry's descendant Prince Charles actually helping to recover some of the amazingly-preserved relics from the seabed. Today, the ship is housed in a specially constructed enclosure at Portsmouth Naval Base, where her timbers are continuously sprayed with seawater to prevent them from drying out and breaking up.

2. THE ROYAL GEORGE

While undergoing a refit off Spithead in 1782, the British man-of-war suddenly keeled over under the strain caused by the shifting of its guns. Over 800 people lost their lives.

3. *The* Victoria

The Royal Navy flagship was accidentally rammed and sunk off the port of Tripoli in 1893, with much loss of life. The queen herself was doubly distressed when her hated prime minister, William Gladstone, refused to replace it.

4. *The* Prince of Wales

Originally intended to be called the *Edward VIII*, this pride of the British fleet survived its historic encounter with the German battleship *Bismarck* in May 1941, only to be sunk by the Japanese off Singapore the following December.

FIVE KINGS WHO WERE KILLED IN BATTLE

1. *Harold II (c. 1020–66)*

The last Saxon King of England, Harold II was killed at the Battle of Hastings on October 14, 1066. His death, which was commemorated in the famed Bayeux Tapestry, seems at first glance to have been caused by an arrow to the eye. Closer inspection, however, reveals that it actually resulted from a blow by a mounted Norman's sword. The original discrepancy came about over confusion as to which of two figures was actually being referred to as king under a caption that read *Harold rex interfectus est* ("Harold the king is killed').

2. *William I, "The Conqueror" (c. 1027–87)*

Died while campaigning in France, after jumping a trench on horseback. Evidently the pommel of his saddle had struck him in the stomach and burst his bowels.

3. *Richard I, "The Lionheart" (1157–99)*

In 1199 the great warrior-king was hit in the shoulder by a crossbow bolt during the siege of an unimportant French castle. The wound, although not serious in itself, quickly became gangrenous and resulted in his death a few days later.

4. *Henry V (1387–1422)*

Died of dysentery while on campaign in France. After his death his body was boiled in a cauldron as a sort of stew, in preparation for burial.

5. RICHARD III (1452–85)

Despite fighting valiantly alongside his men against the forces of Henry Tudor, Richard was ultimately cut down at Bosworth Field on August 22, 1485. He would be the last English king to die in battle.

THREE ROYAL CRUSADERS

Between the eleventh and thirteenth centuries there were a total of nine crusades in all, in which European Christians (led by various warrior kings) attempted to regain control of the holy land from the Moslems. In this they enjoyed a certain measure of success, capturing Jerusalem in 1099 and holding it for some time before finally being driven out.

1. ROBERT, DUKE OF NORMANDY (C. 1053–C. 1134)

The eldest son of William the Conqueror. A brilliant tactician, in 1099 Robert "Curthose" entered Jerusalem at the head of the First Crusade, which had been ordered three years earlier by Pope Urban II.

2. RICHARD I, "THE LIONHEART" (1157–99)

As one of the leaders of the Third Crusade, Richard achieved a number of important victories (including one against the legendary Muslim sultan and warrior Saladin), and although he ultimately failed to recapture Jerusalem he was able to negotiate a treaty that gave Christians the right to visit the city's holy places. A vindictive man, he is reported to have once dined on curried head of Saracen.

3. EDWARD I (1239–1307)

The first Plantagenet king was a legend in his own time, thanks in large measure to his successful four-year sojourn in the Holy Land accompanied by the French king, Louis IX.

FOUR CONQUERING KINGS

1. WILLIAM I, "THE CONQUEROR" (C. 1027–87)

Defeated the Saxon kings in 1066 and managed to hold on to his victory with the aid of strategically placed Norman castles. For all his success, however, William never actually saw himself as a conqueror;

rather, he felt he was merely claiming his legitimate right as heir to the English throne.

2. EDWARD I (1239–1307)

Between 1276-84 Edward waged a brutal, determined and ultimately successful campaign to subjugate the Welsh people. His attempt to do the same in the north was rather less decisive in its outcome (thanks to the efforts of William Wallace), though still sufficient to earn him the name "Hammer of the Scots."

3. EDWARD III (1312–77)

Known for his chivalry, Edward personally masterminded the great English land victories over the French at Crécy (1346) and Poitiers (1356), as well as the on the sea at Sluys (1340).

4. HENRY V (1387–1422)

Fearless in battle, Henry was also a gifted military strategist. His legendary campaign against the French was based upon careful planning as well as the use of new weaponry such as the longbow, and resulted in a sensational victory at Agincourt in 1415. By securing the Channel and forming favourable alliances he made England once more a continental power to be reckoned with.

THREE ROYAL RESPONSES TO TERRIBLE LONDON DISASTERS

1. THE GREAT PLAGUE OF LONDON

In the summer of 1665 an epidemic of bubonic plague swept through the city of London, killing more than 100,000 people by the time it was finished. Charles II and his court were spared, however, by having taken the precaution of fleeing to Oxford for the duration. It is perhaps worth mentioning that, during the much worse Black Death of 1348–50, royalty as usual had fared much better than did their subjects. Although about one-third of the entire population of England died during the pandemic, the only notable royal to succumb was Princess Joan, the daughter of Edward III. Anne of Bohemia (the first wife of Richard II) would also succumb in a slightly later outbreak.

2. THE GREAT FIRE OF LONDON

Still reeling from the devastating epidemic that had hit the capital the year before, on the night of September 1, 1666 a fire broke out in a baker's house on Pudding Lane. The flames quickly spread through a nearby section of wharves and warehouses on the Thames River, and by early the following morning were completely out of control. As the fire ravaged the northern part of the city Charles II himself, along with his brother, had gone out into the streets to hand out gold coins to the fire fighters. By the third day the royal brothers had heroically joined in the bucket brigades, though by then their efforts had become hampered by a lack of water. Pandemonium began to break out as some frightened citizens rose up against the foreigners and Catholics they incorrectly believed to be responsible for the conflagration, while others fled to the safety of the outlying fields. On the fourth day the fire finally burned itself out, though not before almost totally destroying the London of the Middle Ages. Yet, for all its destructiveness, the fire had not been entirely bad; in the process, the plague had been finally obliterated as well, and a newer, more sanitary city was able to grow from the ashes.

3. *The Blitz*

"The children will not leave unless I do. I shall not leave unless their father does, and the King will not leave the country in any circumstances whatever."

Queen Elizabeth

Much has been made of the royal family's refusal to abandon their country during the terrible bombing by the German *Luftwaffe* in 1940-41, though often overlooked is the fact that each night (just before the raids generally began) the king and queen would quietly return to the relative safety of Windsor Castle. Nevertheless, their inspection of bomb-damaged cities such as London and Coventry did much to boost public morale, and on at least one occasion they did narrowly escape injury during a daylight raid when Buckingham Palace was hit by a bomb.

EIGHT THOROUGHLY UNMILITARY ROYALS

1. *Ethelred II (c. 968–1016)*
Known for his practice of paying out protection money (or "Danegeld") to Viking raiders.

2. JOHN *(1166–1216)*

Although originally dubbed "Lackland" by his father owing to the difficulty in finding suitable provision for him, the epithet would later prove to be highly appropriate for the king who failed to hang on to the Angevin Empire. His warrior brother, Richard I, once said of John that, "he was not a man to win land if there was the merest show of resistance."

3. HENRY VI *(1421–71)*

Somehow managed, through his own military incompetence, to lose all the French territories (except for Calais) that had been gained during the Hundred Years' War. In fairness to Henry, however, it was during his watch that the English would face the "divinely-inspired" French heroine Joan of Arc.

4. WILLIAM III *(1650–1702)*

Not only was the king at the head of the coalition forces in their defeat at Landen in 1693, but he also suffered a more personal humiliation by his French foe. During the height of the battle, one bullet passed through his garter sash while another shot the wig from his head.

5. ALBERT VICTOR, DUKE OF CLARENCE *(1864–92)*

An army officer who was utterly incapable of carrying out even the most basic of orders, let alone issuing them.

6. EDWARD VIII *(1894–1972)*

During World War I the then Prince of Wales served as aide-de-camp to General Sir John French and was actually present at the Battles of Loos, the Somme and Passchendaele, though he was never allowed anywhere near the frontline trenches. In fairness it would appear that he was as fully prepared to lay down his life as anyone else, but as Lord Kitchener explained, "I cannot take the chance of the enemy taking (him) prisoner."

By the beginning of the Second World War the by-then former king's willingness to fight Germans had lessened considerably. Assigned a cushy staff job at the French Army HQ, he and his wife fled to neutral Portugal when the Nazis invaded where, inexplicably, they refused to be evacuated back to England. The duke soon outraged his superiors further (not to mention his own people) by publicly stating "the English must be mad not to see that they were doomed." Afterwards considered something of a security risk, he was ultimately packed off to the Bahamas for the duration, though he would continue to be in contact with Germany (through a Spanish intermediary) for the remainder of the war.

The Duke and Duchess of Windsor in the Bahamas during World War II.
(photo courtesy Stanley Toogood)

7. EARL LOUIS MOUNTBATTEN OF BURMA (1900–79)

"Well, that's the end of the *Illustrious*!"

George VI
(*on hearing that Mountbatten was to be given*
command of an aircraft carrier)

A cousin of George VI, it was Mountbatten's career as a Royal Navy captain in the Second World War that served as the basis for an important allied propaganda coup, the Noël Coward movie *In Which We Serve*. Yet contrary to his heroic portrayal in the film the former was actually something of a military disaster; after losing his first destroyer command owing to his own incompetence, he would promptly go on to mastermind the ill-fated Dieppe raid — arguably the worst allied fiasco of the entire war. He later became supreme allied commander in Asia and first sea lord, and after the war served as the last viceroy of India.

8. EDWARD, EARL OF WESSEX (1964–)

Washed out of the Royal Marines in 1987, much to the consternation of his gung-ho father Prince Philip. Part of the impetus for his quitting was no doubt the unflattering nickname ("Mr. Puniverse") that his fellow cadets had bestowed upon him; the media, for their part, began to refer to him, rather more bluntly, as "the royal wimp." He joined a theatre company soon afterwards.

THREE MONARCHS WHO MADE FRONTLINE VISITS

1. ELIZABETH I (1533–1603)

In 1588 Philip II of Spain decided to press his rather tenuous claim on the English crown (through his marriage to Mary I), in order to both curtail English interference in the Spanish Netherlands and to restore freedom of worship for the country's Catholic subjects. Accordingly, a vast armada of 130 ships (carrying some 17,000 soldiers) was assembled, which set off for the south coast of England in early summer. The invasion force was first sighted on July 19, heading towards the Channel for a planned linkup with forces belonging to the Duke of Parma, Philip's regent in the Netherlands. London was immediately alerted with the aid of messages carried by hilltop beacons, but the situation looked bleak indeed; for England had only a handful of ships to counter the threat.

On August 8, 1588, at the height of the crisis, the queen herself travelled to Tilbury and made a speech to her soldiers in the hopes of strengthening their resolve to fight. It included the memorable lines: "I know I have the body of a weak and feeble woman, but I have the heart and stomach of a king, and of a king of England too." Her words would seem to have had the desired effect. With the aid of a veritable forest of fireships (coupled with some very bad weather), the English would inflict upon Spain the most humiliating naval defeat in its history. More importantly, the victory helped to establish England as a world power.

2. GEORGE V (1865–1936)

During a troop inspection on the Western Front in 1915, the king was thrown from a mare he had been riding after it had been startled by the cheers of the men. To make matters worse the horse actually landed on top of him and would surely have crushed him if not for the sogginess of the ground. Agonized and indignant (he had suffered a fractured pelvis and three broken ribs), it would be several days before he was able to return to England.

3. GEORGE VI (1895–1952)

Although he was able to make a quick visit to the British Expeditionary Forces in France at the beginning of the Second World War, it wasn't until 1943 that the military situation was deemed safe enough for the king to make further tours of inspection. He then began to make up for lost time in earnest. Despite being ultimately talked out of taking part in the Normandy invasion fleet on D-Day in June 1944 (he had wanted to witness the proceedings from one of his battleships) he was able to go ashore there ten days later, where he toured the various beachheads in an amphibious truck and visited General Montgomery at his headquarters. For the remainder of the war he managed to put in similar, morale-boosting appearances in France, North Africa, Italy, Malta, and the Low Countries.

TWO ROYAL DECORATIONS

1. THE VICTORIA CROSS

Created by Prince Albert on his wife's wishes, the Victoria Cross was instituted in 1856 to recognise outstanding bravery in battle among all ranks. Awarded sparingly, each medal is made out of bronze from Russian cannons captured during the Crimean War.

2. THE GEORGE CROSS

Based on George VI's own design, and used to commemorate the conspicuous valour of civilians during wartime. In 1942 the king awarded it to the entire population of the island of Malta.

THREE WARTIME SACRIFICES MADE BY ROYALS

1. EXPERIENCED WORKERS

With the blessing of George V and Queen Mary, during the First World War the male workers of the Sandringham estate formed their own company of soldiers and went off to fight at Gallipoli. No trace of any of them was ever found again, the presumption being that they were slaughtered to a man and buried in a mass grave.

2. HOUSEHOLD LUXURIES

In order to save energy, during the Second World War all the baths at Buckingham Palace were painted with a 13-centimetre-high line, beyond which you were not allowed to fill. Central heating was also banned (much to the consternation of such high-profile visitors as Eleanor Roosevelt), and simple foods were invariably served at table — albeit on golden plates.

3. SKI HOLIDAYS

During the Gulf War of 1991, the younger members of the royal family demonstrated their solidarity with the troops by temporarily abstaining from expensive Swiss ski holidays.

FIVE EXAMPLES OF DYNASTIC WARFARE

1. THE NORMAN CONQUEST

In 1066 William the Conqueror led the Norman invasion of England, which culminated in the defeat of Harold II and his forces at the Battle of Hastings. Once secure in his position as the new king he then showed himself to be as ruthlessly efficient an administrator as he was a military leader, by entrenching the system of feudalism in England that persists, arguably, to this very day.

2. THE HUNDRED YEARS' WAR

In 1340 Edward III formally assumed the title King of France, which he claimed through his mother Queen Isabella, thus initiating a series of bloody conflicts known collectively as the Hundred Years' War. Though for the most part pointless attrition with an inconclusive end, the important port city of Calais would be captured as a more or less permanent prize.

3. THE WARS OF THE ROSES

The most famous of all dynastic conflicts began in the mid-fifteenth century, and hinged around which of Edward I's descendants had a better claim to the throne. The combatants were Henry VI of the House of Lancaster (whose emblem was the red rose) and the Duke of York and his son (whose emblem was a white one). In the almost thirty years that followed in which a state of war existed there was only ever actual conflict for about 15 months, with the level of disruption to English life being minimal. During this period however the crown did change a total of six times, until the situation was finally resolved for good with the marriage of Henry Tudor to Elizabeth of York. It is worth noting that the conflict was not widely known as the Wars of the Roses until over three centuries later, when Sir Walter Scott used the term in one of his novels.

4. THE ENGLISH CIVIL WAR

Not so much a dynastic conflict as a political and religious one, the English Civil War (actually, wars) nevertheless saw the end of Charles I's reign and the short-lived ascendancy of parliamentary / military rule under Oliver Cromwell. The king's supporters, called cavaliers because of their dashing appearance, believed in the monarchy and the Church of England; parliament's champions, known as roundheads because of their short-cropped hair, wanted to limit or destroy the monarchy and replace the Church of England with one along more puritanical lines. The first two years of the war produced no appreciable advantage for either side. By the end of 1643 the king's forces controlled three quarters of the country, but early the following year parliament signed a treaty with Scotland that brought her in as a powerful ally. Thanks to this — and to the military leadership of Cromwell — the balance gradually swung towards the roundheads, with major victories being won at the battles of Marston Moor (July 1644) and Naseby (June 1645). The king was put to death, and for the next 11 years the country was nominally a republic and in actuality a dictatorship, led by religious zealots who ultimately undermined their own power through sheer intolerance and lack of respect for the rule of law.

In 1660 the monarchy was restored (in a slightly more constitutionally-limited form) under Charles II, much to relief of virtually everyone who had lived through this troubled time.

5. THE JACOBITE RISINGS

During the early eighteenth century the Hanoverian settlement was challenged by a succession of "Jacobite" pretenders, descendants of the deposed Stuart king James II. Though popular in Scotland, the staunch Catholicism of the latter prevented them from ever being much of a threat in England itself.

*Law
and
Order*

SIX ROYAL WILLS

The contents of royal wills are no longer (intentionally) made available to the public.

1. EDRED (C. 923–955)
Left a massive fortune of several thousand pounds to his two heirs, along with a further £1600 to the people of England. The latter amount was to be set-aside for the express purpose of paying off any invading heathen armies.

2. HENRY IV (1366–1413)
Perhaps feeling guilty about the violent means by which he originally came to the throne, in his will the king declared, "I, Henry, sinful wretch, ask my lords and true people forgiveness if I have misentreated them in any wise."

3. GEORGE I (1660–1727)
Had his will suppressed by his son George II, for reasons that are not precisely known to this day.

4. GEORGE IV (1762–1830)
During one of his periodic nervous breakdowns as Prince of Wales George had a will drawn up, in which he left everything he had to "Maria Fitzherbert who is my wife in the eyes of God and who is and ever will be such in mine." He later came to his senses and put the will aside.

5. VICTORIA (1819–1901)

Left a personal fortune of nearly £2 million, primarily to her younger children. After specifically bequeathing her two private residences (Balmoral and Osborne House) to her eldest son, Edward VII, the queen wound things up with the words, "I die in peace with all fully aware of my many faults relying with confidence on the love...of my Heavenly Father...and earnestly trusting to be united with my beloved Husband...in the mausoleum at Frogmore."

6. DIANA, PRINCESS OF WALES (1961–97)

It was reported that Diana's family, the Spencers, altered her £21-million will to include a £50,000 bequest to her butler, Paul Burrell. She had evidently left nothing to charity, and precious little to her godchildren.

SIX MONARCHS WHO IMPOSED UNUSUAL LAWS

Perhaps the most tangible royal impact on Britain's legal system is to be found in the garb of its barristers, who are still officially in mourning for Queen Mary II.

1. EDWARD III (1312–77)

In order to upgrade the fighting skill of the peasantry, in 1349 Edward banned all sports from England save one — archery.

2. HENRY VII (1457–1509)

Henry VII ordered that all the mastiffs in the land should be destroyed, for the reason that they could potentially attack a lion (the King of Beasts).

3. HENRY VIII (1491–1547)

Henry's Act of Succession in 1534 made it a capital crime to question the validity of his marriage to Anne Boleyn or the legitimacy of their children.

4. EDWARD VI (1537–53)

Passed a law in 1548 banning any man below the rank of lord from displaying "his privy member and buttokkes." At the time it was considered the height of fashion for men to expose their genitals below short-fitting tunics.

5. CHARLES II (1630–85)

By the late seventeenth century London had become so blighted by large advertising signs that the king at last proclaimed, "No signs shall be hung across the streets shutting out the air and light of the heavens."

6. GEORGE III (1738–1820)

Largely responsible for the Royal Marriages Act of 1772, which forbade any future royal marriages not sanctioned by the sovereign. Coming about as it did as a response to his own brother Henry's squalid divorce and remarriage, the measure had the unfortunate effect of increasing the already dangerously high level of royal inbreeding.

EIGHT ROYALS SUSPECTED OF PREMEDITATED MURDER

1. CANUTE (C. 995–1035)

Helped to secure his throne by murdering Eadwig, son of his predecessor Ethelred II.

2. JOHN (1166–1216)

In 1203 the king was suspected of murdering — with his own hands — his 16-year-old nephew (and rival for the throne) Arthur of Brittany.

3. ISABELLA OF FRANCE (1292–1358)

Popularly known as the "She-Wolf of France," Isabella was directly responsible for the downfall and murder of her husband, Edward II. After his death she is said to have had the king's heart removed and placed inside a silver case, which was later buried with her.

4. HENRY IV (1366–1413)

Believed to have been involved in the whacking of his cousin and predecessor, Richard II.

5. EDWARD IV (1442–83)

Believed to have ordered the death of his predecessor, Henry VI.

6. RICHARD III (1452–85)

(For the story of the "little princes in the Tower," see chapter 4 — "Seven Successful Royal Usurpers").

7. GEORGE I (1660–1727)

A notoriously cruel man who kept his wife Sophia Dorothea prisoner (as punishment for adultery) in a German castle for the last 32 years of her life, George was also suspected of having murdered her Swedish lover, Count Philip von Königsmarck. Years after the latter's mysterious disappearance in 1694, his dismembered body was discovered beneath his wife's dressing room floor.

8. ALBERT VICTOR, DUKE OF CLARENCE (1864–92)

The elder son of Edward, Prince of Wales (later King Edward VII), "Eddy" was often described during his short lifetime as a half-witted degenerate. In the late 1880s contemporary gossip even went so far as to connect "a member of the royal family" — a veiled allusion to the prince — with the infamous Jack the Ripper slayings. Eddy's possible involvement in the case was not directly aired until the 1970s, when the theory enjoyed a brief vogue. Subsequent research, however, revealed that he had solid alibis for at least some of the murders.

SIX ROYALS WHO ORDERED MASSACRES (AND ONE WHO DID NOT)

1. ETHELRED II (C. 968–1016)

On St Brice's day, 1002, the king ordered the massacre of all the Danes in his realms. Among the more prominent victims was the sister of King Sweyn Forkbeard.

2. RICHARD I (1157–99)

Richard's siege and capture of the city of Acre during the Third Crusade was unfortunately marred by his subsequent massacre of its inhabitants.

3. EDWARD, PRINCE OF WALES (1330–76)

Unchivalrously destroyed the town of Limoges in 1370, and slaughtered the inhabitants.

4. HENRY V (1387–1422)

Caused by his own order the deaths of at least 12,000 non-combatant civilians and prisoners of war during his campaigns in France.

5. WILLIAM III (1650–1702)

It would appear that it was the Dutch-born king's imperfect ability with English (rather than mere ruthlessness) that was responsible for the infamous massacre of the Macdonald clan at Glencoe in 1692, in which dozens of men, woman and children were brutally slaughtered by troops loyal to the English. The order to carry out the action had been signed, unwittingly, by the king himself, he having been either too busy to read it through or unsure as to the precise meaning of the word "extirpate." In any event he was as shocked as anyone by the way the order had been carried out.

6. WILLIAM, DUKE OF CUMBERLAND (1721–65)

Better-known to the Scots as "Butcher" Cumberland for his infamous leadership of the English army at the Battle of Culloden in 1746, William was the third son of George II. This battle — the last ever fought on British soil — saw the complete destruction of the greatly outnumbered Jacobite forces under Bonnie Prince Charlie, but the bloodshed was even then far from over; indeed, it was the bloated, 24-year-old duke himself who authorized reprisals by his men against Highland families in the vicinity, regardless of whether they were Jacobite or not. (This persecution of the clan system and Gaelic culture would continue for years to come; indeed, for a time it was even forbidden to wear tartan).

AND ONE WHO DID NOT...

EDWARD III (1312–77)

Angry at the prolonged resistance by the inhabitants of the French town of Calais, the king had determined, when the town finally did surrender, upon mass slaughter by way of retribution unless six prominent citizens offered up their lives. Fortunately for all concerned Edward was ultimately talked out of the plan by his gentle wife, Queen Philippa.

SEVEN RUTHLESS ROYALS

1. WILLIAM II, "RUFUS" (C. 1056–1100)

Once personally executed an enemy by throwing him off the top of a castle turret.

2. HENRY I (1068–1135)

When one of Henry's court favourites was found to have been plotting his assassination, rather than simply have the man put to death the king decreed that he be castrated and have both his eyes put out.

3. JOHN (1166–1216)

Once, when he suspected that his wife had taken a lover, the king had the man killed and his corpse suspended over her bed.

4. HENRY VIII (1491–1547)

The king routinely executed anyone who questioned his remarriage to Anne Boleyn, the favoured methods being decapitation, burning, drawing and quartering, and even boiling alive. It is estimated that Henry personally ordered the deaths of some 17,000 people during the course of his reign.

5. MARY I (1516–58)

Known to history as "Bloody Mary" for her vigorous persecution of Protestants, many of whom were burned at the stake.

6. JAMES I (1566–1625)

A nasty piece of work, James once had a man condemned to hang — without benefit of trial — for a simple act of thievery.

7. ELIZABETH, THE QUEEN MOTHER (1900–)

Belying her rather doughy appearance, the Queen Mum was actually a ruthless manipulator in her day who, once crossed, neither forgave nor forgot (as Wallis Simpson and Princess Diana were both to find out).

THREE OBJECTS STOLEN BY ROYALS

1. THE STONE OF SCONE

Between the eighth and thirteenth centuries, Scottish and Irish kings were traditionally crowned while sitting upon this rather ordinary-looking, rectangular block of stone, which resided in a Scottish monastery. In 1296, however, it was stolen by Edward I and taken to Westminster Abbey, where it was placed beneath the seat of King

Edward's chair (the throne still used in coronations) as a symbol of fealty. Negotiations to get it back went on for most of the twentieth century, culminating in its return to Scotland in November 1996 in a ceremony presided over by Prince Andrew.

2. MONEY AND PERSONAL EFFECTS
As a youth Henry V enjoyed mugging his courtiers.

3. A PERSIAN CARPET
While still a boy in Greece, Prince Philip once removed an expensive Persian carpet from the family residence and attempted to sell it in the street to passers-by.

FIVE ROYALS WHO WERE THEMSELVES ROBBED (AND ONE SPECIAL ROBBERY)

1. EDWARD THE CONFESSOR (C. 1005–66)
The saintly king was said to have knowingly allowed a burglar to plunder his royal treasure chest, in the belief that the thief had greater need of the money than he did.

2. GEORGE II (1683–1760)
Relieved of his watch and other items by a robber one morning while walking in the gardens of Kensington Palace.

3. CHARLOTTE OF MECKLENBURG-STRELITZ (1760–1820)
Wife of George III. After being caught trying on the royal jewels in 1771, an enterprising servant girl named Sarah Wilson was banished for life to the American colonies — though not before first managing to steal a few of the items along with one of the queen's dresses. Once in America she promptly proceeded to impersonate the latter's sister, Princess Susanna, accepting a vast amount of gifts from rich southern gentlemen in exchange for bogus royal appointments.

4. WALLIS, DUCHESS OF WINDSOR (C. 1896–1986)
Had a trunk stolen from under her bed while visiting a friend's country house in 1947 with her husband. Though the contents of the former were never publicised, it was widely believed to have contained the exquisite "Queen Alexandra's emeralds" among other,

equally irreplaceable items. The final insurance settlement was in the region of £2 million.

5. ANNE, THE PRINCESS ROYAL (1950–)

In 1989 four embarrassing love letters, written by the queen's equerry Timothy Laurence to her (still married) daughter, were presented to the *Sun* tabloid by an unidentified Buckingham Palace source.

AND ONE SPECIAL ROBBERY…

CHARLES II (1630–85)

On May 9, 1671, an Irish highwayman named Thomas Blood almost managed to steal the British crown jewels. After somehow gaining access to the royal treasure room in the Tower of London, the swashbuckling thief and two accomplices overpowered a guard and then proceeded to stash sundry regalia — including St Edward's crown, which they flattened out with a mallet — into a sack before fleeing. Unfortunately for them they were quickly captured, yet their audacity so intrigued Charles II that he not only commuted the mandatory death sentence but gave Blood himself a lifetime pension as well (not surprisingly, rumours abounded that the king, in hard financial straits, had actually ordered the robbery himself).

SEVEN ROYALS WHO WERE IMPRISONED

1. STEPHEN (C. 1097–1154)

Captured by the forces of the Empress Matilda at the Battle of Lincoln, and afterwards imprisoned in Bristol Castle for seven months.

2. MATILDA, "THE EMPRESS" (1102–67)

King Stephen's rival was herself taken prisoner (twice) during their lengthy struggle over the throne. On both occasions she managed to escape by her own initiative and daring, the first time while disguised as a corpse. The second escape (from Oxford Castle) was even more dramatic, involving as it did a lengthy trek through deep snow and across the frozen Thames.

3. ELEANOR OF AQUITAINE (1121–1204)

Imprisoned by her husband Henry II, after being caught attempting to join her rebellious sons at the French court. The latter were endeavouring to increase their own continental dukedoms at the expense of their father.

4. HENRY III (1207–72)

In 1264 Henry was captured and held prisoner in the dungeon of Hereford Castle by Simon de Montfort, after the latter's victory at the Battle of Lewes. He was later freed with the help of his son, the future Edward I.

5. HENRY VI (1421–71)

Imprisoned twice in the Tower of London by his rivals during the Wars of the Roses, where he would ultimately be murdered. His widow, Margaret of Anjou, was herself imprisoned for a time in Wallingford Castle, before finally being ransomed off and returned to France for good.

6. ELIZABETH I (1533–1603)

Suspected by her sister Queen Mary of complicity in the Wyatt Rebellion of 1554, the young princess was confined for two months in a dark, dank room of the Tower of London, before finally being released.

7. CHARLES I (1600–49)

The king spent nine months imprisoned in Newcastle before ultimately being "sold" back to the English in 1647. Later he would be held for a time at Carisbrooke Castle on the Isle of Wight, where his one attempt at escape was sadly undone when he became stuck between the bars of his window.

FOUR ROYALS WHO WERE KIDNAPPED (OR WHO EVADED CAPTORS)

Holding fellow kings hostage — particularly those who had been captured in battle — was standard procedure during the Middle Ages throughout Europe. Indeed, numerous foreign royals, such as David Bruce of Scotland and John II of France (to name but two) were so held by British monarchs at one time or another. Although they themselves were generally treated well (in keeping with their royal status), their unfortunate subjects back home were liable for raising "a king's ransom."

1. RICHARD I (1157–99)

Kidnapped in Austria on the way home from the crusades, and afterwards held by the Holy Roman Emperor Heinrich VI for the astronomical sum of almost 150,000 marks. In order to secure his release every man in England was required to contribute a fourth of his income, every sheep was shorn and its fleece sold, and church plate had to be pawned. It is interesting to note that, between his crusading and his imprisonment, the king spent only ten months of his ten-year reign in his own country.

2. JAMES I (1566–1625)

In 1582, at the age of 15, the then Scottish king was abducted by a trio of earls and held captive at Ruthven Castle. His kidnappers then proceeded to rule the country with the support of the church until his escape ten months later.

3. WILLIAM IV (1765–1837)

In 1782 George Washington personally approved a plan to kidnap George III's son William, who was then serving as a Royal Navy midshipman in British-occupied New York. The plot came to nothing when the guard around William's home was stepped-up.

4. ANNE, THE PRINCESS ROYAL (1950–)

In March 1974, while travelling back from a film premiere, the princess and her husband were attacked by a man who had swerved his car in front of theirs just outside Buckingham Palace. The assailant, Ian Ball, proceeded to fire several shots at the royal limousine and managed to wound four men in the process, before unsuccessfully attempting to drag his intended victim from her seat. Ball then fled into St James's Park where he was quickly apprehended. The would-be kidnapper (who was later charged with attempted murder) had planned to hold the princess for a ransom of £3 million.

TEN ROYAL REFUSALS

1. A ROYAL PARDON

Edward IV twice refused to issue Sir Thomas Mallory (the author of *Morte d'Arthur*) a pardon from imprisonment. The latter had been serving time on a rape charge.

2. SEXUAL FAVOURS

Henry VIII's then mistress Anne Boleyn refused to put out for him until he agreed to make her a queen.

3. MIRRORS

Horrified by the deterioration in her personal appearance, in old age Elizabeth I refused to allow mirrors in any of her rooms.

4. FINGER-BOWLS

When it was discovered that Jacobites were using them to toast "The King Over the Water" (the pretender, James Stuart), George I had all finger bowls banished from court. Ironically, it was only during Edward VIII's reign that the finger bowls made their return; after *his* exile in 1937, the toast to "The King Over the Water" would also be revived in certain quarters.

5. OFFICIAL RECOGNITION

George IV refused to read a parliamentary speech proclaiming the recognition of some new South American states, on the excuse that he had mislaid his false teeth.

6. BURIAL IN POET'S CORNER

Irritated by the impertinent tone of William Thackeray's (magnificent) *The Four Georges*, Queen Victoria refused to allow him burial in Westminster Abbey.

7. ALCOHOL CONSUMPTION

On the advice of David Lloyd George, during the First World War George V banned all alcohol from the royal households "as an example to the nation." The restriction did not prevent the king, however, from enjoying a bottle of port or two for himself after meals.

8. MARRIAGE PROPOSALS

The future Queen Mother turned down the future George VI twice before finally accepting his offer of marriage.

9. A ROYAL TITLE

On the day of the Duke of Windsor's marriage to Wallis Simpson he was informed by telegram from his brother, George VI, that his bride would not be allowed (in the face of all precedent) to use a royal title. Greatly distressed by this spiteful decision on the part of his own family, for the remainder of his life the ex-king always made a point of referring to his wife as Her Royal Highness anyway.

10. Permission to Marry

Many believe it was the queen's dogmatic refusal to grant permission for her 25-year-old sister, Princess Margaret, to marry Group-Captain Peter Townsend in 1955 that was largely responsible for the bitterness that has been the princess' trademark ever since. Although the palace did its best to put a positive spin on the situation, it appears that the gentlemanly Townsend (a true hero of the Battle of Britain) was considered unsuitable owing to a previous divorce — on the grounds of his wife's adultery. Ironically, Princess Margaret was to become divorced herself in 1978.

PERSONAL MOTTOES OF SIX BRITISH ROYALS

1. Edward, Prince of Wales (1330–76)

The personal motto of every Prince of Wales — "*Ich Dien*" ("I serve") — was first adopted by "the Black Prince" at the Battle of Crécy. It is said to have originated during an encounter with the dying King John of Bohemia.

2. Elizabeth I (1533–1603)

"*Semper eadem* " ("Ever the same").

3. Albert, Prince Consort (1819–61)

"Never relax, never relax, never relax." (*Not surprisingly, Albert died at the relatively young age of 42, after essentially working himself to death*).

4. Mary of Teck (1867–1953)

"One must move with the times." (*Provided of course that the times remained firmly Victorian*)

5. George VI (1895–1952)

"Look after the children and the country will look after itself."

6. ELIZABETH, THE QUEEN MOTHER (1900–)

"Your work is the rent you pay for the room you occupy on Earth."

FOUR ROYAL EXECUTIONS

1. ANNE BOLEYN (C. 1500–36)

Henry VIII's second wife was tried and found guilty of high treason on May 15, 1536, the stated crimes being adultery and incest with her brother. Condemned to be beheaded, she was however to be given an honourable death on Tower Green and the king even went so far as to bring in a professional swordsman all the way from Calais (at the cost of £23) for the job, rather than rely on the traditional axe-man.

The actual execution took place four days later after having been postponed twice, Anne remaining stoic throughout; at one point, she was heard to remark with a laugh that, "I heard the executioner is very good, and I have a little neck." Escorted from her cell, she mounted the scaffold and faced the crowd with perfect composure, exhorting them all to pray for her. An embroidered handkerchief was then tied over her eyes, and a linen cap held up her hair. Commanded to kneel at the block, she began to repeat the phrase, "To Jesus Christ I commit my soul. O Lord, have mercy on me..." over and over until her voice was suddenly silenced with one solid chop. As the swordsman held up the decapitated head for the onlookers to see, the lips and eyes continued to move for several seconds in the same, now silent, prayer.

2. KATHERINE HOWARD (C. 1525–42)

Henry VIII's fifth wife. Attainted for high treason and executed on February 13, 1542 at the Tower of London. Interestingly, the queen actually practised her role in her own beheading the day before, having requested that the executioner's axe and block be brought to her cell.

3. JANE (1537–54)

Remembered as the "Nine Days Queen", Lady Jane Grey was deposed by her Catholic cousin Mary I and held in the Tower of London until her execution on February 12, 1554. Just hours before her death the devout, 16-year-old ex-queen had bade farewell to her young husband, Lord Guildford Dudley, then watched from her cell window as his head and body were brought back to the Tower chapel in a cart. Prayer book in hand, she prayed all the way to Tower Green and, before declaring her innocence, loosened her gown and blindfolded herself. "What shall I do?" she asked. A bystander helped her find the block. "Pray dispatch me quickly," she pleaded.

Lady Jane Grey, the "Nine Days' Queen,"
from a portrait by L. De Heere.

4. *Charles I (1600–49)*

After his defeat in the English Civil War by the forces of Oliver Cromwell, Charles was taken to London and put on trial for high treason by puritan fanatics. Within a week he would be pronounced guilty and the sentence read: "that he, the said Charles Stuart, as tyrant, traitor, murderer, and public enemy to the good people of this nation, shall be put to death by the severing of his head from his body."

On January 30, 1649, the king met his fate with a dignity and a regal demeanour often lacking in his 24 years upon the throne. Since the day was bitterly cold, before making his way to the place of execution he put on two shirts because he was worried that if he shivered on the black-draped scaffold, people would think he was afraid. "I fear not death," he went on, "...Death is not terrible to me. I bless my God. I am prepared." On his arrival at the block he was asked by the executioner for the customary pardon before raising the axe, to which the condemned man replied, "I forgive no subject of mine who comes deliberately to shed my blood." When the executioner's assistant held up the bloody head afterwards, a great groan was said to have gone up from the crowd at the enormity of the act.

Death

FIVE ROYAL DEATHS FROM STRANGE CAUSES

1. RICHARD, DUKE OF BERNAY (C. 1054–C.1081)

William the Conqueror's second son was gored to death by a stag in the New Forest.

2. GEORGE, DUKE OF CLARENCE (1449–78)

According to tradition, the traitorous duke died when his brother, Edward IV, had him drowned in a barrel of Malmsey wine at the Tower of London.

3. GEORGE II (1683–1760)

Died after falling off his toilet and smashing his head on a cabinet. The king suffered from severe constipation and had evidently worked himself into a stroke.

4. FREDERICK, PRINCE OF WALES (1707–51)

Here lies poor Fred, who was alive and is dead.
We had rather it had been his Father,
Had it been his brother, better'n any other,
Had it been his sister no one would have missed her,
Had it been the whole generation, all the better for the nation,
But as it's just poor Fred, who was alive and is dead,
There's no more to be said.
> (*Jacobite jingle on the death of Frederick, Prince of Wales*)

The eldest son of George II (who detested him) and the father of George III, the prince was killed as the result of being struck by a cricket ball. The injury had evidently resulted in an abdominal abscess that continued to grow until finally bursting three years later.

5. GEORGE V (1865–1936)

According to the private papers of his attending physician, Lord Dawson, George V was euthanized in order to meet a media deadline. It seems that, as the terminally stricken king lay comatose on the evening of Monday, January 20, 1936, the former was anxious to ensure that his patient expired before midnight so that his death could be announced in the morning *Times*, rather than in the less respectable evening papers. After releasing a brief bulletin to the waiting press ("The life of the King is moving peacefully to its close"), at 11:55 P.M. the doctor hastened things along by administering a lethal injection of cocaine and morphine.

FOUR ROYALS WHO DIED FROM OVEREATING

1. HENRY I (C. 1068–1135)

Reputedly died of an intestinal illness resulting from "a surfeit of lampreys." The king had unwisely gorged himself, against the advice of his physician, while on a hunting trip in the Forest of Lyons.

2. JOHN (1166–1216)

Died of dysentery following a "a surfeit of peaches and cider."

3. ANNE (1665–1714)

Died from a stroke brought on by overeating.

4. GEORGE I (1660–1727)

Felled by a massive stroke after overindulging in a meal of various fruits. Coincidentally, he had been on a visit home to his native Hanover at the time and died in the very room where he had been born.

EIGHT FEMALE ROYALS WHO DIED AS A RESULT OF CHILDBIRTH

1. ETHELFLEDA THE FAIR (D. C. 963)
2. ISABELLA OF VALOIS (1387–1409)

3. *MARY DE BOHUN (C. 1370–94)*
4. *KATHERINE OF VALOIS (1401–37)*
5. *ELIZABETH OF YORK (1466–1503)*
6. *JANE SEYMOUR (C. 1505–37)*
7. *KATHERINE PARR (C. 1513–48)*
8. *PRINCESS CHARLOTTE (1796–1817)*

SIX ROYALS WHO DIED OF TUBERCULOSIS

Also known as the white plague or consumption; until the advent of antibiotics tuberculosis continued to be one of the most deadly diseases in history.

1. *ANNE OF WARWICK (1456–85)*

Though some accounts suggests she was poisoned by her husband Richard III, it would appear that the queen actually died of tuberculosis.

2. *HENRY VII (1457–1509)*

Died from a combination of gout and tuberculosis at the age of 52.

3. *ARTHUR, PRINCE OF WALES (1486–1502)*

Henry VIII's elder brother died of the disease at age 16.

4. *EDWARD VI (1537–53)*

Although there can be little doubt that the boy-king was riddled with tuberculosis, it is worth mentioning that, when he died, he had neither hair nor fingernails and his body was covered with a terrible rash — symptoms more typically associated with syphilis.

5. *ANNE OF DENMARK (1574–1619)*

Wife of James I. Some historians speculate that the couple's first-born son and heir, Prince Henry, may also have died of the disease, although typhoid was the immediate cause.

6. *PRINCESS AMELIA (1783–1810)*

It was the death of George III's youngest and favourite child, Amelia, from tuberculosis at the age of 27 that finally unhinged his mind for good.

THREE MONARCHS WHO DIED OF SMALLPOX

During the Middle Ages virtually everyone got this terrible disease; it has been responsible for the deaths of tens of millions of people. The most that one could hope for was to survive and not to be too badly pockmarked in the process; women who were thus spared were known thereafter as "fair."

1. *EDWARD I (1239–1307)*
2. *EDWARD II (1284–1327)*
3. *MARY II (1662–94)*

SIX ROYALS WHO DIED ACCIDENTALLY

1. *SWEYN, "FORKBEARD" (C. 990–1014)*
   Died after falling from his horse.

2. *WILLIAM III (1650–1702)*
   Fell from his horse after it stumbled over a molehill in Richmond Park, broke his collarbone and died of the resulting pleurisy two weeks later. Afterwards, Jacobites used to toast the "little gentleman in the velvet coat" who caused the accident.

3. *LEOPOLD, DUKE OF ALBANY (1853–84)*
   Queen Victoria's youngest son. A hemophiliac, Leopold bled to death after slipping on a polished staircase at his hotel in Cannes. Ironically, he had come to the south of France to improve his health.

4. *GEORGE, DUKE OF KENT (1902–42)*
   Killed in a mysterious R.A.F. plane-crash in northern Scotland on August 25, 1942, along with over a dozen passengers. To this day the precise circumstances of the disaster remain shrouded, though it has been suggested that the duke may have been piloting the aircraft himself while drunk when it slammed into a hillside. Another (rather more far-fetched) theory asserts that he was assassinated by his own government, owing to his scandalous lifestyle.

5. *WILLIAM, DUKE OF GLOUCESTER (1942–72)*
   Killed while participating in an air race on August 28, 1972.

6. DIANA, PRINCESS OF WALES (1961–97)

Killed in a car crash in Paris on August 31, 1997, after her drunken chauffeur recklessly attempted to evade a group of paparazzi.

TWO ROYALS WHO EXPLODED
(AND ONE NEAR CATASTROPHE)

1. HENRY VIII (1491–1547)

Having already undergone one mishap while en route to his funeral (when dogs were discovered licking the body during an overnight stop), soon after Henry's corpse was placed inside St George's Chapel, Windsor, his lead coffin burst open once more. According to one witness, "all the pavement of the church was with the fat and the corrupt and putrefied blood foully imbued."

2. CAROLINE OF BRANDENBURG-ANSBACH (1683–1737)

"Here lies wrapt in forty thousand towels
The only proof that Caroline had bowels"

Alexander Pope

Queen Caroline (wife of George II), from a contemporary portrait.

In 1737 the long-suffering wife of George II fell mortally ill after a badly bungled attempt to repair an umbilical rupture. While laying in bed after the operation her bowel suddenly burst open, showering excrement throughout the room. One of the courtiers present, recovering from his shocked silence, ventured the hope that the relief would do the queen some good. Caroline bravely replied that she hoped so too, as it would doubtless be the last evacuation she'd ever have.

AND ONE WHO CAME CLOSE...

GEORGE IV (1762–1830)

The deceased king was badly embalmed, the result being that the body swelled up and threatened to explode through his lead-lined coffin. Fortunately for his mourners, the danger was averted in time by drilling a hole in the latter to let out some of the fetid air.

FIVE ROYAL REACTIONS TO THE DEATH OF OTHERS

1. HENRY VIII (1491–1547)

When informed that his former wife of almost 24 years, Katherine of Aragon, had passed over, Henry immediately threw up his arms and shouted, "God be praised. The old harridan is dead!" He then spent much of the following day dancing while dressed in festive clothing.

2. JAMES I (1566–1625)

(*On hearing the news that his mother, Mary Queen of Scots, had been executed by the English*) "I am now sole king." He was referring (rather coldly) to his then position as undisputed King of Scotland.

3. GEORGE II (1683–1760)

(*On the death of Frederick, Prince of Wales*) "I have lost my eldest son, but I was glad of it."

4. GEORGE IV (1762–1830)

In 1821 a messenger came to inform George of Napoleon's death: "I have, Sir, to congratulate you...your greatest enemy is dead." "Is she, by God?" came the king's cheerful reply, in the belief that his irksome wife Queen Caroline was at long last out of his hair.

5. VICTORIA (1819–1901)

(*On the death of her husband Prince Albert*) "I never, never shall be able to bear that chilling, dreadful, weary, unnatural life of a widow."

LAST WORDS OF 21 ROYALS

1. HENRY II (1133–89)

(*After learning that his favourite son John had been plotting against him*) "Enough; now let things go as they may; I care no more for myself or for the world…Shame, shame on a conquered king."

2. RICHARD I, "THE LIONHEART" (1157–99)

(*After being shot with a crossbow bolt*) "Youth, I forgive thee. Take off his chains, give him 100 shillings and let him go."

3. RICHARD III (1452–85)

(*At Bosworth Field*) "I will die King of England, I will not budge a foot! Treason! Treason!" There is no evidence, incidentally, that he ever said "A horse! A horse! My Kingdom for a horse!"

4. KATHERINE HOWARD (C. 1525–42)

(*Before her execution*) "I die a Queen, but I would rather die the wife of Culpepper (her lover). God have mercy on my soul. Good people, I beg you pray for me."

5. HENRY VIII (1491–1547)

"Monks! Monks! Monks!"

6. EDWARD VI (1537–53)

"Oh my Lord God, defend this realm from papistry and maintain their true religion."

7. ELIZABETH I (1533–1603)

"All my possessions for one moment of time."

8. CHARLES I (1600–49)

(*To his executioner*) "Stay (wait) for the sign."

9. CHARLES II *(1630–85)*

"Let not poor Nelly starve" (*in reference to his favourite mistress, Nell Gwynne*).

10. MARY II *(1662–94)*

"I am not afraid to die."

11. WILLIAM III *(1650–1702)*

"Can this last long?"

12. ANNE *(1665–1714)*

(*When asked by doctors how she felt*) "Never worse. I am going."

13. CAROLINE OF BRANDENBURG-ANSBACH *(1683–1737)*

Wife of George II. "Pray louder that I may hear."

14. FREDERICK, PRINCE OF WALES *(1707–51)*

"I feel death!"

15. GEORGE IV *(1762–1830)*

(*To his physician*) "Wally, what is this? It is death my boy. They have deceived me."

16. ALBERT, PRINCE CONSORT *(1819–61)*

(*To his wife Queen Victoria*) "Good little woman."

17. VICTORIA *(1819–1901)*

"Oh that peace may come. Bertie!" Interestingly, the queen died in the arms of her grandson (and Britain's soon-to-be enemy) Kaiser Wilhelm II of Germany.

18. EDWARD VII *(1841–1910)*

(*On hearing the news that one of his horses, "Witch of the Air," had won the 4:15 at Kempton Park races*) "I am very glad."

19. GEORGE V *(1865–1936)*

Either "How is the Empire?" or "Bugger Bognor," depending upon whom you believe (Bognor is the name of a Sussex coastal resort town, where his doctor suggested he would soon be recuperating).

20. EDWARD VIII (1894–1972)

"Mama...mama...mama...mama."

21. DIANA, PRINCESS OF WALES (1961–97)

Although French authorities denied that Diana uttered any last words at all after being mortally wounded in a Paris car crash, one emergency worker on the scene did report that the semi-conscious princess uttered the words "My God, what's happened?" before lapsing into a coma.

*In
Memoriam*

EIGHT MEMORABLE ROYAL FUNERALS

Up until Queen Victoria's funeral in 1901 it had been customary for most royal burials to take place privately, at night. Victoria, however, left detailed instructions for a daytime funeral and official lying-in-state, and it is this pattern that has been followed ever since. One element that has remained unchanged is the tradition, just before burial, of breaking the late sovereign's staff of office in two and throwing it into the open grave.

1. WILLIAM, "THE CONQUEROR" (C. 1027–87)

William's funeral was one hardly fit for a king. First a fire broke out while his body was being carried into the monastery of St Stephen for burial, and the pallbearers had to abandon the coffin in order to fight the blaze. Then a man named Ascelin interrupted the ceremony, shouting that William had no right to be buried there since he had stolen from him the land on which the monastery had been built. The final indignity was that the marble sarcophagus proved to be much too small to accommodate the corpse; the latter would only just barely be squeezed in with the aid of a pair of soldiers, who accomplished their grim task by jumping up and down on it. Unfortunately they also managed to tear a hole in the stomach in the process, causing it to rupture with a loud bang. The resulting stench was so overpowering that it forced the mourners to evacuate the premises.

2. ELEANOR OF CASTILE (1244–90)

After her unexpected death near Lincoln in 1290, the queen's husband Edward I brought the body home for burial at Westminster Abbey. So devoted to her was he that, at each of the twelve places where the bier rested on its way to London, he erected one of the famous "Eleanor Crosses," three of which still stand (this is also where Charing Cross in London got its name). Once she was interred, the king arranged for two wax tapers to burn forever by her tomb. They continued to do so until the Reformation, three hundred years later.

3. CHARLES I (1600–49)

After the king's execution his head and corpse was loaded onto a cart and taken in the greatest of secrecy to Windsor Castle for entombment. Although there was no state funeral allowed (indeed, public mourning was actually banned) there was a dismal little procession of royalists, who accompanied the body to St George's Chapel. As they did so it began to snow, and soon the black pall of the coffin began to turn white — a reminder of the king's coronation when, against all precedent, he had worn a suit of "unlucky" white velvet.

4. VICTORIA (1819–1901)

The funeral of Britain's longest-reigning sovereign was also history's first truly global media event, with services held throughout every corner of the empire. Victoria had died at her south-coast island retreat, Osborne House, on January 22 1901, in the arms of her beloved grandson Kaiser Wilhelm II of Germany. Two weeks later, her oak coffin was taken aboard the royal yacht *Alberta* and, accompanied by a convoy of destroyers, made its way for Portsmouth through an avenue of Royal Navy warships that stretched for 13 kilometres. From there it was slowly taken by the royal train to London's Victoria Station, and then on in a solemn procession watched by thousands to its final resting place at Windsor Castle. Meanwhile, every minute for an hour and twenty-one minutes, cannon fire echoed from Hyde Park, one for each year of the queen's life. Immediately behind the gun carriage bearing her coffin came the cream of European royalty; a veritable army of emperors, kings, princes and grand dukes, most of whom were related directly to the deceased by blood. For the vast majority of those who witnessed it, Victoria's funeral represented the passing of an age, one unsurpassed in pomp and prosperity.

5. EDWARD VII (1841–1910)

The king's simple coffin (made from one of the oaks in Windsor great park) was escorted to its final resting place by no less than nine reigning European kings, five heirs apparent, forty imperial or royal highnesses, and seven queens. It remains the greatest assemblage of royalty ever seen in one place.

6. GEORGE V (1865–1936)

After his death at Sandringham on January 20, 1936, the king's body was taken by way of a handcart that evening in an eerie, torch-light procession, led by a single Scottish piper, to a small, nearby church. From there it was transported by train to London to lie in state at Westminster Hall, where the new king, Edward VIII, held an extend-ed vigil along with his three younger brothers, each prince standing at a corner of the bier (the line of mourners, incidentally, extended for five kilometres). On the day of the actual funeral all four sons walked behind the casket, the route to Westminster Abbey being thronged with an estimated crowd of three million.

7. EDWARD VIII (1894–1972)

Having been cut out of royal life entirely ever since his abdication 35 years earlier, in May 1972 the dying duke was visited at his Paris home by his niece Elizabeth II, just a few days before his death. His body was subsequently flown back to England for a state funeral at St George's chapel, Windsor, and afterwards buried in the gardens at Frogmore. As a final gesture of reconciliation, his hated widow was invited by the queen to stay on at Buckingham Palace for the duration of the proceedings.

8. DIANA, PRINCESS OF WALES (1961–97)

The tragic death of the "people's princess" in 1997 resulted in an extraordinary outpouring of grief around the world, with the queen's ini-tial refusal to lower the flag at Buckingham Palace or to address her sub-jects resulting in an unprecedented backlash against the royal family. Worried about the security of her throne, the queen was ultimately per-suaded to allow, as she put it, "A unique service, for a unique individual" — to be held at Westminster Abbey in front of the eyes of the world.

THREE ROYALS INTERRED IN THE TOWER OF LONDON

The largest (and oldest) permanently occupied fortress in Europe, throughout its almost ten centuries of history the Tower of London has guarded the north bank of the Thames while simultaneously serving as a prison for the most dangerous foes of the state, the most recent of whom was the Nazi Rudolf Hess in 1941. Among royal circles it was considered to be a great privilege to be beheaded there in the peace and seclusion of Tower Green (as were three queens of England) instead of before the mob at Tower Hill. The latter were subsequently interred in the tiny chapel of St Peter-ad-Vincula.

1. *ANNE BOLEYN (C. 1500–36)*
2. *KATHERINE HOWARD (C. 1525–42)*
3. *JANE (1537–54)*

FOUR ROYALS INTERRED AT FROGMORE

Built on the grounds of Windsor Castle near Frogmore House, the Royal Mausoleum at Frogmore was originally intended solely as a shrine for Queen Victoria's husband Prince Albert. Nowadays two famous royal couples are buried there, although Duke and Duchess of Windsor have admittedly been relegated to outside plots among a host of minor royals.

1. *VICTORIA (1819–1901)*
2. *ALBERT, PRINCE CONSORT (1819–61)*
3. *EDWARD VIII (1894–1972)*
4. *WALLIS, DUCHESS OF WINDSOR (C. 1895–1986)*

30 ROYALS INTERRED AT WESTMINSTER ABBEY

Begun under the command of Edward the Confessor in the mid-eleventh century, and finally completed in 1745. Nearly all of Britain's monarchs have been crowned at Westminster Abbey over the centuries, with a considerable number having been buried there as well — each in his or her own elaborate stone tomb set within the vast gloomy interior.

1. *EDWARD THE CONFESSOR (C. 1004–66)*
2. *EDITH OF WESSEX (C. 1020–75)*
3. *MATILDA OF SCOTLAND (1080–1118)*
4. *HENRY III (1207–72)*
5. *EDWARD I (1239–1307)*

6. *ELEANOR OF CASTILE (C. 1244–90)*
7. *EDWARD III (1312–77)*
8. *PHILIPPA OF HAINAULT (1314–69)*
9. *ANNE OF BOHEMIA (1366–94)*
10. *RICHARD II (1367–1400)*
11. *HENRY V (1387–1422)*
12. *KATHERINE OF VALOIS (1401–37)*
13. *ANNE OF WARWICK (1456–85)*
14. *HENRY VII (1457–1509)*
15. *ELIZABETH OF YORK (1466–1503)*
16. *EDWARD V (1470–C. 1483)*
17. *ANNE OF CLEVES (1515–57)*
18. *MARY I (1516–58)*
19. *ELIZABETH I (1533–1603)*
20. *EDWARD VI (1537–53)*
21. *JAMES I (1566–1625)*
22. *ANNE OF DENMARK (1574–1619)*
23. *CHARLES II (1630–85)*
24. *ANNE HYDE (1637–71)*
25. *WILLIAM III (1650–1702)*
26. *GEORGE OF DENMARK (1653–1708)*
27. *MARY II (1662–94)*
28. *ANNE (1665–1714)*
29. *GEORGE II (1683–1760)*
30. *CAROLINE OF BRANDENBURG-ANSBACH (1683–1737)*

FIVE ROYALS INTERRED AT CHRISTCHURCH CATHEDRAL, CANTERBURY

The first of England's great Norman cathedrals; despite suffering heavy damage in World War II Christchurch continues to be the undisputed centre of English Christianity.

1. *EDGIVA OF KENT (C. 905–968)*
2. *ISABELLA OF GLOUCESTER (C. 1175–1217)*
3. *EDWARD, PRINCE OF WALES (1330–76)*
4. *HENRY IV (1366–1413)*
5. *JOAN OF NAVARRE (C. 1370–1437)*

16 MONARCHS INTERRED AT ST GEORGE'S CHAPEL, WINDSOR

"A strange busload to be travelling through eternity together."
George V (*on his ancestors buried at St George's chapel*)

One of the noblest buildings in all of England, St George's Chapel at Windsor Castle was begun by Edward IV in 1475 (sadly, he did not live to see it completed). Featuring elegant stained-glass windows, a high vaulted ceiling and intricately carved choir stalls; with the exception of Westminster Abbey it is the single most important royal burial site, the various tombs being located beneath the floor. It is also the place where monarchs have traditionally invested new knights at the annual Order of the Garter ceremony each June 24. For over five centuries, heraldic banners of the latter have hung in the choir, giving the whole place an unforgettably medieval appearance.

1. HENRY VI (1421–71)

2. EDWARD IV (1442–83)

3. ELIZABETH WOODVILLE (C. 1437–92)

4. HENRY VIII (1491–1547)

5. JANE SEYMOUR (C. 1508–37)

6. CHARLES I (1600–49)

7. GEORGE III (1738–1820)

8. CHARLOTTE OF MECKLENBURG-STRELITZ (1744–1818)

9. GEORGE IV (1762–1830)

10. WILLIAM IV (1765–1837)

11. ADELAIDE OF SAXE-MEININGEN (1792–1849)

12. EDWARD VII (1841–1910)

13. ALEXANDRA OF DENMARK (1844–1925)

14. GEORGE V (1865–1936)

15. MARY OF TECK (1867–1953)

16. GEORGE VI (1895–1952)

THREE KINGS INTERRED AT GLASTONBURY ABBEY

The ancient town of Glastonbury is steeped in both Arthurian and Christian Legend, supposedly being the place where Joseph of Arimathea brought the Holy Grail (the chalice used by Christ during the Last Supper). The actual abbey, as well as housing the remains of three, historically documented early English kings, is also believed by many to be the final resting place of King Arthur and Queen Guinevere, whose "tomb" was alleged to have been discovered there in 1191. It would seem more likely, however, that the latter was merely an elaborate archaeological fake, perpetrated by the monks in order to bring home fame and riches.

1. *EDMUND I (C. 921–946)*
2. *EDGAR (C. 943–975)*
3. *EDMUND II (C. 990–1016)*

14 BRITISH MONARCHS BURIED IN FRANCE

1. *WILLIAM I, "THE CONQUEROR" (C. 1027–87)*
2. *MATILDA OF FLANDERS (C. 1032–83)*
3. *ADELIZA OF LOUVAIN (C. 1105–1151)*
4. *MATILDA, "THE EMPRESS" (1102–67)*
5. *HENRY II (1133–89)*
6. *ELEANOR OF AQUITAINE (1122–1204)*
7. *RICHARD I, "THE LIONHEART" (1157–99)*
8. *BERENGARIA OF NAVARRE (1165–C. 1230)*
9. *ISABELLA OF ANGOULÊME (1186–1246)*
10. *ISABELLA OF VALOIS (1387–1409)*
11. *MARGARET OF ANJOU (1429–82)*
12. *HENRIETTA MARIA OF FRANCE (1609–69)*
13. *JAMES II (1633–1701)*
14. *MARY OF MODENA (1658–1718)*

NINE MONARCHS INTERRED AT WINCHESTER CATHEDRAL

Founded in the mid-seventh century, Winchester Cathedral contains some of the best surviving examples of Norman architecture along with the tombs of many early English monarchs.

1. *ETHELSWITHA (D. 905)*
2. *EDWARD THE ELDER (C. 871–924)*
3. *ELFLEDA (D. 920)*
4. *EDRED (C. 923–955)*
5. *EDWY (C. 942–959)*

6. *Emma of Normandy (c. 986–1052)*
7. *Canute (c. 995–1035)*
8. *Harthacanute (c. 1018–42)*
9. *William II, "Rufus" (c. 1056–1100)*

THREE AMBITIOUS ROYAL MEMORIALS

1. *The George III Statue*

This enormous copper statue of the king is situated on a hill at the end of the 5-km Long Walk at Windsor Castle. He is shown mounted on a horse, in rather unlikely Roman costume.

2. *The Albert Memorial*

This sombre and somewhat vulgar monument in Kensington Gardens continues to be among the most beloved landmarks in London. Erected on the orders of Queen Victoria to commemorate the loss of her husband, the Albert Memorial stands on the site where his Great Exhibition amazed the world. The centrepiece of the structure is a huge bronze statue of the Prince Consort (the metal coming from thirty-seven melted-down cannons) under a vast stone canopy and spire, in turn surrounded by granite steps, life-sized animal statues and Venetian mosaics. After deteriorating for much of the twentieth century — during the First World War it even suffered the indignity of being painted entirely black to deter its detection by zeppelins — in recent years the edifice has undergone a much-needed renovation.

3. *Althorp*

Located in Northamptonshire, Althorp is the ancestral home of Lady Diana Spencer. Here, on a tiny island within the estate park, can be found the final resting place of the girl who grew up to become Princess of Wales and arguably the most famous woman who ever lived. Since her death in 1997 this beautiful site (which Horace Walpole described in 1765 as "one of those enchanted scenes which a thousand circumstances of history and art endear to a pensive spectator") has been converted into a cheesy (if financially lucrative) tourist trap by the present Earl Spencer, complete with visitors' centre.

EIGHT ROYAL EXHUMATIONS

1. EDWARD THE CONFESSOR (C. 1004–66)

The founder of Westminster Abbey would find little rest there after his death, with his corpse being repeatedly exhumed and tampered with over the next several centuries. In 1098 the future Henry I had the coffin opened, in order to prove the holy king's "incorruptibility." According to a contemporary account, the body was found to be "fresh and rosy-cheeked, with soft skin and flexible joints." An attending bishop even managed to pluck out a hair from the long white beard, for which he received a stern scolding.

Sixty-five years later the coffin was moved to a new shrine in the abbey by Henry II, and again opened (it was then that the king's burial robes and sapphire ring were removed for safekeeping). Henry III, for his part, had the abbey completely renovated and paid particular attention to creating an even more glorious, jewel-encased shrine for Edward in 1269. The former not only personally helped to carry the new casket to its re-interment but also decreed that, on his own death, he was to be buried in the old one. Sadly, during Henry VIII's reign the shrine was plundered and largely destroyed, though his daughter Mary I would do much to restore its former splendour.

The last disinterment came in 1685, as a result of activities surrounding the coronation of James II. It seems that, as workmen were removing scaffolding used during the ceremony, part of it suddenly crashed down and broke open the sarcophagus below. During repairs a crucifix and gold chain were subsequently discovered within, which where coincidentally presented to Edward's distant successor on the very day of his victory at the Battle of Sedgemoor. These artifacts, unfortunately, were later stolen during James' initial attempt to escape England after his forced abdication 1688. Yet for all the tampering and tomb raiding, the shrine itself continues to be the holy centre of the abbey to this very day.

2. WILLIAM I, "THE CONQUEROR" (C. 1027–87)

Until recently it had been thought that the king's remains, originally interred in a monastery in France, had long since been dispersed by vandals. However, in 1987 French officials discovered a thighbone there, believed to be genuine, which has since been reburied under a new tombstone.

3. Edward I (1239–1307)

On May 2, 1774, Edward's tomb at Westminster Abbey was opened and his body found to be largely intact, four and a half centuries after his death.

4. Henry IV (1366–1413)

According to an account first published in 1691, when the king's body was being taken by boat from London for burial at Canterbury Cathedral, a great storm suddenly arose. Fearing it was the wrath of God, the superstitious sailors decided to throw the corpse overboard and later substituted another in the king's coffin. When the latter was opened in 1832, however, the story was debunked, its well-preserved occupant bearing an unmistakable resemblance to Henry.

5. & 6. Edward V (1470–c. 1483) and Richard, Duke of York (1473–c. 1483)

In 1674 a chest was unearthed beneath the stairs leading to the White Tower in the Tower of London, containing the skeletons of two young boys that were believed to belong to the murdered Edward V and his brother Richard. The bones were later re-interred in a marble urn in Westminster Abbey by order of Charles II.

7. Katherine Parr (c. 1513–48)

During the English Civil War Katherine's casket disappeared from its resting place at Sudeley Castle, only to be rediscovered a century and a half later by a local farmer who had been digging on the grounds. Forcing open its lead-lined seals, the man found the queen's corpse to be perfectly preserved, though the sudden exposure to the elements quickly caused it to deteriorate before his very eyes. He decided to rebury the coffin on the spot, and it would be yet another century before it was finally returned to the castle's chapel.

8. George I (1660–1727)

After his death the king's remains were interred in the Chapel of the Leine Schloss in his native Hanover, where they would be brutally disturbed by a British bombing raid some two centuries later. After the Second World War they were transferred to the chapel vaults of Schloss Herrenhausen.

13 MONARCHS WHOSE BODIES WERE LOST, STOLEN OR DESTROYED

1. ALFRED THE GREAT (C. 849–C. 899)

The present site of the king's grave is unknown, although it is thought that his bones may possibly lie in one of the mortuary chests at Winchester Cathedral.

2. EDWARD THE MARTYR (C. 963–978)

The whereabouts of the king's alleged remains, which were unearthed by a gardener in the ruins of Shaftsbury Abbey in 1931, are presently unknown. At last report they were in the possession of the Midland Bank in Croydon.

3. ETHELRED II (C. 968–1016)

Originally buried in Old St Paul's Cathedral in London, his tomb was lost in the Great Fire of 1666.

4. HAROLD I (C. 1016–40)

Originally buried in Westminster Abbey, Harold was afterwards disinterred by his successor Harthacanute, who had the body decapitated and thrown into the Thames. It was later dragged up again in a fisherman's net and reburied at St Clement Danes.

5. & 6. STEPHEN (C. 1097–1154) AND MATILDA OF BOULOGNE (C. 1104–1152)

In common with many other medieval monarchs, the tombs of King Stephen and his consort at Faversham Abbey (along with their contents) were destroyed during the Reformation.

7. RICHARD II (1367–1400)

For several centuries the king's tomb in Westminster Abbey (which he shared with his beloved queen, Anne of Bohemia) had a hole in it, through which visitors could reach in and touch his skull. In 1776 a schoolboy stole his jawbone and subsequently passed it down as a family heirloom; it was finally returned to the abbey in 1906.

Richard II (painting by J. Randall after a contemporary portrait).

8. RICHARD III (1452–85)

After his death at Bosworth Field the last Plantagenet was buried on the cheap at Greyfriar's Abbey in Leicester, in an unmarked grave. During the Reformation his bones were dug up and thrown into the River Soar, the empty coffin thereafter being used as a horse-trough and, later, to make cellar steps at an inn.

9. HENRY VIII (1491–1547)

During the king's interment in the royal vault at St George's Chapel, a workman removed one of his finger-bones and subsequently used it to make a knife handle.

10. ANNE BOLEYN (C. 1500–36)

After she was beheaded the queen's heart was stolen and secretly hidden in a church near Thetford in Suffolk. Rediscovered in 1836, it was reburied under the church organ.

11. KATHERINE OF ARAGON (1485–1536)

The tomb of Henry VIII's first wife in Peterborough Cathedral was destroyed in 1642, but its site may still be seen and her bones still lie beneath the flagstones.

12. CHARLES I (1600–49)

After his execution the king's body was quietly buried in St. George's Chapel, Windsor, where it would remain until the restoration of the monarchy under his son Charles II in 1660. It was then that the idea for a grand new monument in Westminster Abbey befitting the "royal martyr," to be designed by Christopher Wren, was first proposed by the government. Unfortunately, before this could be undertaken Charles II appropriated the £70 000 allocated for the reburial, and a mysterious disappearance of the original casket was quickly arranged to prevent a scandal. Its precise whereabouts would remain a mystery until April 1, 1813, when workmen accidentally broke through the wall of Henry VIII's burial vault. There, beside the coffins of Henry, his wife Jane Seymour and one of Queen Anne's stillborn babies was one covered entirely in black velvet, inscribed "King Charles 1648." Although the date was incorrect (Charles died in January 1649) it was undoubtedly genuine.

In any event, the coffin was soon opened in front of a small group of court observers. The various wrappings surrounding the severed head were removed, revealing a face that closely resembled the Charles I depicted in portraits by Van Dyck, though according to royal surgeon Sir Henry Halford the skin was understandably discoloured and the nose decayed. Amazingly, the pointed beard was more or less intact. After these sombre examinations were concluded, the skull was returned to its former place and the vault was closed up once more. Yet this was not the end of the story, for unbeknownst to the others Halford had stolen a portion of the king's fourth cervical vertebra during the exhumation, which he later had made into an amusing novelty salt holder. The doctor's heirs, however, didn't find the relic quite so humorous and eventually returned it to Queen Victoria for re-interment.

13. JAMES II (1633–1701)

After his death while in exile in France the king was temporarily buried in the Church of the English Benedictines in Paris, whilst hopefully awaiting eventual transportation back to England for burial in Westminster Abbey. Unfortunately the body (along with that of his wife) seems to have disappeared during the French Revolution, although there are reports that it was later found and re-interred at the Château of St Germain-en-Laye by order of George IV.

Uneasy
Lies the
Head ...

FOUR ROYAL PRETENDERS

1. LAMBERT SIMNEL (C. 1475–1525)

In 1487 this twelve-year-old Yorkist pretender to Henry VII's throne was proclaimed as "Edward VI" at a cathedral in Dublin. Evidently, his handlers tried to pass him off as the heir to the late Duke of Clarence, though in actual fact he was merely the son of an organ-maker. Their small force of German mercenaries was quickly defeated in battle, however, and Simnel was captured alive. Instead of hanging the latter for treason the king decided on an arguably much worse fate for the unfortunate child — a lifetime of menial work in the royal kitchens.

2. JAMES SCOTT, DUKE OF MONMOUTH (1649–85)

One of Charles II's many bastard sons, the Protestant duke led an uprising in 1685 against his unpopular Catholic uncle James II with the intention of seizing the throne for himself. The rebellion was ruthlessly put down at the nighttime Battle of Sedgemoor, after which the chief justice, Lord Jeffreys, conducted the infamous Bloody Assizes to try both rebels and sympathizers. In the mass executions that followed the duke himself was put to the axe (it would take half a dozen chops to separate his head from his body). It was only then someone realised that, as the — albeit illegitimate — son of a king, it was important that his portrait should be painted. The head was promptly sewn back onto the body, the corpse was dressed up in finery, and the painting was made. It now hangs in the National Portrait Gallery in London.

3. JAMES STUART, "THE OLD PRETENDER" (1688–1766)

The only surviving (legitimate) son of James II, James Stuart styled himself James III and did much to stir up Jacobite aspirations during his lengthy exile in France. After his final defeat in 1715 he spent the remaining fifty years of his life in Rome, where on his death he was accorded the funeral of a reigning Catholic monarch and burial in St Peter's.

4. CHARLES STUART, "THE YOUNG PRETENDER" (1720–88)

The son of James Stuart (see above), the man who styled himself "Charles III" has gone done in history by the more familiar name of "Bonnie Prince Charlie." In 1745 he led an initially successful invasion in an effort to claim his inheritance, during which he was actually able to hold court at Holyrood Palace in Edinburgh for over a month, in suitably regal fashion. The English quickly regrouped however and were soon marching north, culminating in the terrible Jacobite massacre that was Culloden. Charles himself managed to escape (dressed as a woman), and like his father spent the remainder of his life in exile, a dissolute alcoholic. He was buried in St Peter's Basilica.

FOUR NOTABLE ROYAL FEUDS

1. GEORGE II VS. FREDERICK, PRINCE OF WALES

Both the king and his wife Queen Caroline despised their eldest son Frederick, Prince of Wales, to the point where the former considered disinheriting him altogether. The feeling was entirely mutual.

Frederick, Prince of Wales (from a painting by Philip Mercier).

2. THE QUEEN MOTHER VS. THE DUCHESS OF WINDSOR

The Queen Mother never forgave Wallis Simpson for her part in the abdication of Edward VIII in 1936, which resulted in the unwanted succession (and early death) of her own weak husband George VI. Aside from shutting them both out entirely from royal society in the years that followed Elizabeth also made some highly unflattering remarks about the duchess — remarks that ultimately got back to the duke's ears. Thereafter, he tended to refer to his sister-in-law by such derogatory names as "The Monster of Glamis," "Cookie" or "that fat Scotch cook."

3. QUEEN ELIZABETH II VS. PRINCESS MICHAEL OF KENT

The queen has always hated the Czech-born wife of her cousin Prince Michael, mainly owing to her embarrassing outspokenness. Perhaps the most memorable example of this occurred during a television interview in the late 1970s, when she suggested that Elizabeth's beloved corgis should all be shot.

4. PRINCESS ANNE VS. PRINCESS DIANA

Aside from the fact that the two princesses had virtually nothing in common Anne was always a little jealous of her younger rival as well, not to mention mortified by her often sordid lifestyle. The Princess Royal particularly disagreed with Diana's approach to child rearing, which she described as "gooey."

15 ROYAL OPINIONS REGARDING EACH OTHER

1. "A blushing rose without a thorn." *(HENRY VIII, ON KATHERINE HOWARD)*

2. "A miserly martinet with an insatiable sexual appetite." *(FREDERICK, PRINCE OF WALES, ON HIS FATHER GEORGE II.)*

3. "Fretz might be a Wechselbag or changeling." *(GEORGE II, ON PRINCE FREDERICK.)*

4. "The lowest stinking coward in the world...I wish the ground would open this minute and sink the monster into the lowest hole in hell." *(QUEEN CAROLINE, ON PRINCE FREDERICK.)*

5. "Too disgusting, because his face was covered with grease paint." (QUEEN VICTORIA, ON HAVING TO KISS HER UNCLE, GEORGE IV, AS A CHILD.)

6. "A thoroughgoing lazybones!" (PRINCE ALBERT, ON EDWARD VII.)

7. "Oh! Bertie, alas! Alas! That is too sad a subject to enter on." (QUEEN VICTORIA, ON EDWARD VII).

8. "I never left her presence without a sigh of relief" (EDWARD VII, ON QUEEN VICTORIA).

9. "What a curious child he is." (QUEEN ALEXANDRA, ON HER GRAND-SON, THE FUTURE EDWARD VIII.)

10. "Mother dear is the most selfish person I have ever known." (GEORGE V, ON QUEEN ALEXANDRA.)

11. "How horribly boneless it felt!" (EDWARD VIII, ON HAVING TO HOLD THE HAND OF HIS GREAT-GRANDMOTHER, QUEEN VICTORIA, AS A CHILD.)

12. "He is intelligent, has a good sense of humour and thinks about things the right way." (GEORGE VI, ON PRINCE PHILIP.)

13. "As tedious in death as she had been in life." (THE QUEEN MOTHER, ON THE RECENTLY-DECEASED PRINCESS DIANA.)

14. "Precious, extravagant and lacking in the dedication and discipline he will need if he is to make a good king." (PRINCE PHILIP, ON HIS SON PRINCE CHARLES.)

15. "The vulgar view of King George III is quite simply that he was mad, and to make matters worse, that he also succeeded in losing the American colonies. The fact that he had wide and civilised interests, was a great patron of the arts and sciences and devoted a vast quantity of time to affairs of State has been conveniently neglected." (PRINCE CHARLES, ON GEORGE III.)

NINE ROYAL ASSASSINATIONS

For God's sake let us sit upon the ground
And tell sad stories of the death of kings -
How some have been deposed, some slain in war,
Some haunted by the ghosts they have deposed,
Some poisoned by their wives, some sleeping killed,
All murdered....

William Shakespeare
Richard II

1. EDMUND I (C. 921–946)

Fatally stabbed in a fracas on May 26, 946, by an outlaw named Liofa. The latter was immediately torn limb from limb by the king's attendants.

2. EDWARD THE MARTYR (C. 963–978)

Ambushed and murdered on March 18, 978 at Corfe Castle, Dorset, most likely on the orders of his stepmother, Queen Elfrida of Devon.

3. EDMUND II (C. 990–1016)

This formidable Saxon king was actually killed while sitting on a toilet. The story goes that his unknown assassin had hidden in the pit below waiting for his opportunity, before ultimately thrusting a long sword up his victim's anus.

4. WILLIAM II, "RUFUS" (C. 1056–1100)

Killed by an arrow in the back while hunting in the New Forest on August 2, 1100, by a knight named Walter Tyrel. The latter, who claimed it had been an accident (conveniently, there were no witnesses) may in fact have been acting on orders from the king's brother Henry (later Henry I). The alleged site of the murder is still marked by the so-called Rufus Stone.

5. EDWARD II (1284–1327)

Deposed by his French consort, Queen Isabella, and her paramour Roger Mortimer, Earl of March. After months of humiliation, torture and near starvation by his captors, the ex-king was ultimately killed in his cell at Berkeley Castle on September 22, 1327, by having a red-hot poker thrust up his rectum.

6. RICHARD II (1367–1400)

There has been much speculation over the years as to the precise cause of Richard's death. Though it is a fairly safe bet that he was murdered on the orders of his usurper, Henry IV, some historians have theorized that he died from depression-related anorexia. The more popular view was that he was hacked to death or, according to Shakespeare, pole-axed by his prison guards at Pontefract Castle (neither of which theory was born out by an examination of his skeleton in 1871). Imposed starvation would seem to have been the most likely cause.

7. HENRY VI (1421–71)

Deposed in 1461, Henry was briefly restored to the throne nine years later but was soon returned by his enemies to a cell in the Tower of London. It was there that he was stabbed to death by an unknown assailant on May 21, 1471, probably on the orders of Edward IV or one of his men.

8. EDWARD V (1470–C. 1483)

Believed smothered to death in his sleep along with his younger brother, most likely on the night of September 3, 1483, while imprisoned in the Tower of London.

9. EARL LOUIS MOUNTBATTEN OF BURMA (1900–79)

While on holiday in Ireland, the 79-year-old Mountbatten was killed instantly when his fishing boat was blown up by an IRA bomb. His grandson and two others also died.

EIGHT ROYALS WHO SURVIVED ASSASSINATION ATTEMPTS

1. EDWARD I (1239–1307)

Attacked and wounded with a dagger by an assassin while on crusade in Joppa. He made a complete recovery with the help of his wife Eleanor of Castile, who (legend has it) heroically sucked the pus out of his septic wound.

2. ELIZABETH I (1533–1603)

When a shot fired from shore wounded one of her royal bargemen, the queen was said to have comforted the man with the words, "Be of good cheer, for you will never want. For the bullet was meant for me."

3. JAMES I *(1566–1625)*

In 1605, a notorious conspiracy (known to history as the Gunpowder Plot) to blow up both the king and the English parliament was hatched and very nearly carried out. It seems that a group of IRA-like Catholics, among them a mercenary named Guido Fawkes, had managed to smuggle two-dozen barrels of gunpowder into the cellars beneath the Houses of Parliament, with the intention of setting them off during the state opening. The plot was ultimately foiled when one of the conspirators sent off an anonymous letter of warning, though the affair is still commemorated with fireworks each November 5, in the national holiday known as Guy Fawkes Day.

4. GEORGE III *(1738–1820)*

The king survived a number of attacks upon his person throughout his almost sixty-year reign. Perhaps the most notorious of these occurred in 1786, when a housemaid named Margaret Nicholson attempted to stab him as he was arriving at St James's Palace for a reception. She was easily overpowered, however, and when the crowd began to attack her the king mercifully shouted out, "The poor creature is mad! Do not hurt her! She has not hurt me!" The woman was later declared insane and sent to an asylum.

Other attempts on George III's life occurred in 1795 (when a shot was fired at his coach during the state opening of parliament) and in 1800, when a man unsuccessfully tried to shoot him during a performance of Mozart's *Le Nozze di Figaro* in London.

5. VICTORIA *(1819–1901)*

During the queen's long reign there were no less than seven attempts made on her life, mostly from mentally disturbed adolescents with unloaded guns. Arguably the most serious incident occurred in 1840, when a young man fired two pistols at her while she was out driving with Prince Albert in an open carriage (both shots missed). Ten years later, a man brutally beat her about the head with a walking stick.

6. EDWARD VII *(1841–1910)*

On April 4, 1900, while the royal train had stopped briefly at the station in Brussels on its way to Copenhagen, a 15-year-old tinsmith's apprentice named Jean-Baptiste Sipido fired several shots through the window of the royal carriage and somehow missed both the Prince and

Princess of Wales. The would-be assassin — a Boer sympathizer — later disappeared while on parole.

7. EDWARD VIII (1894–1972)

In 1925, while watching a horserace, the then Prince of Wales was attacked and slightly wounded by a shawled woman wielding a hatpin. Perhaps more unsettling was an incident in 1936, when a deranged Irish journalist threw a loaded gun under the king's horse during a ceremony in Hyde Park.

8. ELIZABETH II (1926–)

In 1981 the queen narrowly escaped death when she visited a Scottish oil terminal where, soon after, three kilos of gelignite exploded. Earlier that same year, a youth named Marcus Sergeant had fired six blank shots at her during the Trooping of the Colour ceremony on The Mall. He was charged under the Treason Act of 1842 and later sentenced to five years in prison.

FIVE ROYALS WHO FACED DOWN INTRUDERS

1. ELIZABETH I (1533–1603)

In 1584 a Welsh assassin named William Parry stole into the queen's garden at Richmond, with the intention of killing her. According to legend, when he actually set eyes on her however he was "so daunted with the majesty of her presence" that he couldn't do it.

2. VICTORIA (1819–1901)

In 1840 a 17-year-old intruder known to history as "the boy Jones" was discovered hiding under a sofa in the room adjoining the queen's bedroom. He had evidently been in Buckingham Palace for three days, living off any food he had found lying about, at one point even managing to sit on the throne. In the years to come he would make two more uninvited visits to the palace (in between stints in a house of correction) before eventually being sent off to sea, never to be heard from again.

3. ELIZABETH, THE QUEEN MOTHER (1900–)

At Windsor Castle one night during the Second World War, a mentally disturbed army deserter suddenly leapt from behind some bathroom curtains and threw himself at the queen's feet. Although terrified, she managed to keep both herself and him reasonably calm as she slowly edged towards the alarm bell.

4. ELIZABETH II (1926–)

One morning in July 1982, a young man named Michael Fagan hopped the wall at Buckingham Palace and proceeded to crawl through an unlocked window, undetected by anyone. Incredibly, he was then able to gain access to the queen's private quarters, where he found her still fast asleep. The latter was promptly awakened, and to her credit was able to handle the situation in much the same deft way as her mother had forty years before (see above). Evidently, the mentally disturbed Fagan didn't intend any harm, and had merely wanted to talk. The incident served to highlight serious flaws in palace security, though perhaps the most interesting facet of this case was the revelation that the queen and Prince Philip sleep in separate rooms.

5. CHARLES, PRINCE OF WALES (1948–)

While stationed at the Royal Navy barracks at Portland, Dorset in 1974, Charles was awakened one morning by an armed intruder who proceeded to attack him. Alarmed by the sound of the struggle, a detective rushed in just in time to prevent the man — a deranged naval lieutenant — from bringing a chair down on the prince's head.

FIVE ROYALS WHO DESPISED ENGLAND

1. WILLIAM III (1650–1702)

The cold, Dutch-born William had little appreciation for the kingdom he jointly-inherited and never took the time to try and understand his subjects. Fortunately for him his warm-hearted wife Mary did much to make up for his lack of popularity.

2. GEORGE I (1660–1727)

England's first Hanoverian king never attempted to hide his preference for his native country and took almost no interest in running the British government, spending much of his time instead abroad.

3. GEORGE II (1683–1760)

Another narrow-minded Hanoverian with little use for England or its customs; once, in a temper, the king was heard to consign the whole island to the devil.

4. CAROLINE OF BRUNSWICK-WOLFENBÜTTEL (1768–1821)

Though they were by then long separated, George IV's refusal to allow her to take part in his coronation in 1821 so humiliated the princess that she immediately fell ill and died a month later in her native Germany. Bitter to the end, her final wish was to have the words "Caroline of Brunswick, the injured Queen of England" inscribed upon her crimson coffin.

5. DIANA, PRINCESS OF WALES (1961–97)

Came to dislike England owing to the sheer intrusiveness of the press. It is believed that she was planning a move — possibly to the United States or France — in the months prior to her death.

THREE MONARCHS WHO HATED THE JOB

1. VICTORIA (1819–1901)

A recluse for much of her reign who rarely showed her face to her subjects, the queen frequently refused to greet visiting heads of state for no apparent reason.

2. GEORGE V (1865–1936)

Despite a firm (if somewhat abstract) sense of duty, George V nevertheless looked upon the everyday realities of kingship as an unpleasant nuisance. He particularly hated anything to do with matters of state, not the least of which being the annual opening of parliament.

3. EDWARD VIII (1894–1972)

Although he clearly enjoyed the power and perks that came with his social position, the Prince of Wales spent much of his time rebelling against the often meaningless ceremony and stuffiness of court life. Indeed, ten years before he acceded to the throne (and then abandoned it) he actually threatened to renounce his royal rights entirely in a letter to his father, and was only prevented from doing so by an easing off in his schedule of duties. To his closest friends he often stated his desire to "bring the monarchy into the twentieth century," though as it turned out he wasn't king long enough to achieve his aims.

SIX INCREDIBLY UNPOPULAR ROYALS

1. JOHN (1166–1216)

John was utterly devoid of tact and managed to alienate just about everyone with his generally bad administration, brutal behaviour and high taxation. So reviled was he, in fact, that many actually considered him to be a werewolf; according to at least one Norman chronicler, after his death monks supposedly heard sounds emanating from his grave and promptly had his body removed from consecrated ground.

2. ELEANOR OF PROVENCE (1222–91)

Owing to her blatant preference for foreigners and refusal to assimilate, the French-born wife of Henry III was one of the most hated queens in English history.

3. JAMES II (1633–1701)

A most unlikable individual, James was noted for his arrogance and complete absence of either tact or humour. Though his constant, outspoken claims to absolute power ("I am above the law") helped to earn him the hatred of his people, it was mainly his ill-timed efforts to impose Roman Catholicism upon his Protestant subjects that brought about his downfall.

4. GEORGE IV (1762–1830)

George IV was so hated by his people that he was literally unable to step outside his door for fear of being pelted with filth. Uniquely, by his very nature he had managed to alienate not just one but *every* segment of British society, from the starving masses to the idle rich.

5. ERNEST, DUKE OF CUMBERLAND (1771–1851)

Rivalled his brother George IV for the title of most detested British royal ever. Widely booed in the streets whenever he was foolish enough to venture out, on one occasion he was actually dragged from his horse by a would-be lynch mob.

6. WALLIS, DUCHESS OF WINDSOR (C. 1896–1986)

During and even long after the abdication crisis of 1936 the British public hated Wallis Simpson, and it was not uncommon for her to receive death threats and even the occasional brick through her window. Widely perceived as crude and ambitious, it was her American background however that was the most serious bone of contention.

FOUR MONARCHS WHO ABDICATED

1. EDWARD II (1284–1327)

Forced by an illegally convened "parliament" to abdicate the throne in favour of his son, Edward III, in 1327. He was afterwards murdered.

2. RICHARD II (1367–1400)

Formally abdicated on September 29, 1399, after being deposed by his cousin Henry Bolingbroke.

3. JAMES II (1633–1701)

Deemed by parliament to have abdicated on December 11, 1688 and formally deposed two weeks later.

4. EDWARD VIII (1894–1972)

"After I am dead the boy will ruin himself in twelve months."
George V (on his son and heir)

Much has been written about how Edward VIII, constitutionally unable to marry the twice-divorced, Catholic American Wallis Simpson, reluctantly chose love over a crown. What is less widely known is that, in reality, there really wasn't an insurmountable constitutional problem to the match. The king did not need the consent of parliament regarding his choice of bride, and alternatives — such as a morganatic marriage (whereby Wallis would become his wife but not his queen) — were available. Indeed, the real reason for the abdication had much more to do with the king's alarmingly anti-democratic politics, which alienated his own ministers to the point where they all but forced him out. In any event, with his country deeply divided, on December 11, 1936 Edward VIII astonished the world by announcing his decision to voluntarily relinquish the throne.

FIVE MONARCHS WHO WERE EXILED

1. ETHELRED II (C. 968–1016)

Driven from the throne by King Sweyn Forkbeard of Denmark in 1013. After a year of exile in Normandy Ethelred returned on the early death of the former to rule for another couple of years.

2. EDWARD THE CONFESSOR (C. 1004–66)

An exile in Normandy for 28 years, prior to his brief restoration of the royal house of Wessex.

3. CHARLES II (1630–85)

When his father was executed in 1649 by parliamentary forces Charles was already in exile in Holland. From then until the restoration of the monarchy in 1660 he would live a life of insecurity in France as well as on Jersey in the Channel Islands where, according to his puritan enemies, he indulged in much "fornication, drunkenness and adultery."

4. JAMES II (1633–1701)

Deposed during the bloodless "Glorious Revolution" of 1688–89, as a result of his unabashed Catholicism, and replaced by the Protestant joint-sovereigns William and Mary. Fearing that he would be murdered like his father Charles I, on the night of December 11, 1688 the ex-king hastily fled London in disguise, stopping only to toss the Great Seal of England into the Thames at Vauxhall. Unfortunately for him he was soon captured by sailors and returned to the capital in a state of collapse, in the belief that he was a Catholic priest. He managed to get away once more and this time made it to the safety of France. It was there, aside from a failed attempt to regain the throne at the Battle of the Boyne in 1690, that he would spend the remaining years of his life.

5. EDWARD VIII (1894–1972)

With the exception of a brief wartime spell when he was governor of the Bahamas and occasional visits to the United States and England, after his abdication Edward and his wife remained in exile in France for the remainder of their long, vacuous lives.

MONTHLY HIGHLIGHTS FROM
THE QUEEN'S *ANNUS HORRIBILIS* ("YEAR OF HORRORS")

The year 1992 was a particularly bad one for the royal family, with each month bringing forth fresh examples of scandal and disaster in the county's tabloid press. The queen herself acknowledge this in her famous "annus horribilis" speech at year's end, in which she revealed that it was "not one I shall look back upon with undiluted pleasure."

JANUARY:

Prince Charles is besieged by anti-hunt demonstrators in Derbyshire, who taunt and heckle him until he loses his temper. Meanwhile, photos of the **Duchess of York** and her lover Steve Wyatt, taken during a vacation together in Morocco, are printed in the tabloids. The palace officially denies that the Yorks' marriage is in trouble.

FEBRUARY:

Princess Diana is slammed in the press for exchanging her British Jaguar for an expensive new German Mercedes. She will ultimately give up the unpatriotic automobile several months later after repeated urgings from the queen. **The queen** marks forty years on the throne.

MARCH:

The palace officially announces the separation of the **Duke and Duchess of York**. The father of **Princess Diana** dies of a heart attack.

APRIL:

Princess Anne divorces Mark Phillips after a three-year separation. Meanwhile, a paternity suit concerning Anne's former husband and a schoolteacher is resolved through a one-time cash settlement.

MAY:

Princess Anne is reported to be romantically involved with her equerry; many royalists object when it is revealed that he is part Jewish. The palace offers its standard denial, though the couple will nevertheless be married seven months later. **Prince Charles** humiliates himself on national television by singing off-key with a group of Celtish crofters. Newspaper polls indicate the **royal family's** popularity is at an all-time low — a situation not helped by that month's release of two major tell-all books.

JUNE:

Prince Edward, the queen's 28-year-old unmarried son, once again publicly denies that he's gay. He then denies making the denial.

JULY:

Princess Diana's massage therapist tells reporters that the former wants to end her marriage; he is promptly fired.

AUGUST:

Candid photos appear in the tabloids of a topless **Duchess of York** and her lover John Bryan (*see chapter 1, "Three Female Royals Who Have Been Photographed Nude"*). Just days later, **Princess Diana's** humiliating "Squidgygate" tapes are released in transcript form (*see chapter 13, "Two Infamous Cell-Phone Interceptions"*).

SEPTEMBER:

The palace officially denies that the **Prince and Princess of Wales** are having problems with their marriage.

OCTOBER:

During a visit to Dresden **the queen** is booed and rotten eggs are hurled at her limousine. The negative outpouring was prompted by her recent unveiling in Britain of a statue to the murderous Arthur "Bomber" Harris, who directed the firebombing of German cities during the Second World War.

NOVEMBER:

While still reeling from the release of the so-called "Camillagate" tapes, **fire breaks out at Windsor Castle**, destroying much of St George's Hall, the queen's private chapel and numerous state apartments. The disaster is seen as symbolic of the state of the royal family itself.

That same day, November 20th, is **the queen's** 45th wedding anniversary; her husband had chosen to commemorate the occasion with a trip to Argentina with a young female friend.

DECEMBER:

A firestorm of a different sort begins to blaze, owing to **the queen's** expectation that British taxpayers should foot the £37 million bill for the restoration of Windsor Castle. Under enormous pressure, she later agrees to cover the cost herself (by opening up Buckingham Palace as a money-making tourist attraction) and to start paying taxes on the income generated by her immense fortune. On a sadder note, The **Prince and Princess of Wales** officially announce their separation.

Public
Relations

NINE INDIVIDUALS OR GROUPS THAT PRINCE PHILIP HAS INSULTED

"If anyone asks me, 'Is it true that Prince Philip said, or did, such and such a thing?' I immediately answer, 'Yes, yes, yes, of course it is.'"

(*An anonymous British ambassador, on Prince Philip*)

1. THE CANADIANS

During a visit to Ottawa in 1969 the prince gave a speech in which he stated, in part: "The monarchy exists not for its own benefit, but for that of the country. We don't come here for our health. We can think of better ways of enjoying ourselves."

2. NON-FASCISTS

During a visit to Paraguay, Philip remarked to Dictator Alfredo Stroessner that it was, "a pleasant change to be in a country that isn't ruled by its people."

3. THE DUTCH

During a visit to Holland the prince was heard to observe (in the presence of a bilingual Dutch chauffeur), "What a po-faced lot these Dutch are."

4. THE EGYPTIANS

Complaining about the traffic in Cairo during an official visit, the prince remarked to his hosts, "The trouble with you Egyptians is that you breed too much."

5. THE PERUVIANS

After being presented during a state visit with a history of the city of Lima, Philip quickly passed the book to an aide with the remark, "Here, take this. I'll never read it."

6. THE SCOTS

Once in Scotland the prince asked a driving instructor, "How do you keep the natives off the booze long enough to get them to pass the test?"

7. THE ARCHBISHOP OF CANTERBURY

During his son Charles' confirmation, the then archbishop Michael Ramsey was greatly annoyed to see the prince reading a book rather than paying attention to the ceremony. "Bloody rude, that's what I call it," he later remarked.

8. AQUARIUM HOBBYISTS

Philip was once heard to caution: "Be very, very careful of people who have tropical fish in their homes. Such people are usually suffering from some psychiatric problem."

9. THE UNEMPLOYED

During an appearance on a British radio show in 1981, Philip offered the following bit of wisdom: "A few years ago everybody was saying we must have much more leisure, everybody is working too much. Now that everybody has got so much leisure — it may be involuntary, but they have got it — they are complaining they are unemployed. People do not seem to be able to make up their mind what they want, do they?" After twenty Labour MPs subsequently tabled a Commons motion protesting his insensitive remarks, the prince was forced to apologize.

FIVE ROYAL VIEWS ON TRAVEL DESTINATIONS

1. MARY I ON CALAIS

(*After losing England's last French possession in 1558*) "When I am dead and opened, you shall find 'Calais' lying in my heart."

2. EDWARD VII ON ROME

"You look at two mouldering stones and are told it's the temple of something."

3. GEORGE V ON NAPLES

The xenophobic king abhorred all things foreign. "Abroad is awful," he once declared, "...I know because I've been there." He particularly hated Naples, once noting (perhaps by way of explanation) that its harbour was full of dead dogs.

4. PRINCE PHILIP ON BEIJING

Once, during an official visit to China, the prince was heard to describe his hosts' capital as "ghastly."

5. PRINCE CHARLES ON THE TAJ MAHAL

When asked if he had been touched by this romantic Indian mausoleum, the prince replied, "Well, I did bang my head against the ceiling at one point."

THREE KINGS WHO MAY NOT HAVE BEEN WHAT THEY SEEMED

1. RICHARD III (1452–85)

Thanks to a small number of militant apologists (the most notable being the Richard III Society), since the eighteenth century the king's image has been transformed from that of Shakespeare's evil manipulator to one more historically ambivalent. The former have not only been able to cast doubts on his complicity in the murder of Edward V and his brother, but have also successfully emphasised his administrative and military skill.

2. HENRY VIII (1491–1547)

Although known to history as a tyrant in the truest sense, in actual fact Henry was a careful student of the law and the constitution, and always scrupulously observed both to the letter.

3 GEORGE III (1738–1820)

Ironically, apart from his well-known bouts of madness George was perhaps the most stable ruler his family ever produced. Unlike the other Hanoverian kings he was a amiable man with a strong sense of duty, who wasn't reckless with money, sexually promiscuous or freakishly overweight. Nevertheless, he is still remembered by most people today (and particularly by Americans) as a despotic lunatic.

SIX ROYAL REPRIMANDS

1. "WE ARE NOT AMUSED." (**Queen Victoria** to her groom-in-waiting Alexander Yorke, after he had performed an unflattering imitation of her. In later life she denied ever making the catchphrase remark)

2. "IF YOU DON'T COME AT ONCE YOU WON'T BE CROWNED QUEEN." (**Edward VII** to his tardy wife Alexandra on the morning of their coronation)

Queen Alexandra (wife of Edward VII).

3. "YOU DRESS LIKE A CAD. YOU ACT LIKE A CAD. YOU ARE A CAD. GET OUT!!!" (**George V** to his thirty-something son, the future Edward VIII)

4. "YOU CAN CALL ME THAT ONCE A DAY, AND NO MORE. I'M SICK OF IT." (**George VI**, to a gardener who kept calling him "Your Royal Highness")

5. "SWITCH THAT BLOODY THING OFF, YOU SILLY FUCKER." (**Prince Philip**, to a member of his official police escort in Panama who had turned on his siren)

6. "LESS OF THE WISECRACKS AND STICK TO THE COMMENTARY." (**Prince Charles**, to cricket commentator Tom Oxley)

SEVEN ROYALS WHO PUBLICLY LOST THEIR TEMPER

1. CANUTE (C. 995–1035)

A hard man, Canute once killed one of his household servants in a fit of anger. He is said to have expiated the crime by paying a fine equal to nine times the man's worth.

2. HENRY II (1133–89)

Henry's fits of temper were legendary. Once, when a servant spoke well of one of his enemies in his presence, the king threw off his clothing in response and began to chew madly on pieces of straw.

3. EDWARD I (1239–1307)

Had to pay compensation to one of his pages after striking and wounding the boy badly during his daughter's wedding. Another time he angrily threw his crown into a fireplace.

4. RICHARD II (1367–1400)

A man with a violent temper; in 1385 Richard had to be physically restrained from hacking the archbishop of Canterbury to death with his sword when the latter dared to register a complaint about the king's courtiers.

5. JAMES I (1566–1625)

On one occasion the king, who had nothing but contempt for the public at large, was told by his courtiers that his subjects only wanted to have a look at him. "God's wounds!," came the reply, "...I will pull down my breeches and they shall also see my arse!"

6. GEORGE II (1683–1760)

A man with a terrible temper at the best of times; when suffering from one of his frequent attacks of piles the king would often resort to kicking his wig and coat about in rages, to the astonishment of his courtiers.

7. ANDREW, DUKE OF YORK (1960–)

On numerous occasions the prince was observed to tell his boorish wife to "shut up," evidently to prevent her from embarrassing them both further.

NINE OPINIONS ABOUT ROYALS BY FAMOUS PEOPLE

1. SIR THOMAS MORE ON RICHARD III
"Malicious, wrathful and envious."

2. MARTIN LUTHER ON HENRY VIII
"Junker Heinz will be God and does whatever he lusts."

3. SIR ROBERT WALPOLE ON FREDERICK, PRINCE OF WALES
"A poor, weak, irresolute, false, lying, dishonest, contemptible wretch, that nobody loves, that nobody believes, that nobody will trust."

4. W. M. THACKERY ON GEORGE IV
"…This George, what was he? I look through all his life, and recognise but a bow and a grin. I try and take him to pieces, and find silk stockings, padding, stays, a coat with frogs and a fur collar, and star and blue ribbon, a pocket-handkerchief prodigiously scented, one of Truefitt's best nutty-brown wigs reeking with oil, a set of teeth and a huge black stock, underwaistcoats, more underwaistcoats, and then nothing."

5. CHARLOTTE BRONTË ON QUEEN VICTORIA
"A little stout, vivacious lady, very plainly dressed — not much dignity or pretension about her."

6. KAISER WILHELM II ON EDWARD VII
"He is Satan. You cannot imagine what a Satan he is!"

7. COLE PORTER ON EDWARD VIII
"They had to get rid of him as king. He's simple." (*the two men were old friends*)

8. ADOLF HITLER ON QUEEN ELIZABETH (THE FUTURE QUEEN MOTHER)
"The most dangerous woman in Europe." The Fuehrer also had some words regarding the future Elizabeth II: "*Ein fabelhaftes kind*" ("a marvelous child")

9. CLIVE JENKINS (TELEVISION HOST) ON PRINCE PHILIP
"He's the best argument for republicanism since George III."

SEVEN ROYAL AUDIENCES WITH FAMOUS PEOPLE

1. CHARLES I MEETS "OLD PARR"

Reputed to be the oldest man who ever lived, Thomas Parr had an audience with the king just before he died at the age of 152 or so. Charles was so impressed that he later permitted the man to be buried in Westminster Abbey.

2. GEORGE III MEETS SAMUEL JOHNSON

Johnson, compiler of the monumental *Dictionary of the English Language,* ran into George III late one night while browsing in the royal library at Buckingham House (the nucleus of the British Library). The unlikely pair enjoyed a brief informal chat, during which the king suggested the author undertake a history of England. This was not the latter's first encounter with a British sovereign, incidentally; as a young child he was once ceremonially "touched" for scrofula by Queen Anne, whom he always remembered as an "old lady in a black cloak and diamonds."

3. QUEEN VICTORIA MEETS GENERAL TOM THUMB

During a tour of England in 1864 with Barnum & Bailey Circus, the 64 cm-high midget Tom Thumb was presented to the queen. The unusual meeting of minds was recorded in the Court Circular as follows: "His impersonation of the Emperor Napoleon elicited great Mirth...The General danced a nautical hornpipe and sang several of his favorite songs" (one of which was reported to have been "I'm a Yankee Doodle Dandy.")

4. GEORGE V MEETS CHARLES LINDBERGH

After his historic first solo flight across the Atlantic Lindbergh was presented to the king, whose first question to him was, "What did you do about peeing?"

5. ELIZABETH, THE QUEEN MOTHER MEETS THE BEATLES

After their triumphant Royal Variety show in 1964, the Queen Mum met the four lads from Liverpool backstage. "And where are you playing next?" she inquired. "Slough," replied John Lennon. "Oh," said the Queen Mother, "...That's near us."

6. ELIZABETH II MEETS LADY DIANA COOPER

Once, while chatting with an unknown if nevertheless friendly little woman at a Festival Hall reception, the elderly, high-society eccentric suddenly realized it was in fact the queen that she was addressing. "Oh, I'm so sorry," she apologised at once, "...I didn't recognise you without your crown."

7. PRINCE WILLIAM MEETS BON GELDOF

When William was six, the recently knighted Irish rock star Bob Geldof paid a visit to his parents, Charles and Diana. Never having seen anything like him before, the boy's reaction was one of complete bewilderment: "Why does he have such dirty hair, daddy? Why is he wearing gym shoes?"

TWO ROYAL P.R. TRIUMPHS

1. QUEEN VICTORIA'S DIAMOND JUBILEE

In 1897 Victoria celebrated 60 years on the throne, a milestone that marked both the zenith of her personal popularity as well as the symbolic highpoint of the British Empire itself, with nearly one-quarter of the world's people then acknowledging her as sovereign. For the occasion the ailing and normally reclusive queen was even persuaded to drive in state (through streets lined with millions) for a service of thanksgiving at St Paul's.

2. THE REHABILITATION OF THE ROYAL FAMILY IMAGE

Borrowing on an idea first put forward by his grandfather Prince Albert, George V was successfully able to transform the long-sullied image of the British monarchy into one epitomizing the values of duty, honour and family values. In the process he even managed to force his more peripheral relations — the Von Tecks, Battenbergs and so on — to anglicize their surnames in the way he himself had been forced to do. This moral straightjacket of sorts would endure (with the help of a deferential press) for much of the twentieth century, until finally being revealed for the illusion it was in the early 1990s.

THREE ROYAL P.R. DISASTERS

1. *The Anonymous Letter*

The future King Edward VII wrote an anonymous letter to *The Times* in 1874, in which he suggested that more government money from the civil list should be made available to "that fine fellow, the Prince of Wales." The revelation of the letter's true origins was a considerable embarrassment to the royal family.

2. *The Royal Family's Game Show Debacle*

For many years one of the most popular shows on British television was *It's a Knock-Out!*, in which opposing teams competed in bizarre contests involving obstacle courses and mock gladiatorial combat. In 1987 viewers tuned in — to their astonishment — to see two members of the royal family — Prince Edward and Sarah, Duchess of York — cavorting among other "celebrities" in the most undignified manner imaginable, each dressed in medieval-style costume, as Princess Anne and Prince Andrew cheered them on. To compound the embarrassment, the show (which had even gone so far as to change its name for the special to *It's a Royal Knockout!*) had chosen as its location the grounds of a venerable old English castle that had recently, owing to hard economic times, been converted into an amusement park.

3. *The Infamous Princess Diana Television Interview*

In November 1995 the estranged wife of Prince Charles gave a controversial interview for British television, watched by millions of viewers worldwide. Mixed among frank discussions of her bulimia, adultery, suicide attempts and the pressures of being royal the princess made a special point of talking about her ex-husband's failings as well, leaving no doubt that she thought him unsuitable for the position of king. So damaging was the interview, in fact, that the palace press office afterwards tried to dismiss it as the paranoid ravings of an unbalanced woman.

The
Class
System

FIVE ROYAL RACISTS

1. WILLIAM IV (1765–1837)
The king would frequently embarrass himself and his ministers in the House of Lords by making long, incoherent speeches in defense of slavery.

2. GEORGE V (1865–1936)
As far as George was concerned there were only three types of people in the world: "blacks, whites and royals."

3. EDWARD VIII (1894–1972)
While serving as governor of the Bahamas during World War II, the former king forced blacks to use the back door of his official residence.

4. ELIZABETH, THE QUEEN MOTHER (1900–)
In keeping with her age and class the Queen Mother was (and is) not fond of black people, and over the years has been excused on these grounds for referring to the latter as "blackamoors" and "nig-nogs."

5. PHILIP, DUKE OF EDINBURGH (1921–)
During a state visit in 1986 the prince warned a Scottish student in China, "If you stay here much longer, you'll go back with slitty eyes." On another occasion, when asked by an interviewer how he would feel if one of his children married a "coloured person," the prince hesitated considerably before finally dismissing the question as "difficult to answer."

FIVE ROYALS WHO WERE ANTI-FEMINIST

1. JAMES I (1566–1625)

(*On his refusal to allow his daughter to learn Latin and Greek*) "To make women learned and foxes tame has the same effect — to make them more cunning."

2. WILLIAM III (1650–1702)

When his English wife (and cousin) Mary inherited the throne in 1689, the chauvinistic Dutchman insisted on ruling with her in a so-called "duel monarchy." Evidently he refused to be the mere consort of a woman.

3. VICTORIA (1819–1901)

(*On voting rights for women*) "A mad, wicked folly."

4. EDWARD VII (1841–1910)

Despite his preference for the company of worldly, intelligent women, like most of his subjects the king was against granting women the vote.

5. GEORGE V (1865–1936)

Frequently protested for his anti-feminist stance. At the 1913 Derby horse race a suffragette named Emily Davison threw herself under the king's horse, and later died from her injuries. Another young woman, while being presented at court, boldly shouted out (in mid-curtsy) "For God's sake, Your Majesty, stop persecuting women!" George was heard to wonder aloud afterwards just what things were coming to.

TWO FAMILY MEMBERS GEORGE V REFUSED TO HELP (FOR POLITICAL REASONS)

1. PRINCE LOUIS OF BATTENBERG (1854–1921)

The king stood by quietly as his first cousin was vilified simply because of his German name. A naturalized British subject, at the beginning of the First World War Battenberg was first sea lord and in that position was responsible for the efficient mobilization of the Royal Navy. Despite his total loyalty to the crown and to his adopted country, however, he quickly became a target of anti-German hysteria. For expediency's sake the king not only forced him to give up his position and title but had him change his surname as well (to the more politically correct Mountbatten).

2. Czar Nicholas II (1868–1918)

In March 1917 the king's look-alike first cousin, Nicholas II of Russia, was forced to abdicate by his subjects and appealed to George for asylum. Concerned about the state of his own throne at the time, the latter ultimately wrote back and informed him that he did not think it "advisable that the Imperial Family should take up their residence in this country," at the same time cowardly placing the blame for the decision on the shoulders of the prime minister. Thus assured that Britain would do nothing to protect the hated czar, communist revolutionaries promptly seized his entire family and later murdered them.

NAZI ASSOCIATIONS OF SEVEN PROMINENT ROYALS

1. Edward VIII (1894–1972)

"Of course, if I'd been king, there'd have been no war."

Edward, Duke of Windsor

A longtime Nazi sympathizer and apologist, during the 1930s the Prince of Wales kept in regular contact with his British-born cousin Charles, Duke of Coburg (an SS officer and one of Hitler's diplomats) as well as other high-ranking officials of the regime. In common with those who believed in appeasement it was his goal to try and avert another terrible European war, preferably by the peaceful transplantation of Nazi policies into England. Towards this end, in October 1937 the by then Duke of Windsor and his odious wife Wallis Simpson traveled to Germany where, to the horror of the British government, they proceeded to fawn over its dictatorial leaders. Aside from being captured by newsreel photographers giving the stiff-armed Nazi salute everywhere they went — not to mention warmly clasping the *führer's* hand — the latter were privately entertained by such future war criminals as Hermann Göering, Rudolf Hess, Joseph Goebbels and Joachim von Ribbentrop (to their obvious delight, wherever the couple went they were invariably greeted with cries of "Heil Windsor!") The ex-king's actions during the subsequent war were naïve at best, with many suggesting that, if not for his royal status, he would most likely have been charged with treason. Indeed, it has long been suggested that the duke had secret aspirations of regaining the throne in the event of a successful German invasion of England. What is beyond dispute is that, even years after the war had ended, he was still heard to insist to his friends, "I never thought Hitler was such a bad chap."

2. George, Duke of Kent (1902–42)

Edward's VIII's younger brother, like many pre-war British aristocrats, saw in fascism a solution to the social and economic ills of the 1930s — a solution moreover that didn't threaten their own privileged positions. Both the duke and the king considered Hitler to be an important bulwark against communism, and sympathised with the British fascist movement of their good friend Sir Oswald Mosley.

3. & 4. George VI (1895–1952) and Elizabeth, The Queen Mother (1900–)

Though not actually sympathetic to the Nazis, both the king and his wife were nevertheless enthusiastic supporters of Neville Chamberlain's pre-war policy of appeasement with Hitler.

5. Philip, Duke of Edinburgh (1921–)

During the 1930's four of Philip's older sisters married German noblemen, all of whom went on to support the Nazis. One eventually became an SS Colonel on Himmler's personal staff, while another even went so far as to name his son after Hitler himself. A third — his brother-in-law Prince Christopher — was head of Hermann Göering's secret phone-tapping branch (a unit that eventually evolved into the dreaded Gestapo). But perhaps most embarrassing of all for the future prince consort, the man for whom he himself was named, Prince Philip of Hess, actually served as Hitler's personal messenger and functioned so effectively in the position that the *führer* made him an honorary *obergruppenfürer* in his Storm Troopers. Significantly, none of Philip's sisters or their husbands would be invited to his wedding to Princess Elizabeth in 1947.

6. Princess Michael of Kent (1945–)

In 1985 it was revealed that the German father of the wife of Prince Michael of Kent (the queen's cousin) had in fact been a devout Nazi with links to the SS. When asked about this at the time the remarkably Nordic-looking princess commented, rather unconvincingly: "I didn't know..."

7. DIANA, PRINCESS OF WALES (1961–97)

The princess was a distant cousin of Reich Marshal Hermann Göering.

SIX MONARCHS WHO DISLIKED THEIR PRIME MINISTERS

1. GEORGE II (1683–1760)

Initially disliked Robert Walpole, England's powerful first prime minister.

2. GEORGE IV (1762–1830)

Particularly loathed Sir Robert Peel. Once, on encountering the latter at Ascot, the king was heard to say to a friend: "I would have as soon expected to see a pig in church." The king's hatred for another prime minister, George Canning, was equally intense.

3. VICTORIA (1819–1901)

The queen made no secret of her dislike for the Liberal William Gladstone and his anti-imperialist policies. After one of his many re-elections, she actually tried to avoid sending for him to form a government and when the Liberals complained, commented: "The Queen does not the least care but rather wishes it should be known that she has the greatest possible disinclination to take this half-crazy & really in many ways ridiculous old man…"

Her Majesty wasn't particularly fond of Viscount Palmerston (another Liberal) either, once declaring emphatically: "I NEVER liked him." The reason perhaps had something to do with the latter's attempted rape of one of her ladies-in-waiting during a visit to Windsor Castle.

4. GEORGE V (1865–1936)

George V despised his wartime prime minister, David Lloyd George, who in return felt nothing but contempt for the king.

5. EDWARD VIII (1894–1972)

During the abdication crisis of 1936, puritanical Prime Minister Stanley Baldwin's refusal to accept the compromise solution of a morganatic marriage did little to endear him to the king.

6. ELIZABETH II (1926–)

The queen relished telling private jokes about Margaret Thatcher, whom she never really warmed to and often disagreed with over Commonwealth matters. Her son Prince Charles, for his part, actively hated the prime minister and her radical-conservative policies, which he felt were "ruining the country."

FOUR ROYAL HOMOPHOBES

1. HENRY VIII (1491–1547)

Personally outlawed (on pain of death) "the detestable and abominable Vice of Buggery."

2. EDWARD VII (1841–1910)

The king was deeply shocked when one of his close associates was involved in a homosexual scandal. In his friend's defense he argued "that any man addicted to such a filthy vice must be regarded as an unfortunate lunatic (rather than a criminal)."

3. GEORGE V (1865–1936)

On hearing that an elderly acquaintance of his was gay, the king was heard to mutter: "I thought chaps like that shot themselves." He also steadfastly refused to knight "buggers" (sic).

4. ANNE, PRINCESS ROYAL (1950–)

In 1988 the princess gave an ill-considered speech in which she described the Aids epidemic as a "classic own goal" — a roundabout way of saying that those afflicted by the deadly disease had nobody to blame but themselves.

SEVEN ROYAL EXCURSIONS INTO FOREIGN POLICY

According to the Victorian constitutional expert Walter Bagehot, Britain's monarchs have three main areas of influence; the right to be consulted, the right to encourage, and the right to warn the country's government.

1. EDWARD I (1239–1307)

In 1290 the temporarily leaderless Scots asked Edward to deliberate from a list of candidates on who should be their next king. He quite naturally chose the one that seemed the most easily dominated.

2. HENRY VIII (1491–1547)

In June 1520 a historic meeting took place between former enemies Henry VIII and Francis I of France on the Field of Cloth-of-Gold near Calais. Essentially a magnificent, 17-day festival of alliance (complete with temporary pavilions and wine flowing from fountains), the conference culminated with the two young kings sealing their uneasy truce with bouts of wrestling and jousting.

3. WILLIAM IV (1765–1837)

Once strained Anglo-French relations by referring to the king of France as "an infamous scoundrel." He later excused the comment by claiming he was drunk at the time.

4. ALBERT, PRINCE CONSORT (1819–61)

Single-handedly prevented the British government from entering the American Civil War on the side of the Confederacy (from whom they received most of their cotton).

5. EDWARD VII (1841–1910)

Far more traveled than any of his ancestors, the king considered himself something of an expert on foreign policy. Known as "Edward the Peacemaker," it was he that was primarily responsible for the *Entente Cordiale* with France in 1904, as well as the 1907 Anglo-Russian alliance against Germany.

6. GEORGE V (1865–1936)

It was George V's continual political interfering that was largely responsible for prolonging the pointless slaughter that was the First World War. The British army in France had been hobbled by incompetent leadership from the start, with commander-in-chief Sir John French being among the worst offenders. When French was finally replaced in 1915, however, it was only by the equally disastrous Sir Douglas Haig — an appointment received solely on the merits of his friendship with the king. Haig continued with his predecessor's futile policy of attrition, protected from his growing number of detractors by George V. When the war finally ended in an inglorious stalemate three years later, nearly a million British servicemen were dead and two-and-a-half million were wounded.

7. GEORGE VI (1895–1952)

The king appears to have been the only person in England in 1939 who still believed that war could be averted, having twice offered at the time to write to Adolf Hitler personally "as one ex-serviceman to another." So out of touch was he in fact that, on April 20 of that year, he actually sent the *führer* a warm birthday greeting.

THREE SOVEREIGNS WHO SHOWED CONTEMPT FOR DEMOCRACY

Democratic parliament in England had its origins in the medieval Curia Regis ("royal council"), a sort of advisory board to the king. From that time forward it would continue to develop as rival governing body, becoming ever more inclusive and powerful.

1. JAMES I (1566–1625)

The Scottish-born king once told the Spanish ambassador: "The House of Commons is a body without a head. The members give their opinions in a disorderly manner. At their meetings nothing is heard but cries, shouts and confusion. I am surprised that my ancestors should even have permitted such an institution to come into existence. I am a stranger and found it here when I arrived, so that I am obliged to put up with what I cannot get rid of."

2. CHARLES I (1600–49)

Utterly convinced of his "divine right" to rule, it was Charles' undisguised contempt for democratic principles during his "Eleven Years' Tyranny" (1629–40) that was directly responsible for his country being plunged into civil war. In his clumsy attempts to increase his own power at the expense of the people he imposed illegal taxes, dissolved parliament four times and even arrested its leaders — moves which, ultimately, cost him both the crown and his head.

Charles I.

3. VICTORIA (1819–1901)

In 1839 Victoria (then a dogmatic Whig partisan) refused to let the Tory Sir Robert Peel, named to be prime minister, replace her ladies of the bedchamber with his own choices, as per tradition. He was ultimately forced to step aside, though he would win back the office two years later. This so-called "Bedchamber Plot" was the last time a British sovereign successfully overruled a prime minister.

FIVE ROYALS WHO BROKE DOWN SOCIAL BARRIERS

1. JAMES I (1566–1625)

James was the first English monarch to use a fork; prior to that, use of the utensil was considered to be effeminate.

2. CAROLINE OF BRANDENBURG-ANSBACH (1683–1737)

In 1721 the then Princess of Wales became the first mother in England to inoculate her children against smallpox.

3. VICTORIA (1819–1901)

In 1853 the queen allowed herself to be chloroformed while giving birth to her seventh child, Prince Leopold, thereby setting an example for other women to follow.

4. EDWARD VII (1841–1910)

Once, during an official dinner in England, the German delegation objected to King Kalakaua of the Hawaiian Islands taking precedence over their own crown prince in the seating order. Edward's response was remarkably democratic: "Either the brute is a king or else he is an ordinary black nigger, and if he is not a king, why is he here at all?"

5. DIANA, PRINCESS OF WALES (1961–97)

During her brief lifetime the princess did much to help make the royal family more accessible and, in the process, socially relevant. In the spring of 1987 for instance she made a highly publicised visit to the new Aids ward at Middlesex Hospital, London. Back then the disease was still little known and greatly feared, yet Diana nevertheless made a point of shaking hands with patients without benefit of gloves. Subsequently published photos of the event helped to convince many that Aids cannot be spread through casual social contact.

EIGHT ROYAL FORAYS AMONG THE COMMON PEOPLE

1. ALFRED THE GREAT (C. 849–C. 899)
The legend of Alfred and the cakes is one of the most enduring of all royal anecdotes. The story goes that the king, while in temporary hiding with his army in Somerset after their dispersal by invading Danes, took shelter in a swineherd's hut. One day he was sitting by the kitchen fire restringing his bow when the swineherd's wife, unaware she was addressing the king, soundly berated him for forgetting to turn the cakes she had asked him to watch and allowing them to burn. The shaken Alfred accepted the scolding as his due.

2. EDWARD II (1284–1327)
The king preferred the company of unsuitable commoners, in particular sailors and actors. He once missed holy mass because he was too busy digging ditches.

3. GEORGE III (1738–1820)
For a pair of articles he had contributed to the *Annals of Agriculture* in 1787, the king went by the pen name of Ralph Robinson.

4. EDWARD VII (1841–1910)
While serving on a royal commission looking into the plight of London's aged poor in the 1890s, the then Prince of Wales personally investigated some of the city's worst slums.

5. GEORGE V (1865–1936)
In 1924, the king received the ministers of the first-ever socialist government in Britain wearing a tie in the traditional Labour Party colour, red. Commented the normally arch-conservative royal: "We are all socialists nowadays."

6. EDWARD VIII (1894–1972)
Shortly after his accession the king visited a Welsh mining district in which unemployment was soaring, an experience that moved him to make the famous remark "Something must be done!" Although noth-

ing of course ever was, the comment did temporarily raise the spirits of the locals.

7. PRINCESS ELIZABETH (1926–) AND PRINCESS MARGARET (1930–)

On VE night, 1945, the two daughters of George VI anonymously joined the throng of revellers outside Buckingham Palace, with the future queen of England at one point mischievously knocking off a policeman's helmet. Explaining his decision to allow this unprecedented freedom to the princesses, George is reported to have said, "With the war and everything, they've never had any fun."

8. PRINCE WILLIAM (1982–)

Although entitled, since his 18th birthday, to be called His Royal Highness, the prince still insists on using his old name "William Wales." He also steadfastly refuses to allow people to bow or curtsy to him or to address him as Sir, in the belief that to do so would be to place barriers between himself and others.

NINE MONARCHS WHO FACED OUTRIGHT REBELLIONS

"Nothing of importance happened today."
(*George III's diary entry for July 4, 1776*)

1. WILLIAM I, "THE CONQUEROR" (C. 1027–87)

In the winter of 1069–70, William personally crushed rebellions in northern England in a bitter campaign known as the Harrying of the North. It is said that it took the country generations to recover.

2. HENRY II (1133–89)

The king's final years were marred by a series of rebellions led by his sons and urged on by his own wife, Eleanor of Aquitaine.

3. JOHN (1166–1216)

In the summer of 1216 sixty knights loyal to King John held Windsor Castle against a ferocious assault by a great army of rebel barons. The latter were angry because, after signing the *Magna Carta* the previous year, the king managed to get the pope to cancel it by giving a misleading account. The angry barons rose in rebellion and within a few weeks had captured nearly all of John's castles in southern England, with only Dover and Windsor standing firm. The siege on Windsor itself included assaults with giant catapults (accurately lobbing rocks the size of cars for hundreds of metres), though in the end the castle withstood all efforts to take it. After three months the rebels simply gave up and went after the king himself elsewhere. The rebellion ended when John died soon after, reputedly from his own gluttony.

4. HENRY III (1207–72)

Temporarily deposed by the forces of Simon de Montfort, history's first great "parliamentary" leader.

5. RICHARD II (1367–1400)

In 1381 a revolt of the peasant's erupted under a certain Wat Tyler. Having seized the city of Canterbury the rebels marched on London where, after an unsuccessful attempt to see the boy-king, they proceeded to take the Tower of London, burned public buildings and, later, murdered the archbishop of Canterbury himself. Richard showed a remarkably conciliatory and brave face throughout the crisis, meeting personally as he did with the angry mob on two occasions. The rebellion itself soon petered out after the assassination of its leader.

6. HENRY IV (1366–1413)

Faced with revolts throughout much of his reign, both internal and external. Amazingly (especially for a usurper), the kingdom he left behind on his death was both united and at peace.

7. MARGARET OF ANJOU (1430–82)

In 1450 the formidable, twenty-year-old queen bravely stamped out the Kentish Rebellion in Greenwich, after her husband, Henry VI, ignominiously fled.

8. MARY I (1516–58)

Mary's decision to wed the Catholic King Philip II of Spain resulted in a popular uprising in 1554. Known as the Wyatt Rebellion, it was ruthlessly put down through a series of royal reprisals.

9. GEORGE III (1738–1820)

Strictly speaking the American Revolution was really more of a rebellion, originating as it did among disgruntled taxpayers. In 1775 the British prime minister had actually put forth a number of proposals to address these grievances (including the right of the colonists to tax themselves and provide for their own civil administration and defenses); unfortunately, news of this did not reach America until after the Battle of Lexington, and by then it was too late. It remains true however that George III favoured armed intervention to resolve the crisis, while his advisors preferred a naval blockade. Indeed, it was this very wavering between a land or sea strategy that was largely responsible for Britain's eventual defeat.

Potpourri

12 UNREALIZED ROYAL AMBITIONS

1. *A Royal Pilgramage*
Unable to fulfill a vow to make a pilgrimage to Rome, Edward the Confessor elected to build Westminster Abbey instead.

2. *Edward I's Last Wish*
While dying in Cumbria in 1307 the king asked his son to boil his body after he was gone and to carry his bones with him on all his campaigns, until such time as the Scots were finally conquered. The request was overruled.

3. *Henry VII's Final Crusade*
The king's desire, during his later years, for one last glorious crusade against the Turks was ultimately undone by a complete lack of enthusiasm on the part of his court.

4. *Henry VIII's Desire to be Holy Roman Emperor*
In 1519 Henry ran a badly mismanaged "campaign" to become Holy Roman Emperor. Central European leaders elected the king of Spain instead.

5. *Elizabeth I's Alchemy Lab*
Encouraged by the Dutchman Cornelius Lannoy's claims that he could turn ordinary base metal into gold, the queen had a fully equipped laboratory constructed for him. When no actual gold was forthcoming, however, a different kind of room was made available for him at the Tower.

6. JAMES I'S SILKWORM ENTERPRISE

In 1609 the king decided to try and produce silk for weaving, ordering some 30,000 black mulberry trees to be planted on the grounds where Buckingham Palace now stands. Unfortunately, no one had bothered to inform him that silkworms only feed on the leaves of *white* mulberries, and the enterprise came to nothing.

7. CHARLES I'S CONVERSION OF THE SCOTS

In 1637 the king tried (unsuccessfully) to foist the Anglican Church on Presbyterian Scotland.

8. GEORGE I'S TURNIP FARM

Once considered planting turnips in St James's Park, though the idea was never acted upon.

9. VICTORIA'S DESIRE FOR A KING NAMED ALBERT

After her husband's death the queen decreed that every future male heir to the throne should be given the name Albert. Though Edward VII, Edward VIII and George VI were all bestowed with this as at least one of their names, each chose a different one for his respective reign. Edward VII's firstborn son Albert Victor died before reaching the throne (leaving George V to take his place), and Elizabeth II abandoned the idea altogether when naming her sons.

10. EDWARD VII'S ASPIRATION TO CROSS NIAGARA FALLS ON A TIGHTROPE

During his North American tour of 1860, the 19-year-old prince had to be prevented from accepting an offer by famed tightrope walker Charles Blondin to be conveyed across the falls in a wheelbarrow.

11. A SECRET IMPULSE

Toward the end of her life Mary of Teck claimed that her only regret was that she had never climbed over a fence. Queen Victoria, incidentally, once admitted that she was often seized with the urge to roll on the lawns at Osborne, though she too never actually acted upon it.

12. AN EPSOM DERBY-WINNING HORSE

Despite decades of trying, the present queen has yet to come up with a horse that can win this most prestigious of equestrian trophies.

FOUR COMMON ROYAL MISCONCEPTIONS

1. THE ROYAL FAMILY CANNOT VOTE

It is only the sovereign who is constitutionally not allowed to vote. Other members of the royal family are free to do so, but choose to demonstrate their "royal disinterest in politics."

2. THE SOVEREIGN IS THE RULER OF HER COUNTRIES

The sovereign symbolically rules *over* Britain, but does not actually govern it. Although theoretically the present queen still retains a great deal of power over the political and legal life of her subjects (such as the right to dismiss government or to declare war), in actual practice her role is essentially that of an umpire.

3. THE MONARCHY IS VITAL FOR TOURISM

France (to name but one example) managed to rid herself of monarchy without unduly affecting the number of visitors to, say, the Palace of Versailles.

4. THE MONARCHY IS A STABILIZING INFLUENCE

(*See Chapter 21, "Monthly Highlights From the Queen's Annus Horribilis"*).

FIVE THINGS LOST OR DESTROYED BY ROYALS

1. THE CROWN JEWELS

According to legend, in 1216 King John took a shortcut across the Wash of the Thames and lost his baggage train (which contained the crown jewels) when caught out in the tide. As a consequence his son and successor, Henry III, had to be crowned with his mother's circlet.

2. CARLTON HOUSE

After years of lavishing expense upon it, in 1827 George IV ordered this spectacular London residence to be demolished for the simple reason that he preferred Buckingham Palace instead. Today, all that remains of the structure (which was once intended to rival Versailles itself) are the original entrance columns, which have since been incorporated into the portico of the new National Gallery.

3. QUEEN VICTORIA'S DIARIES

Throughout her long life the queen kept detailed and highly intimate diaries, which in later years were left to her youngest daughter Princess Beatrice to edit. The latter routinely doctored the journals as she copied them out, destroying the original manuscripts as she went. Thus, what would doubtless have been the most important memoirs of a major 19th century figure (next to those of Lord Byron's, which incidentally were also destroyed) were for all intents and purposes lost to history. To make things even worse, her own son Edward VII set about after her death to track down her correspondence to and from family members, political leaders, and the like and had them all burned.

4. MEMENTOES OF JOHN BROWN

On the death of his mother Queen Victoria, Edward VII smashed a number of memorial statuettes and busts of her jumped-up Highland ghillie, whom he had despised, with his own hands. He also systematically destroyed all other traces of John Brown that he could find, including a vast portrait of him at Balmoral that he first poked in the heart with his cane.

5. HOUSEHOLD BELONGINGS OF THE PRINCE AND PRINCESS OF WALES

Shortly after the couple's divorce became finalised in 1996, two entire truckloads of household belongings (which neither of them wanted any longer) were taken out to Highgrove, the prince's country estate, and burned.

PHYSICAL PECULIARITES OF 15 ROYALS

1. EDWARD THE CONFESSOR (C. 1005–66)

Historical descriptions (for example, long white hair and pale skin) indicate that Edward may have been an albino.

2. WILLIAM I, "THE CONQUEROR" (C. 1027–87)

Said to have been so physically strong that he could vault onto his horse's back, clad in full armour.

3. EDWARD I (1239–1307)

Had a droopy eyelid like his father, Henry III.

4. HENRY IV (1366–1413)

Towards the end of his life the king developed a terrible skin disease that, although often described as leprosy, was most likely a serious case of eczema. Regardless, the condition would become so bad that he would eventually be unable to appear in public.

5. EDWARD IV (1442–83)

Regarded as a giant in his time. When the king's coffin was opened in 1789 it revealed a skeleton 1.9 metres long (he would have significantly exceeded this measurement in life), thus confirming him as Britain's tallest-ever monarch. The tallest female monarch, incidentally, was Anne of Denmark (James I's queen), who herself approached the two metre mark.

6. RICHARD III (1452–85)

In spite of his occasionally used epithet "crouchback" (hunchback), the king's much-publicised deformity was most likely a mere irregularity of the shoulder blade.

7. KATHERINE OF ARAGON (1485–1536)

Had loosely flowing straight hair that almost reached down to her feet.

8. ANNE BOLEYN (C. 1500–36)

The queen had three nipples, along with a small extra finger on her left hand which she managed to keep hidden most of the time in her skirts. It was Henry VIII's intention, in the event that his trumped-up charges of incest and adultery against her should fail, to use her supernumerary breast in particular as evidence and have her burned as a witch.

9. CHARLES I (1600–49)

Based upon his surviving suits of armour, the king evidently stood only 1.4 metres tall. Matilda of Flanders (the wife of William the Conqueror) was however the shortest royal by far, having only attained an adult height of around 1.2 metres.

10. CHARLOTTE OF MECKLENBURG-STRELITZ (1744–1818)

In her later years the queen was subject to attacks of erysipelas, which left her face swollen and purple.

11. WILLIAM IV (1765–1837)

Had a head shaped like a pineapple — a fact that may help to account for the eighteen different women known to have rejected his marriage proposals.

12. VICTORIA (1819–1901)

Although a tiny woman (standing as she did at just 1.5 metres in height), the queen nevertheless had enormous breasts.

13. ALEXANDRA OF DENMARK (1844–1925)

In contract to her mother-in-law, the wife of Edward VII was said to have been "flat as a board."

14. ALBERT VICTOR, DUKE OF CLARENCE (1864–92)

Had a greatly elongated neck.

15. GEORGE V (1865–1936)

Extremely knock-kneed.

CHARLES I's 12 GOOD RULES TO LIVE BY

1. *URGE NO HEALTHS*
2. *PROFANE NO DIVINE ORDINANCES*
3. *TOUCH NO STATE MATTERS*
4. *REVEAL NO SECRETS*
5. *PICK NO QUARRELS*
6. *MAKE NO COMPARISONS*
7. *MAINTAIN NO ILL OPINIONS*
8. *KEEP NO BAD COMPANY*
9. *ENCOURAGE NO VICE*
10. *MAKE NO LONG MEALS*
11. *REPEAT NO GRIEVANCES*
12. *LAY NO WAGERS*

12 CURIOUS FACTS ABOUT QUEENS

1. EMMA OF NORMANDY (D. 1052)

The only queen to have been successively married to two different

English kings (Ethelred II and Canute).

2. ELEANOR OF AQUITAINE (1121–1204)

Henry II's queen presided over one of history's most unusual institutions, the medieval Courts of Love. Its function was to resolve abstruse questions regarding romance and passion.

3. ELEANOR OF CASTILE (C. 1244–1290)

First popularized the use of oriental carpets in England.

4. ANNE OF BOHEMIA (1366–94)

It was to Anne — the first wife and queen of Richard II — that medieval women owed the custom of riding sidesaddle.

5. ELIZABETH OF YORK (1466–1503)

A portrait of Henry VII's queen, Elizabeth of York, has appeared eight times on every deck of playing cards for over 500 years.

6. KATHERINE HOWARD (C. 1525–42)

The fifth wife of Henry VIII, Katherine practised her role in her own execution. When informed that she would be beheaded on the following day, the queen requested that the executioner's axe and block be brought to her cell.

7. MARY I (1516–58)

The queen was eleven years older than her husband, Philip II of Spain.

8. ELIZABETH I (1533–1603)

Never once set foot outside of England.

9. ANNE (1665–1714)

Of the queen's eighteen pregnancies, only five of the babies were born alive. Of these five only one, the Duke of Gloucester, actually survived infancy — and he would die when he was eleven of hydrocephalus.

10. VICTORIA (1819–1901)

Victoria's first act after her accession, at the age of eighteen, was to remove her bed from her mother's room.

Queen Anne.

11. ELIZABETH, THE QUEEN MOTHER (1900–)
Owned a pet pig named Satan as a child.

12. ELIZABETH II (1926–)
Once admitted to having watched the Beatles' movie *Yellow Submarine* on at least five separate occasions.

FOUR WELL-KNOWN ROYAL ANECDOTES THAT ARE (UNFORTUNATELY) UNTRUE

1. QUEEN BERENGARIA NEVER ONCE SET FOOT IN ENGLAND
A story that is still frequently quoted regarding the beautiful wife of Richard I, despite the fact that it has no truth to it whatsoever. Indeed, the queen often visited England (particularly during her widowhood) though admittedly much of her time was spent in Italy and France.

2. EDWARD I CONQUERED WALES THROUGH TRICKERY

According to a popular Elizabethan legend, Edward's eventual conquest of Wales was actually arrived about through sheer trickery. The story goes that in 1284 the crafty king, knowing the proud Welsh chieftains would never accept a foreign prince, allegedly promised in exchange for peace to designate a ruler who could speak no word of English. He then sent his pregnant queen, Eleanor of Castile, to the cold stone fortress of Caernarvon Castle to give birth there. When his son (the future Edward II) was at last born, the king triumphantly presented the infant on a shield to the assembled chieftains as their prince "who spoke no English, had been born on Welsh soil, and whose first words would be spoken in Welsh." The ruse worked, and on that day was proclaimed the first English Prince of Wales. (In actual fact Edward II did not receive the principality of Wales until he was nearly 17, and his birth there had been nothing more than a fluke).

3. JAMES I INVENTED THE TITLE "SIRLOIN BEEF"

It has often been told how James I, being pleased once at dinner by a particularly good cut of beef, allegedly knighted it with the words, "Arise, Sir Loin" (in actual fact, the word is just a misspelling of the Old French *surloigne*, meaning "top of the loin").

4. GEORGE III ONCE HAD A CONVERSATION WITH AN OAK TREE

One of the more persistent apocryphal stories concerning George III and his madness concerns the time when he supposedly approached an oak tree in Windsor Great Park, shook hands with it and proceeded to discuss continental politics in the belief that it was the King of Prussia.

THREE UNUSUAL PLACES TO FIND BRITISH ROYALTY

1. AT THE VATICAN

Somewhere among the countless religious tracts contained in the Vatican Library in Rome are to be found a number of passionate love letters, written by Henry VIII for his then mistress Anne Boleyn.

2. IN AN OAK TREE

During his flight from Cromwell's forces after his crushing defeat at Worcester, Charles II was forced at one point to hide out in the branches of an enormous oak to avoid detection.

3. ON THE WATERGATE TAPES

One of the many Oval Office conversations that President Nixon recorded on these infamous tapes was a rather lengthy one between himself and Prince Charles, which took place in 1970.

THREE REASONS WHY IT'S GOOD TO BE THE KING (OR QUEEN)

1. UNIMAGINABLE WEALTH AND PRIVILEGE

Servants at your beck and call, rent-free living in some of the grandest homes in the world, and a guaranteed annual income (not to mention the almost complete lack of taxation).

2. NO SUBPOENAS

The sovereign is not required to give evidence in court, and cannot be sued.

3. EASE OF TRAVEL

Since all British passports are technically issued by the sovereign, they do not require one themselves.

THREE DRAWBACKS TO BEING ROYAL

1. FORMALITY

No end to dull ceremonies and stifling restrictions on your personal behaviour. Being royal has been likened to going to a wedding every single day of your life; indeed, so ingrained does the formality become that many royals (such as the Queen Mother) are known to dress up for dinner even when eating alone.

2. ENFORCED IDLENESS

This is particularly true for the heir to the throne, who may have to spend the better part of his lifetime waiting for a chance to reign without anything meaningful to do in the interim.

3. LACK OF PRIVACY

Life in a goldfish bowl. Paparazzi wherever you go, just waiting for you to make a mistake so that they can transmit it all over the world and wreck your life.

Royal
Records

THE FIVE LONGEST REIGNS

Honorable mention in this category must go to James I who, prior to his 22-year-reign in England, ruled for 35 years in Scotland as James VI.

1. *VICTORIA*   *63 years, 216 days*
2. *GEORGE III*   *59 years, 96 days*
3. *HENRY III*   *56 years, 1 month*
4. *ELIZABETH II* (since 1952)
5. *EDWARD III*   *49 years, 9 months*

THE FIVE SHORTEST REIGNS

1. *JANE*   *9 days*
2. *SWEYN, "FORKBEARD"*   *"a few weeks"*
3. *EDWARD V*   *77 days*
4. *EDMUND II*   *7 months*
5. *EDWARD VIII*   *326 days*

THE FIVE OLDEST SOVEREIGNS TO ASCEND THE THRONE

1. *WILLIAM IV*   *64 years, 10 months*
2. *EDWARD VII*   *59 years, 2 months*
3. *GEORGE IV*   *57 years, 5 months*
4. *GEORGE I*   *54 years, 2 months*
5. *JAMES II*   *51 years, 3 months*

THE FIVE YOUNGEST SOVEREIGNS TO ASCEND THE THRONE

1. *Henry VI*	*c. 9 months*
2. *Henry III*	*9 years, 18 days*
3. *Edward VI*	*9 years, 3 months*
4. *Ethelred II*	*10 years*
5. *Richard II*	*10 years, 6 months*

FIVE MONARCHS WHO DIED YOUNGEST

1. *Edward V*	*12 years, 8 months*
2. *Edward VI*	*15 years, 9 months*
3. *Edward the Martyr*	*c. 16 years*
4. *Jane*	*16 years, 4 months*
5. *Edwy*	*c. 19 years*

FIVE MONARCHS WHO LIVED THE LONGEST

1. *Elizabeth, the Queen Mother*	*(101 years and counting)*
2. *Eleanor of Aquitaine*	*82 years*
3. *Victoria*	*81 years, 243 days*
4. *George III*	*81 years, 239 days*
5. *Edward VIII*	*77 years, 11 months*

THE FIVE BEST BRITISH SOVEREIGNS
(AS SELECTED BY THE AUTHOR)

(Ranked chronologically)

1. *Alfred the Great (c. 849–899)*
2. *William I, "the Conqueror" (c. 1027–87)*
3. *Henry II (1133–89)*
4. *Edward I (1239–1307)*
5. *Elizabeth II (1926–)*

THE FIVE WORST BRITISH SOVEREIGNS (AS SELECTED BY THE AUTHOR)

(Ranked chronologically)

1. *ETHELRED II (C. 968–1016)*
2. *HENRY III (1207–72)*
3. *HENRY VI (1421–71)*
4. *JAMES II (1633–1701)*
5. *EDWARD VIII (1894–1972)*

THE FIVE MOST UNDERRATED BRITISH SOVEREIGNS (AS SELECTED BY THE AUTHOR)

1. *CANUTE (C. 995–1035)*
2. *HENRY VIII (1491–1547)*
3. *GEORGE III (1738–1820)*
4. *GEORGE IV (1762–1830)*
5. *EDWARD VII (1841–1910)*

THE FIVE MOST OVERRATED BRITISH SOVEREIGNS (AS SELECTED BY THE AUTHOR)

1. *HENRY V (1387–1422)*
2. *ELIZABETH I (1533–1603)*
3. *VICTORIA (1819–1901)*
4. *GEORGE V (1865–1936)*
5. *GEORGE VI (1895–1952)*

28 ROYAL FIRSTS AND LASTS

1. *ATHELSTAN (C. 895–939)*
   Generally regarded as the first king of a whole, united England.

2. *EDGAR (C. 943–975)*
   The first king to be crowned (rather than merely consecrated).

3. STEPHEN (C. 1097–1154)

The first (and thus far the last) British king by that name. King John also shares this distinction.

4. RICHARD I, "THE LIONHEART" (1157–99)

The first king to use the now familiar royal heraldry of England.

5. EDWARD III (1312–77)

The first royal to fire a gun.

6. HENRY VI (1421–71)

The first sovereign to use a wooden stamp for his signature; the first (and last) king to be crowned in both England and France.

7. HENRY VIII (1491–1547)

The first king to be called "Your Majesty."

8. ANNE BOLEYN (C. 1500–36)

The first female ever to be created a peer in her own right (she had been proclaimed Marchioness of Pembroke in 1532 by her husband).

9. EDWARD VI (1537–53)

The first king to keep a diary.

10. MARY I (1516–58)

The first woman to rule England in her own right; the first (and last) British monarch to marry a foreign reigning sovereign.

Mary I (painting by Master John).

11. ELIZABETH I (1533–1603)

The first monarch to install a bathroom in her palace.

12. JAMES I (1566–1625)

The first royal to travel in a submarine (albeit a very primitive one).

13. CHARLES I (1600–49)

The last king to enter the House of Commons.

14. KATHERINE HENRIETTA OF BRAGANZA (1638–1705)

The first tea-drinking royal.

15. WILLIAM III (1650–1702)

England's first constitutional monarch.

16. ANNE (1665–1714)

The first sovereign of the new United Kingdom; the last reigning monarch to refuse the assent to an act of parliament.

17. GEORGE II (1683–1760)

The last sovereign to be born abroad; the last to lead troops into battle (he did so — at the age of sixty — against the French at Dettingen in 1743, during the War of the Austrian Succession).

George II.

18. GEORGE III (1738–1820)
The first (and last) British king to strike for better living conditions; to hire a press secretary; the last King of America.

19. WILLIAM IV (1765–1837)
The last British sovereign to dissolve parliament.

20. VICTORIA (1819–1901)
The first sovereign to appear on a postage stamp; to be recorded, filmed and photographed; to travel by train; to have electric lights and a telephone. She was also the first person to send a trans-Atlantic cable message (to US President James Buchanan in 1858), and the first queen regnant to give birth to an heir.

21. EDWARD VII (1841–1910)
The first king to own and operate a car (he took his first drive on December 31,1899); to attend a football match; to meet with the pope; to visit Russia; to endorse a product (Angelus Player Pianos).

22. GEORGE V (1865–1936)
The first king to hire a public-relations officer; to make a Christmas radio broadcast to the nation; to go down a coal mine; to make a "balcony appearance" at Buckingham Palace.

23. EDWARD VIII (1894–1972)
The first royal to make a radio broadcast (he had preceded his father by over a year); to own a television; to pilot an airplane (in 1917).

24. GEORGE VI (1895–1952)
The first reigning British sovereign to visit North America; the first head of the British Commonwealth; the last emperor of India.

25. PHILIP, DUKE OF EDINBURGH (1921–)
The first royal to consent to a live television interview; to visit Antarctica.

26. ELIZABETH II (1926–)
The first sovereign to appear on British bank notes; to visit a leper colony; to fly across the Atlantic; to make a Christmas television broadcast to the nation; to have her own website; to visit a communist coun-

try. She was also the first reigning monarch to visit Australia, China and 10 Downing Street.

27. CHARLES, PRINCE OF WALES (1948–)

The first heir to the throne to attend public school; to earn a university degree; to go skydiving and windsurfing.

28. PRINCE WILLIAM (1982–)

The first heir to the throne to be born in a hospital.

Appendix:

The Kings and Queens of England Since Alfred the Great

Monarch	Marriages(s)	Reigned
Alfred the Great (c. 849–c. 899)	Ethelswitha of Mercia (d. 905)	(871–c. 899)
Edward the Elder (c. 871–c. 924)	1. Egwina (d. c. 901) 2. Elfleda (d. 920) 3. Edgiva of Kent (c. 905–968)	(899–924)
Athelstan (c. 895–939)	(*Unmarried*)	(924–939)
Edmund I (c. 921–946)	1. Elgiva (d. 944) 2. Ethelfleda (d. 975)	(939–946)
Edred (c. 923–955)	(*Unmarried*)	(946–955)
Edwy (c. 942–959)	Elgiva (d. 959)	(955–959)

Edgar (c. 943–975)	1. Ethelfleda the Fair (d. c. 963) 2. Elfrida of Devon (d. 1002)	(959–975)
Edward the Martyr (c. 963–978)	(*Unmarried*)	(975–978)
Ethelred II (c. 968–1016)	1. Elgiva (c. 963–1002) 2. Emma of Normandy (c. 986–1052)	(978–1016)
Sweyn, "Forkbeard" (c. 960–1014)	1. Gunhilda (d. c. 1015) 2. Sigrid, "The Haughty"* (d. 1013)	(986)
Edmund II (c. 990–1016)	Edith (*dates unknown*)	(1016)
Canute (c. 995–1035)	Emma of Normandy (c. 986–1052)	(1016–35)
Harold I (c. 1016–1040)	Elgiva (*dates unknown*)	(1035–40)
Harthacanute (c. 1018–1042)	(*Unmarried*)	(1035–42)
Edward the Confessor (c. 1004–1066)	Edith of Wessex (c. 1020–1075)	(1042–66)
Harold II (c. 1021–1066)	Ealgith of Mercia (c. 1042–c. 1070)	(1066)
William I, "The Conqueror" (c. 1027–87)	Matilda of Flanders (c. 1032–83)	(1066–87)

William II, "Rufus" (c. 1058–1100)	(*Unmarried*)	(1087–1100)
Henry I (1068–1135)	1. Matilda of Scotland (1080–1118) 2. Adeliza of Louvain (c. 1105–1151)	(1100–35)
Stephen (c. 1097–1154)	Matilda of Boulogne (c. 1104–1152)	(1135–54)
Matilda, "The Empress" (1102–67)	1. Heinrich V, Holy Roman Emperor (1105–25) 2. Geoffroy IV, Count of Anjou (*dates unknown*)	(*Disputed*)
Henry II (1133–89)	Eleanor of Aquitaine (1121–1204)	(1154–89)
Richard I (1157–99)	Berengaria of Navarre (c. 1164–c. 1230)	(1189–99)
John (1166–1216)	1. Isabella of Gloucester* (c. 1175–1217) 2. Isabella of Angoulême (c. 1187–1246)	(1199–1216)
Henry III (1207–72)	Eleanor of Provence (c. 1223–1291)	(1216–72)
Edward I (1239–1307)	1. Eleanor of Castile (c. 1244–1290) 2. Margaret of France (c. 1280–1318)	(1272–1307)
Edward II (1284–1327)	Isabella of France (c. 1293–1358)	(1307–27)

Edward III (1312–77)	Philippa of Hainault (1314–69)	(1327–77)
Richard II (1367–1400)	1. Anne of Bohemia (1366–94) 2. Isabella of Valois (1387–1409)	(1377–99)
Henry IV (1366–1413)	1. Mary De Bohun* (c. 1370–94) 2. Joan of Navarre (c. 1370–1437)	(1399–1413)
Henry V (1387–1422)	Katherine of Valois (1401–37)	(1413–22)
Henry VI (1421–71)	Margaret of Anjou (1429–82)	(1422–71)
Edward IV (1442–83)	Elizabeth Woodville (c. 1437–92)	(1461–83)
Edward V (1470–c. 1483)	(*Unmarried*)	(1483)
Richard III (1452–85)	Anne of Warwick (1456–85)	(1483–85)
Henry VII (1457–1509)	Elizabeth of York (1466–1503)	(1485–1509)
Henry VIII (1491–1547)	1. Katherine of Aragon (1485–1536) 2. Anne Boleyn (c. 1500–36) 3. Jane Seymour (c. 1508–37) 4. Anne of Cleves (1515–57)	(1509–47)

5. Katherine Howard
(c. 1525–42)
6. Katherine Parr
(c. 1513–48)

Edward VI   (*Unmarried*)   (1547–53)
(1537–53)

Jane (Lady Jane Grey)   Lord Guildford Dudley   (1553)
(1537–54)   (1536–54)

Mary I   Philip II of Spain   (1553–58)
(1516–58)   (1527–98)

Elizabeth I   (*Unmarried*)   (1558–1603)
(1533–1603)

James I   Anne of Denmark   (1603–25)
(1566–1625)   (1574–1619)

Charles I   Henrietta Maria of France (1625–49)
(1600–49)   (1609–69)

The First Interregnum or Commonwealth — England ruled by Lord Protector **Oliver Cromwell** *(1649–58), who was briefly succeeded by his son,* **Richard Cromwell** *(1658–60).*

Charles II   Katherine Henrietta   (1660–85)
(1630–85)   of Braganza
                   (1638–1705)

James II   1. Anne Hyde   (1685–88)
(1633–1701)   (1637–71)
                   2. Mary of Modena
                   (1658–1718)

Second Interregnum (December 1688 — February 1689)

Mary II   William III   (1689–94)
(1662–94)   (1650–1702)

William III (1650–1702)	Mary II (1662–94)	(1689–1702)
Anne (1665–1714)	George of Denmark (1653–1708)	(1702–14)
George I (1660–1727)	Sophia Dorothea of Celle* (1666–1726)	(1714–27)
George II (1683–1760)	Caroline of Brandenburg-Ansbach (1683–1737)	(1727–60)
George III (1738–1820)	Charlotte Mecklenburg-Strelitz (1744–1818)	(1760–1820)
George IV (1762–1830)	1. Maria Fitzherbert* (1756–1837) 2. Caroline of Brunswick-Wolfenbüttel (1768–1821)	(1820–30)
William IV (1765–1837)	Adelaide of Saxe-Meiningen (1792–1849)	(1830–37)
Victoria (1819–1901)	Albert of Saxe-Coburg-Gotha (1819–61)	(1837–1901)
Edward VII (1841–1910)	Alexandra of Denmark (1844–1925)	(1901–10)
George V (1865–1936)	Mary of Teck (1867–1955)	(1910–36)
Edward VIII (1894–1972)	Wallis Simpson* (c. 1896–1986)	(1936)

George VI Elizabeth Bowes-Lyon (1936–52)
(1895–1952) (1900–)

Elizabeth II Philip of Greece (*Since 1952*)
(1926–) (1921–)

* *Indicates never formally acknowledged either as queen or queen consort*

Bibliography

Anderson, Christopher. *The Day Diana Died*. New York, 1998.

Blitzer, Charles. *Age of Kings*. New York, 1967.

Bradford, Sarah. *The Reluctant King*. New York, 1989.

Brown, Craig and Cunliffe, Lesley. *The Book of Royal Lists*. New York, 1982.

Cannon, John and Griffiths, Ralph. *The Oxford Illustrated History of the British Monarchy*. Oxford, 1988.

Cowie, L. W. *Dictionary of British Social History*. London, 1973.

Cure, Karen (ed.). *Fodor's Great Britain 2000*. New York, 2000.

Delderfield, Eric. *Kings & Queens of England & Great Britain*. London, 1990.

Devere-Summers, Anthony. *War and the Royal Houses of Europe*. London, 1996.

Edmunds, Sarah. *Royal Trivia*. London, 1990.

Falkus, Christopher. *The Life and Times of Charles II*. London, 1972.

Farndon, John. *Royal Castle: The Inside Story of Windsor*. London, 1997.

Fearon, Peter. *Buckingham Babylon*. New York, 1993.

Fraser, Antonia (ed.). *The Lives of the Kings and Queens of England*. London, 1975.

Fulford, Roger. *The Wicked Uncles*. New York, 1933.

Grant, Neil. *Kings & Queens*. London, 1996.

Heald, Henrietta (ed). *Chronicle of Britain*. Farnborough, 1992.

Hibbert, Christopher. *Charles I*. London, 1968.

—. *Queen Victoria in Her Letters and Journals*. Guildford, 1984.

Holden, Anthony. *Charles: A Biography*. London, 1989.

—. *The Tarnished Crown*. New York, 1993.

Hough, Richard. *Born Royal*. New York, 1988.

Hudson, M. E. and Clark, Mary. *Crown of a Thousand Years*. New York, 1978.

Joelson, Annette. *Heirs To the Throne*. London, 1966.

Kelley, Kitty. *The Royals*. New York, 1997.

Latham, Caroline and Sakol, Jeannie. *The Royals*. London, 1987.

Lofts, Norah. *Queens of Britain*. London, 1977.

Longford, Elizabeth (ed.). *Victoria R.I.* London, 1976.

—. *The Oxford Book of Royal Anecdotes*. Oxford, 1989.

Macleod, John. *Dynasty*. London, 1999.

Magnus, Philip. *King Edward VII*. New York, 1964.

Mercer, Derrik. *Chronicle of the Royal Family*. London, 1991.

Montgomery-Massingberd, Hugh (ed.). *The Heritage of Royal Britain*. Toronto, 1984.

Morton, Andrew. *The Wealth of the Windsors*. London, 1993.

—. *Diana: Her True Story*. New York, 1998.

Palmer, Alan. *The Life and Times of George IV*. Glasgow, 1972.

Pearson, John. *The Selling of the Royal Family*. New York, 1986.

Plumb, J. H. *The First Four Georges*. London, 2000.

Sanders, Margaret. *Intimate Letters of England's Kings*. London, 1959.

Shaw, Karl. *Royal Babylon: The Alarming History of European Royalty*. London, 1999.

Softly, Barbara. *The Queens of England*. New York, 1979.

Starkie, Allan. *Fergie: Her Secret Life*. New York, 1996.

Thackeray, W. M. *The Four Georges*. London, 1910.

Vansittart, Peter (ed.). *Happy and Glorious!* London, 1988.

Wallace, Irving and Wallace, Amy and Wallechinsky, David. *The Book of Lists*. New York, 1977.

—. *The Book of Lists 3*. New York, 1983.

Wallace, Irving and Wallace, Amy and Wallace, Sylvia and Wallechinsky, David. *The Book of Lists 2*. New York, 1980.

—. *The Intimate Sex Lives of Famous People*. New York, 1981.

Wallechinsky, David and Wallace, Irving. *The People's Almanac 2*. New York, 1978.

—. *The People's Almanac 3*. New York, 1981.

Weir, Alison. *The Six Wives of Henry VIII*. London, 1991.

—. *Britain's Royal Families*. London, 1996.

—. *Elizabeth the Queen*. London, 1999.

Williams, Neville. *The Life and Times of Elizabeth I*. London, 1972.

Ziegler, Philip. *Diana Cooper*. London, 1981.

—. *King Edward VIII*. London, 1990.

Select Index